Luxury and Public Happiness

Political Economy in the Italian Enlightenment

TILL WAHNBAECK

CLARENDON PRESS · OXFORD

This book has been printed digitally and produced in a standard specification in order to ensure its continuing availability

OXFORD
UNIVERSITY PRESS

Great Clarendon Street, Oxford OX2 6DP

Oxford University Press is a department of the University of Oxford.
It furthers the University's objective of excellence in research, scholarship,
and education by publishing worldwide in

Oxford New York

Auckland Cape Town Dar es Salaam Hong Kong Karachi
Kuala Lumpur Madrid Melbourne Mexico City Nairobi
New Delhi Shanghai Taipei Toronto
With offices in
Argentina Austria Brazil Chile Czech Republic France Greece
Guatemala Hungary Italy Japan South Korea Poland Portugal
Singapore Switzerland Thailand Turkey Ukraine Vietnam

Oxford is a registered trade mark of Oxford University Press
in the UK and in certain other countries

Published in the United States
by Oxford University Press Inc., New York

Reprinted 2006

ISBN 978-0-19-926983-9

Meinen Eltern

ACKNOWLEDGEMENTS

Now that this book is going off to the printer, it is a pleasure to acknowledge the numerous debts I have incurred ever since it began to take shape several years ago at Oxford. Financial support throughout came from the British Academy and the German Academic Exchange Service. Various people in England, Italy, and Germany have talked with me about luxury and political economy and helped me clarify my thoughts: Tim Hochstrasser in London, Robert Evans and David Parrott in Oxford, and Istvan Hont in Cambridge provided constructive criticism at various stages (and delicious dinners in the case of David Parrott). Balliol College has been the perfect place in which to live, row, and write. Balliol—and Maurice Keen in particular—has been exceedingly generous in financing research trips and conference participation.

During a year of research spent in Florence, I was welcomed into the European University Institute by John Brewer. In Italy I profited enormously from conversations with Vincenzo Ferrone, Silvia Sebastiani, Antonio Trampus, and Renato Pasta. Elisabetta and Adriano Guadagni have taught me more about Tuscany and Tuscan culture than many a history book.

A large part of this book was written at the Max Planck Institute for the History of Science in Berlin. I wish to thank its director, Lorraine Daston, for providing what are probably the most luxurious working conditions to be found in Germany. My officemate at the Institute, Abigail Lustig, has taught me a great deal about language and style.

Several friends have shaped my interest in the history of ideas ever since my days as an undergraduate at Freiburg University: I have spent long hours discussing history and many other things with Nick Eschenbruch, Holger Hoock, Thoralf Klein, and Ulrich Gotter. Holger Hoock has been a friend and an ever-intelligent critic for more than ten years now; I owe him a great deal. With Nick Eschenbruch I have probably spoken least about this book, but his sharp mind, his vast knowledge, and his friendship have contributed more to it than he may realize.

My greatest debt, however, is to John Robertson. He was the supervisor of the original thesis out of which this book has grown, as well as my academic editor at Oxford University Press. A more intelligent, caring, and encouraging mentor no history student could wish for.

This book is about luxury and public happiness, but what I have discovered in the last few years is this: the greatest luxury of all is private happiness. For this I thank Carolin Karnath.

T.W.

Geneva
August 2003

CONTENTS

Introduction

> Public virtue has been the concern of thinkers in Antiquity; the subtle examination of reason of state that of the last two centuries . . . But now . . . writers have undertaken to clarify the elements which lead to public wealth.
>
> (*Giornale de' letterati di Pisa*, 1771)

This book is about ideas. It seeks to explain the development of political economy in eighteenth-century Italy, and it argues that the focus on economic thought is characteristic of the Italian Enlightenment at large. By an analysis of the debate about luxury, it attempts to chart the development of a new language of political economy which was inspired by, and contributed to, European debate, but which offered solutions that were as much shaped by local intellectual traditions and socio-economic circumstances as by French or Scottish precedent.[1] Ultimately, those traditions were responsible for the development of very distinct schools of thought across the peninsula, and they led to the development of significantly different cultures of enlightenment spanning Italy from Milan in the north to Naples in the south.

The moral and economic nature of luxury was a topic virtually every major thinker in the eighteenth century engaged with. Montesquieu and Voltaire, David Hume and Adam Smith, Cesare Beccaria and Pietro Verri, stand out as some of the most famous contributors to this cosmopolitan debate, but they were joined by hundreds of *philosophes*, political economists, literary figures, agriculturalists, priests, academicians, and administrators

[1] The most important general accounts are John Sekora, *Luxury: The Concept in Western Thought, Eden to Smollett* (Baltimore, 1977); Ellen Ross, 'The Debate on Luxury in Eighteenth-Century France: A Study in the Language of Opposition to Change', diss., University of Chicago, 1975; M. R. de Labriolle-Rutherford, 'L'Évolution de la notion du luxe depuis Mandeville jusqu'à la révolution', *Studies on Voltaire and the Eighteenth Century*, 26 (1963), 1025–36; Christopher J. Berry, *The Idea of Luxury: A Conceptual and Historical Investigation* (Cambridge, 1994). On Italy, not much has been published. For an account of the Neapolitan discussion which remains a valuable point of reference, see Paolo Frascani, 'Il dibattito sul lusso nella cultura napoletana del '700', *Critica storica*, 11 (1971), 397–424. In the only comprehensive treatment of the Italian debate, Norbert Jonard tells us that Cesare Beccaria 'adds absolutely nothing to the debate'; that Pietro Verri's treatment is 'deprived of all originality'; and that the Tuscans simply repeated physiocratic teachings because they 'naturally had a physiocratic mentality'. The aim of the article in general seems to be to deny the importance of its subject. Norbert Jonard, 'Le Problème du luxe en Italie au XVIIIe siècle', *Revue des études italiennes*, 15 (1969), 295–321.

across Europe. Few of them would have been surprised to hear Cesare Beccaria's argument in his lecture sketches (written when he had just been appointed to one of the first European chairs of political economy in Milan in 1768) that all his reasoning ultimately culminated in an answer to the question of the value of luxury.[2] Luxury was so important to all these thinkers because one of the central concerns of political reformers and philosophers alike was 'public happiness', and that encompassed public wealth. Luxury was one of the major fault lines along which this project was made—or broken. If what the *Giornale de' letterati* in Pisa said in 1771 is true—that public virtue and reason of state were concerns of the past, and that now was the age of the economy—then we should expect the issue of luxury to feature prominently in this new project.[3]

Outside Italy, the Italian Enlightenment is probably the least well known of the peninsula's modern historical periods.[4] The scarcity of studies in English comes despite the fact that Ferdinando Galiani and Antonio Genovesi in Naples were economists and philosophers of the first rank, who were considered by their counterparts in Paris and Edinburgh as some of the prime exponents of the republic of letters; that Cesare Beccaria single-handedly placed Milan on the map of the European Enlightenment with his work *On Crimes and Punishments*, which made him one of the most admired legal thinkers of the century; and finally that Tuscany was the testing ground for physiocracy, with many of the physiocrats' recommendations (such as the liberalization of the grain trade) translated into legislation by the reform-minded grand duke Peter Leopold. In Italy, by contrast, the peninsula's significance for the European Enlightenment has long been recognized, and the intellectual culture of the eighteenth century is now a major field of research.

[2] Cesare Beccaria, *Piano d'istruzioni per la cattedra di scienze camerali o sia di economia civile* (1768), in Beccaria, *Opere*, ed. Sergio Romagnoli (Florence, 1958), i. 344.

[3] 'La virtù pubblica fu per lungo tempo il soggetto de' politici della antichità: i sottili esami sulla ragion di stato occuparano quelli del secolo passato e del decimo sesto . . . da qualche tempo . . . gran copia di scrittori . . . ha intrappreso a schiarire gli elementi, da cui risulta la vera ricchezza pubblica' (*Giornale de' letterati di Pisa*, 4 (1771), 81–3).

[4] For the best accounts in English, see Franco Venturi's collection *Italy and the Enlightenment: Studies in a Cosmopolitan Century*, ed. Stuart Woolf (London, 1972); Dino Carpanetto and Giuseppe Ricuperati, *Italy in the Age of Reason, 1685–1789* (London, 1987), a political, economic, and intellectual history; Stuart Woolf, *A History of Italy 1700–1860: The Social Constraints of Political Change*, new edn. (London, 1991), a social and political history. For the history of ideas, see most recently Vincenzo Ferrone, *The Intellectual Roots of the Italian Enlightenment: Newtonian Science, Religion, and Politics in the Early Eighteenth Century* (New Jersey, 1995; original Italian version, Naples, 1982), and the classic Franco Venturi, *Utopia and Reform in the Enlightenment* (Cambridge, 1971).

Ever since Franco Venturi's lecture at the Society of Risorgimento Studies in 1953, the eighteenth century in Italy has been considered to be a period in its own right.[5] If, prior to this, it had often simply been seen as a forerunner to unification,[6] now the eighteenth century, along with the Enlightenment, had its own identity as a period of cosmopolitanism, reform, and reason. The contest for interpretative hegemony of the period is heated, and Italian historiography about the eighteenth century is increasingly becoming a battlefield between two rival schools of interpretation. One, which can be dubbed the 'Torinese school', gathers around the memory of Franco Venturi, the father of Italian Enlightenment studies. For them, the Enlightenment is a 'civil' project with an eminently cosmopolitan, reformist, and political thrust.[7] It is inspired by the 'attempt—perhaps ingenuous—to learn how to change the world'.[8] Its prime exponents are Giuseppe Ricuperati, Vincenzo Ferrone, Edoardo Tortarolo, and, to an extent, Carlo Capra, all of whom are, or have been, associated with the university of Turin. The second school is less homogeneous, but has recently joined forces. On the one hand, this is the 'Catholic Enlightenment school' pioneered by Cesare Mozzarelli, who holds a chair at the Catholic University of Milan. Rather than European reform projects in an age of declining religion, this school is interested both in the insertion of the Enlightenment into Catholic thought and in the interplay between the absolutist state and local administration.[9] As a consequence of those interests, Mozzarelli is inclined to present the Lombard group around Pietro Verri and Cesare Beccaria more as members of the Milanese patriciate intent on restoring oligarchic hegemony in Lombardy than as social reformers.[10] With this anti-reformist, anti-Enlightenment interpretation of the Milanese Enlightenment, Mozzarelli has indirectly come to the aid of Mario Mirri, the prime exponent of the 'local histories school'. Comparable to the British project of 'enlightenment in regional context' in its potentially anti-cosmopolitan

[5] Franco Venturi, 'La circolazione delle idee', *Rassegna storica del Risorgimento* (1954), 203–22.

[6] Ettore Rota, *Le origini del Risorgimento (1700–1800)*, 2 vols. (Milan, 1938).

[7] Vincenzo Ferrone, Massimo Firpo, Giuseppe Ricuperati, and Edoardo Tortarolo, 'Vita civile e storiografia: contributo per una discussione', *Studi storici*, 1 (1994), 91–8.

[8] Giuseppe Ricuperati, 'Illuminismo e Settecento dal dopoguerra ad oggi', in Ricuperati (ed.), *La reinvenzione dei lumi: percorsi storiografici del Novecento* (Florence, 2000), 201–22: 217.

[9] An example of the first is Mozzarelli's edition of Muratori's *Della pubblica felicità oggetto de' buoni principi* (Rome, 1996). For the latter, see Mozzarelli, *Sovrano, società e amministrazione locale nella Lombardia teresiana (1749–1758)* (Bologna, 1982).

[10] Cesare Mozzarelli, 'Riforme e controriforme', in Aldo Frantoianni and Marcello Verga (eds.), *Pompeo Neri: atti del colloquio di Castelfiorentino (6–7 maggio 1988)* (Castelfiorentino, 1992), 391–400.

thrust, Mirri has argued for the abandonment of the concept of one Italo-European Enlightenment in favour of a return to the history of the Italian states with a focus on its indigenous traditions.[11]

A third school has tried to steer clear of a debate that is increasingly becoming personal.[12] It is represented by Luciano Guerci's work on *l'altro Settecento*, the eighteenth century of conservatism, religion, and anti-Enlightenment, which he first presented in a study on the role of the woman in eighteenth-century Italy and then broadened into a history of Europe in the eighteenth century.[13]

This study is an attempt to overcome the conflict between the differing schools. Indeed, I contend, the Italian Enlightenment was both a cosmopolitan enterprise (acutely aware of, and engaged in, European debate) *and* an eminently regional project. It drew inspiration from Edinburgh to St Petersburg, from Berlin to Madrid. But the ultimate aim of this cross-border intellectual curiosity was to improve local conditions in the region in which the authors lived. This helps to explain why the thought of the different regions has developed in such utterly different directions; why Tuscany could have become one of the prime exponents of physiocracy; why Lombardy was at the forefront of a new language of political economy; and finally, why Naples constantly oscillated between a moral and an economic approach to political economy.

In other words, this book attempts to combine Franco Venturi's conviction that the eighteenth century in Italy was a cosmopolitan age of reform with Mario Mirri's insistence on political history in local context and with Luciano Guerci's view of 'the other eighteenth century', that of religion, conservatism, and anti-Enlightenment. It does so by analysing an area of eighteenth-century thought that has not yet received its due attention in Italian Enlightenment studies: political economy.

The study of political economy does not command the same interest among Italian historians of the Enlightenment as it does in Great Britain.[14]

[11] Mario Mirri, 'Dalla storia dei "Lumi" e delle "riforme" alla storia degli antichi stati italiani', in Frantoianni and Verga, *Pompeo Neri*, 401–540.

[12] See e.g. Giuseppe Ricuperati's characterization of Mozzarrelli's call for a new interpretation of the 18th century as 'impertinent' and 'revisionist': Ricuperati, 'Illuminismo e Settecento', 221.

[13] Luciano Guerci, *La discussione sulla donna nell'Italia del Settecento: aspetti e problemi* (Turin, 1987), and his *L'Europa del Settecento: permanenze e mutamenti* (Turin, 1988), esp. pt. 2.

[14] See, however, Manuela Albertone and Alberto Masoero (eds.), *Political Economy and National Realities* (Turin, 1994), and most recently Maria Luisa Pesante (ed.), *Etiche economiche*, *Quaderni storici*, 105 (2000), and therein Terenzio Maccarelli and Erica Morato, 'Il "bisognevole" e il "superfluo": occupazioni e distribuzione della ricchezza in Giammaria Ortes', 731–66.

This is all the more surprising as contemporaries clearly acknowledged the paramount importance of the study of political economy, as the *Giornale de' letterati* has shown.[15] There is of course ample work on the eighteenth century by historians of economics.[16] The two extreme positions that frame debate in this discipline differ in their interpretation of the importance of Italy in the founding of political economy. Oscar Nuccio's account is a rather self-conscious attempt to ascertain the 'Italian paternity' of capitalism against Max Weber, and offers a diatribe against virtually all previous historiography which has the guts not to acknowledge Italian primacy in the field of economics.[17] Eugenio Zarin, on the other hand, tells the history of political economy from mercantilism to Marx without mentioning Italian contributions.[18] But whereas the aim of historians of economics is often to trace precedent and influence on current economic models,[19] this book remains faithful to a *historical* analysis which is more interested in context, and which seeks to insert economic thought into the framework of the Enlightenment.[20] In fact, the development of a new language of political economy by the prime exponents of the Italian Enlightenment is as much an advance in economic doctrine about value and money (of which historians have already given an account[21]) as it is part of a wider attempt to include economic thinking into the preoccupation with human nature, liberty, and reason which characterized the Enlightenment in France, Scotland, and Italy alike. In particular, I argue, it was one of the major achievements of the Lombard Enlightenment to have found a distinctly economic language for this aspect of enlightened enquiry.

A word on method. I refer not only to the printed texts that shaped the debate but also to the socio-political, economic, and institutional contexts in

[15] See e.g. the *Giornale de' letterati di Pisa*, 4 (1771), 81–3.

[16] For an exhaustive bibliography, see Marco Bianchini and Erica Morato, 'Per una storia della storiografia del pensiero economico italiano del Settecento: l'Italia centro-settentrionale', *Il pensiero economico italiano*, 1 (1993), 17–55.

[17] Oscar Nuccio, *La civiltà italiana nella formazione della scienza economica* (Milan, 1995).

[18] Eugenio Zarin, *Storia dell'economia politica: dai mercantilisti a Marx* (Turin, 1991).

[19] A notable exception is Riccardo Faucci, *L'economica politica in Italia: dal Cinquecento ai nostri giorni* (Turin, 2000), which focuses on influence and precedence between thinkers, but gives ample references to context.

[20] See James A. Tully, 'The Pen is a Mighty Sword: Quentin Skinner's Analysis of Politics', *British Journal of Political Science*, 13 (1983), 489–509, and Skinner's own theoretical work now in James A. Tully (ed.), *Meaning and Context: Quentin Skinner and his Critics* (Princeton, 1988).

[21] See most recently Pier Luigi Porta and Roberto Scazzieri, 'Il contributo di Pietro Verri alla teoria economica', *Pietro Verri e il suo tempo: quaderni di Acme*, 35 (1999), 813–52. More generally, see Alberto Quadrio Curzio (ed.), *Alle origini del pensiero economico in Italia*, ii: *Economia e istituzioni: il paradigma lombardo tra i secoli XVIII e XIX* (Bologna, 1996).

so far as they shed light on the specific turn the Italian debate took in the course of the eighteenth century. In this sense, this is a 'social history of ideas', but a history of ideas nevertheless.[22] The focus determines my choice of sources, most of which are printed treatises on political economy, technical manuals and journal contributions, university lectures, ministerial memorandums, and widely circulated manuscripts. Letters and personal sketches will be used to trace influences more specifically and to illuminate the development of ideas. Reviews, annotated translations, and 'creative readings' of foreign texts will reveal the process of the transmission of ideas. I am of course aware that 'the historian, like a chameleon, is coloured by his sources'.[23] In my case, the type of sources used highlights the economic dimension of the luxury debate. But it is no coincidence that the great majority of published material (and certainly the texts with the greatest repercussions) *are* about economic concerns.

Not all the texts belong to the 'high Enlightenment'. Perhaps only a few of them would qualify for such a characterization. But they certainly constitute the utterings of a social elite. I do not say, for example, what Tuscan peasants thought of luxury's effects on the Tuscan peasantry, and this requires an explanation. My aim is to analyse the cosmopolitan and patriotic origins of a debate and the influence of local contributions on subsequent interventions, and this requires the use of sources whose influence can be traced. We simply do not know how peasant anxieties contributed to a debate that was carried out in public through writing and publishing. But there is also a methodological claim behind my choice of sources. If we visualize these sources as three layers of a pyramid, then the apex is formed by textbooks and treatises on political economy, whose influence often transcended regional borders. They are followed by less ambitious works such as specialized agrarian tracts or reflections on fashion. Dictionaries and encyclopaedias constitute the third layer. They can elucidate how new ideas trickle down into common language. I contend that *Gipfeltexte* ('apex texts') to a large extent cover what is being said in society at large. Hence, they will feature prominently in my account, even though they are often accompanied by more modest and less widely circulated texts which are nevertheless important in order to assess the context in which the *Gipfeltexte*

[22] See Reinhart Koselleck, 'Sozialgeschichte und Begriffsgeschichte', in Wolfgang Schieder and Volker Sellin (eds.), *Sozialgeschichte in Deutschland* (Göttingen, 1987), i. 89–109. If Koselleck seems to view *Begriffsgeschichte* as conducive to elucidating *tatsächliche Geschichte*, I seek to illuminate the history of concepts with the help of social contexts, rather than vice versa.

[23] Peter G. M. Dickson, *Finance and Government under Maria Theresa, 1740–1780*, 2 vols. (Oxford, 1987), i. 15.

took shape and better to bring out their exemplary character. Finally, the reader will look in vain for evidence from administrative bodies. On the level of ideas, scrutiny of archival evidence indicates that administrative papers would not shed a significant amount of additional light on the development of the debate. What they could do is trace the actual implementation, in other words examine the political and economic reforms carried out in this age of reform. But that has been done many times by historians of government, and I do not wish to add to their findings.[24] There is no denying that thought influenced reform, and I have mentioned examples in Tuscany where this was the case. But these should not distract from the central claim of this study: that intellectual debate needs to be taken seriously as what it was meant to be—a process of critical assimilation of the themes of the European Enlightenment by regional elites, embedded in local intellectual tradition and driven by the attempt to sketch the path towards public happiness, not to order the planting of mulberry trees in the Po valley.

Part I of this book first explores the range of meaning the term 'luxury' could be used to express. What could Italians in the eighteenth century *mean* when they *said* the word 'luxury'? An analysis of dictionaries and encyclopaedias from the seventeenth to the nineteenth centuries questions the received notion that the concept of luxury was de-moralized in the course of the eighteenth century.[25] Rather, I argue, the term assumed a range of new meanings without ever completely losing old connotations. This widening of the range of meaning was, I believe, one of the reasons why later Italian thinkers could invoke luxury when they wanted to intervene in many different economic, social, political, and religious debates.

Next, I present the development of the European debate on luxury from Mandeville's *Fable of the Bees* to Adam Smith's *Wealth of Nations*. Even

[24] On Lombardy, see most recently Carlo Capra, 'Il gruppo del "Caffè" e le riforme', in Vincenzo Ferrone and Gianni Francioni (eds.), *Cesare Beccaria: la pratica dei lumi* (Florence, 2000), 63–78, and his 'Riforme finanziarie e mutamento istituzionale nello Stato di Milano: gli anni sessanta del secolo XVIII', *Rivista storica italiana*, 91 (1979), 313–18, and 'Lo sviluppo delle riforme asburgiche nello Stato di Milano', in Pierangelo Schiera (ed.), *La dinamica statale austriaca nel XVIII e XIX secolo* (Bologna, 1981), 161–87. See also Franco Valsecchi, 'Le riforme teresiane in Lombardia', in *Economia, istituzioni, cultura*, i. 27–40; on Tuscany, Giorgio Giorgetti, 'Per uno studio delle allivellazioni leopoldine', *Studi storici*, 2 (1966), 245–90; Mario Mirri, 'Proprietari e contadini nelle riforme leopoldine', *Movimento operaio*, 7 (1955), 173–229; Abele Morena, 'Le riforme e le dottrine economiche in Toscana', *Rassegna nazionale*, 18 (1887), 211–56; Luigi Dal Pane, 'Le riforme economiche e finanziarie di Pietro Leopoldo', *Rassegna storica toscana*, 11 (1965), 229–46; Adam Wandruszka, 'Pietro Leopoldo e le sue riforme in Toscana: dal diario del conte Carlo Zinzendorf', *Archivio storico italiano*, 118 (1960), 286–91.

[25] Berry, *The Idea of Luxury*, ch. 5: 'The De-moralisation of Luxury'.

though I attempt to give a fresh interpretation of some aspects of the debate, this is largely an analysis of 'big texts' which were to become influential in the Italian context, and does not pretend to be exhaustive.

The next chapter (Chapter 3) describes how the debate reached Italy and how it was first assimilated in the context of enlightened Catholicism. It then sketches the development of the unique Neapolitan discussion to elucidate the establishment of political economy and the interplay between moral and economic languages in eighteenth-century Italy. The chapter focuses on Antonio Genovesi and Ferdinando Galiani, but goes back to the beginning of the century and to Paolo Mattia Doria and Carlo Antonio Broggia to place their thought into its local intellectual context.

Parts II and III are case studies of two regions which best serve to illuminate the broader themes of the transmission of ideas and the shaping of political economy. A comparison of the two can teach us something about the relationship between the local and patriotic, and the European and cosmopolitan, in intellectual debate. It shows how different socio-economic and intellectual contexts determine the development of thought and debate and how two regions which at first sight appear similar both economically and politically could develop distinctly differing intellectual interests.

Part II deals with Tuscany, and in this part the straightforward history of ideas gives way to social history of ideas in that it proceeds from intellectual and cultural contexts to individual authors and their texts. An account of the social and political world and the economic reality in which the ideas operated hence precedes the analysis of the development of economic thought in Tuscany. Through case studies of journalistic activity and the practice of debate, the agencies of intellectual socialization and the reception of foreign thought, I attempt to show how ideas were transmitted into the grand duchy, how they related to, and were affected by, Tuscan traditions of economic thought, and how a public culture evolved in the course of the second half of the century.[26] The aim of this part is threefold. Its first objective is to question the received wisdom that Tuscan thought was eclectic and that the undoubted inclination of Tuscan political economists towards physiocracy was merely a somewhat opportunistic echo of Peter Leopold's own preferences. It does so by tracing Tuscan economic thought back to the beginning of the century and by showing its close association with French thought that was a source for later physiocratic thinking. By the time the ideas of the physiocrats reached the grand duchy, it will be

[26] My thought on the transmission of ideas has been informed by Fania Oz-Salzberger, *Translating the Enlightenment: Scottish Civic Discourse in Eighteenth-Century Germany* (Oxford, 1995).

argued, they must have been perceived as almost genuinely Tuscan; their teachings also seemed especially relevant to Tuscany's agricultural economy. The second aim is to show how a culture of ministerial memorandums was transformed into an increasingly public culture around the middle of the century through new media and the new role played by the region's academies. This shift allowed new actors (mainly secular clergy writing in the context of enlightened Catholicism) to contribute to the debate. This broadening of the range of participants in economic debate beyond administrators (concerned with questions of state finance and taxation) to embrace priests (concerned with the salvation of souls) reintroduced, to an extent, moral considerations into the luxury debate. But, and this is the third theme of this part, the 'pragmatic tradition' of Tuscan thought together with the powerful influence of French economic thinking had substantially altered the discussion. Even the enlightened Catholic tradition now had to accept the vocabulary and the concepts of the 'pragmatic school' in order to voice their moral concerns.

Part III deals with Lombardy. Here we see a new language of political economy at work, and it is here that the greatest advances in economic thinking were being made. Through an insertion of the main texts of the Lombard Enlightenment into the political and social context of Habsburg rule, I first seek to explain why political economy became the focus of the Milanese Enlightenment. In a second step I trace the development of a new language of political economy back to a debate about differing visions for economic development in Lombardy. Pietro Verri in particular, I argue, contributed important aspects to an emerging economic science. His approach, which deduced economic rules from a limited set of principles, is one of the major attempts at systematization prior to Adam Smith. Writing at the beginning of the 1770s, Verri emphasized savings and productive investment as the main engine of economic development. This was not only a significant development from his early economic writings, which had still accorded luxury a pivotal role in the running of the economy. It also marked an advance in the European debate about luxury by both addressing, and offering solutions to, its central concerns. By the 1760s the positive economic effects of luxury were commonly accepted, but making it the cornerstone of economic development raised the issue of its moral value—and here the debate had shown that the language used to discuss it was too ambiguous to lend itself to generalization. Verri recognized this and offered a way out of a European debate that had lost its force. He accepted luxury and rescued its public benefits, but he subordinated it to what made wealth grow: the accumulation of money and its productive investment driven by low interest rates.

I

The European Debate about Luxury

I

The Meaning of the Term 'Luxury': Shifts and Extensions

Nous voilà conduits à l'examen du Luxe . . .; l'objet de tant de vagues déclamations.

(J.-F. Melon, *Essai politique sur le commerce*, 1734)

When Jean-François Melon, author of one of the most important reflections on luxury in the eighteenth century, complained about the vagueness of the term, he addressed a common theme. Ever since antiquity, luxury had been a matter of dispute. In the Middle Ages, Christian thinkers elaborated on the range of meaning inherited from Greek and Roman usage. It was only in the eighteenth century, however, that entirely new definitions of 'luxury' began to be proposed. But this development added new meanings without ever quite replacing previous ones. To accept such an enlargement of the range of meaning was not to admit defeat. As subsequent chapters will show, the very vagueness of the term made luxury a most versatile tool in many different debates.

Luxury in Antiquity and the Middle Ages

For the Greek philosophers, 'luxury' (or the term *truphē*) had two meanings: soft and sumptuous living and effeminacy. Both these strands were to last well into the eighteenth century: luxury as related to the flesh (feasting, food) and luxury as rendering man effeminate, weak, and unfit for military action.[1]

Based on these connotations, both Plato and Aristotle rejected luxury. In the *Republic*, Socrates portrayed anarchy as the corollary of luxury because

[1] The following account draws on John Sekora, *Luxury: The Concept in Western Thought, Eden to Smollett* (Baltimore, 1977), 23–62, and Christopher J. Berry, *The Idea of Luxury: A Conceptual and Historical Investigation* (Cambridge, 1994), 45–98. The identification of luxury with effeminacy suggests an early association of luxury with women. Werner Sombart has made this association the built-in principle of his account of capitalism, which originated, he argued, in the luxury of women in court; Werner Sombart, *Luxus und Kapitalismus*, 2nd edn. (Munich, 1922; first edn. 1912).

he saw luxurious man as a creature of impulse and passion, unable to distinguish necessary from unnecessary desires. To prevent anarchy—and thus to hold luxury at bay—was the duty of the virtuous guardians to whose will the multitude must submit.

Aristotle elaborated Plato's arguments against luxury, necessity, and hierarchy. He established a distinction between necessity and virtue on the one hand, and luxury and vice on the other. This distinction, Aristotle argued, was an a priori component of nature. Plato and Aristotle's rejection of luxury gained acceptance, and it was the foundation of the Cynic, Sophist, and early Stoic philosophies, which regarded it as an impediment to self-sufficiency. But luxury was pervasive, they held, because the craving for fame, wealth, and possessions was part of human nature. Against Plato's association with hierarchy they argued that only independent conduct and reason could liberate man from the enslavement of luxury.

The Roman response to this legacy was to have the most long-lasting success. It focused on the political function of luxury by distinguishing between private and public luxury. Like most Roman moralists, Cicero continued the association—already present in Plato—of luxury, softness, and effeminacy. Indebted to Stoic arguments, he endorsed their demand for self-denial, sobriety, and simplicity to overcome the disastrous effects of luxury. But he differentiated between the private and the public realm: 'The Roman people loathe private luxury but they love public splendour.'[2] Luxury, for Romans, represented the use of wealth to serve private satisfaction. In its positive guise (as splendour), it furthered the glory of the commonwealth. Cicero furthermore established a conceptual link between luxury and the city which was to gain tremendous importance: 'The city creates luxury.'[3] As we shall see, the definition of luxury as 'the pleasures of the city' became common in Italy well into the eighteenth century.

Finally, Roman historians presented luxury as the cause for ruin, again a concept that was to prove durable. For Sallust, for example, luxury was the primary factor in the dissolution of the Roman republic. The pattern of Roman history as a whole, Sallust believed, was a constant line of degeneration into luxury and the subsequent loss of republican greatness. Rome was glorious while it was virtuous. With the destruction of Carthage came ambition, avarice, and pride, while justice, honesty, and industry fell into disrepute. From Sallust onwards, historians of Rome gave luxury a prominent role as the cause of republican decline.[4]

[2] Cicero, *Pro Murena*, trans. C. MacDonald (London, 1977), §76.

[3] Cicero, *Pro Roscio Amerino*, trans. John Henry Freese, 27, quoted by Sekora, *Luxury*, 35.

[4] D. C. Earl, *The Political Thought of Sallust* (Cambridge, 1961), 41–59.

This is the understanding of luxury that Christian thinkers inherited from antiquity. St Augustine most prominently embraced the classical attack upon luxury, and he more than anybody else kept alive the Platonic and Stoic condemnations. He endorsed the Greek understanding that luxury was pervasive because it was part of human nature. He even conceded that it was needed to run the *civitas terrena*, the worldly city as opposed to the City of God, and could no more be eliminated than could mortality.[5] But necessary though it may be for worldly success, luxury for Augustine (as well as for Christian theologians after him) signified disobedience to God as well as the love of a degraded world. As such it was still a sin, but it was pardonable by the Church. This is the Augustinian notion of the necessity of luxury to run society, which was to become one of the cornerstones of eighteenth-century debates about luxury. It was precisely this silent toleration of luxury that would later open the door for Bernard Mandeville's claim which outraged his contemporaries, namely that private vices procured public benefits.[6]

A Reassessment in Early Modern Times

The term *luxe*, which began to appear in French usage at the beginning of the seventeenth century, seems to have been less morally charged. In the dictionary of Nicot from 1606, for example, *luxe* was used as a synonym for *superfluidité*. The dictionary of Trevoux, published almost a century later, in 1704, explained the term as 'expenses superflues, somptuosité excessive, soit dans les habits, soit dans les meubles, soit dans la table'.[7] Nevertheless, luxury remained a pejorative term for much of the early eighteenth century. This was true for private luxury, but also for that of the state. The term retained its strong association with licentiousness, corruption, and political enfeeblement. Historical memory continued to associate it with political decline, notably that of the Roman republic.[8] But by the last quarter of the eighteenth century 'luxury' had acquired quite a different meaning, at least at the hands of some writers. As Adam Smith noted in his *Wealth of Nations*: 'Under necessaries therefore, I comprehend, not only

[5] On Augustine's *De Civitate Dei*, see Peter Brown, *Augustine of Hippo: A Biography* (London, 1967), 299–312.

[6] See below, Ch. 2.

[7] M. R. de Labriolle-Rutherford, 'L'Évolution de la notion du luxe depuis Mandeville jusqu'à la révolution', *Studies on Voltaire and the Eighteenth Century*, 26 (1963), 1025–36.

[8] E. J. Hundert, *The Enlightenment's Fable: Bernard Mandeville and the Discovery of Society* (Cambridge, 1994), 198.

those things which nature, but those things which the established rules of decency have rendered necessary to the lowest rank of people. All other things, I call luxuries; without meaning by this appellation, to throw the smallest degree of reproach upon the temperate use of them.'[9] For Smith, this is self-consciously not a moral assessment. The only concession to moral judgement in his definition is the word 'temperate', as Donald Winch has noted.[10] Similar attempts to ban moral considerations from the definition of luxury can be found in Italy in the second half of the century. Gaetano Filangieri from Naples, for example, offered a definition that was limited in scope and economically oriented. He spoke of luxury as 'nothing but the employment of one's wealth and industry in order to achieve a pleasant existence'.[11]

The transition from derogatory notions towards positive definitions with a strong emphasis on the economic effects of luxury took different courses across Europe. While the process was relatively clear-cut in northern Europe and France, Italy offered some resistance to the European attempts at redefinition: the term remained vague and ambiguous.

The Meaning of Luxury

The process of redefinition as well as the broader range of meaning that the term had acquired by the eighteenth century is best assessed through the explanations given in contemporary dictionaries. They provide the conventional range of meaning trickled down into common usage from previous rounds of *Gipfeltexte*—and against which intellectual innovation can be measured.

Dictionaries compiled by English, French, and German authors only began to abandon the old moral notions of luxury in the course of the eighteenth century. In the century before, not much had changed: seventeenth-century editions took over the same definitions they had given at the end of the sixteenth century and associated 'luxury' with superfluity, excess, and riot, as well as 'lust, lechery, or rankness'.[12] Equally long-lived was

[9] Adam Smith, *An Inquiry into the Nature and Causes of the Wealth of Nations* (1776), ed. R. H. Campbell and A. S. Skinner (Oxford, 1976; repr. Indianapolis, 1982), bk. v, ch. ii.k, para. 3.

[10] Donald Winch, *Riches and Poverty: An Intellectual History of Political Economy in Britain, 1750–1834* (Cambridge, 1996), 84 n. 74.

[11] Gaetano Filangieri, *La scienza della legislazione* (1780; rev. 1781), 3 vols. (Milan, 1822), 276.

[12] John Florio, *Vocabolario italiano & inglese / A Dictionary, Italian and English*, repr., rev., corr. (London, 1688), s.v. 'Lusso' and 'Lussuria'.

the Greek notion of luxury as rendering man effeminate and given to pleasures.[13]

Around the turn of the century we begin to encounter less judgemental accounts of luxury. To be sure, the negative connotations of excess and superfluous spending are still to be found, but the examples given turn the attention away from the effects of luxury on man, for example to less controversial subjects such as biology: the 'Vine, if not pruned, will run out and spend it self in fruitless luxury'.[14] While this example still has negative undertones, German dictionaries of the beginning of the eighteenth century were less concerned with moral judgement. For Matthias Kramer, who edited an Italian–German dictionary in 1724, *lusso* simply became 'a great abundance of food, drink, clothes and furniture'. Translating the expression *spender le entrate del Regno in lussi*, he chose the neutral 'to use' (*verwenden*) rather than the morally charged 'to waste' (*verschwenden*).[15] The identification of luxury with *lussuria*, lechery, begins to fade until it disappears from most dictionaries towards the end of the first half of the century.[16]

It is around this time that new effects of luxury come to the fore when the term is explained in dictionaries, and in the 1750s and 1760s French philosophical dictionaries begin to devote more and more attention to the economic nature of luxury. Two insights in particular are used to reassess the meaning of luxury. One builds on the needs of modern, commercial society, which were intricately linked to luxury. The 'spirit of commerce', we are told, introduces luxury on a grand scale. Luxury, in turn, enriches large states. Alongside the old notion of luxury as morally corrupting, thus, we begin to encounter a new assessment that presents luxury as economically enriching.[17] It would prove to be a durable coexistence.

The second insight is the link between luxury and the unequal distribution of wealth. For this line of argument, luxury is not reproachable as such (and the explicit reason seems to be that it is natural for man to spend what he has in order to make life more agreeable to him). It is, however, a telltale

[13] Antoine Furetiere, *Dictionnaire universel*, new, corr., and augm. edn. (The Hague, 1694), s.v. 'Luxe'.

[14] Guy Miege, *The Short French Dictionary, in Two Parts. I. English and French, II. French and English; According to the Present Use, and Modern Orthography*, 4th edn. (The Hague, 1699), s.v. 'Luxuriousness, or Luxury'.

[15] Matthia Kramer, *Neu ausgefertigtes Italienisch–Teutsches Sprach- und Wörterbuch* (Nuremberg, 1724).

[16] e.g. Niccolò Castelli, *Dizionario italiano–tedesco e tedesco–italiano*, 2 vols., new edn. (Leipzig, 1749), s.v. 'Lussuria', which is translated solely with *Geilheit* (lewdness).

[17] *Dizionario filosofico o sia introduzione alla cognizione dell'Uomo: traduzione dal francese* (Venice, 1756), s.v. 'Lusso' and 'Commercio'.

sign of the unequal distribution of wealth within society. Such inequality will plunge a large part of society into poverty while others prefer indulgence in luxury to cultivation of land. Hence, it is not luxury as such which needs to be remedied politically, but inequality, the condition that has given rise to it.[18] We encounter here for the first time in a dictionary of wide circulation an argument that was to become prominent in Italian treatises on political economy: the connection between luxury and the morally and economically reproachable unequal distribution of wealth within society.

If 'luxury' increasingly acquired new, economic layers of meaning in England, France, and Germany alike over the course of the eighteenth century, the Italians offered some resistance to this development. Even though well aware of the new meaning of the term (all the major dictionaries were in circulation in Italy), the Italians themselves became more and more cautious about giving too rigid a definition and assigning too specific a connotation to the term. In fact, the definitions offered by Italian authors of language dictionaries became standardized in the second half of the century and followed the definition given by the main authority on the correct use of Italian since the seventeenth century, the Accademia della Crusca.[19] Already in the edition of 1691 we find the definition of luxury as 'superfluity of food, clothes, or other'. This definition was not to change throughout the eighteenth century, or indeed throughout the nineteenth.

In Italian dictionaries of the eighteenth century luxury was thus identified with superfluity in respect to clothing, furniture, and food. Beyond the realm of spending on purchased goods, it came to denote a series of traits ranging from indulgence through pride to arrogance.[20] Sometimes the emphasis tended more towards excess and immoderation,[21] sometimes more towards innocent pleasure and decency,[22] but definitions in general acquired a striking similarity that left room to accommodate the various economic, moral, political, and social facets of the term that we have

[18] *Dizionario del cittadino, o sia ristretto storico, teorico e pratico del commercio . . . Tradotto dal Francese. Edizione novissima. Accresciuta di moltissimi articoli tralasciati nelle altre*, 2 vols. (1765; French original, Nice, 1762), vol. ii, s.v. 'Lusso'.

[19] The academy was founded in 1582; on its influence from the 16th to the 18th centuries, see Eric Cochrane, *Tradition and Enlightenment in the Tuscan Academies, 1690–1800* (Chicago, 1961).

[20] *Nuovo Dizionario italiano–tedesco e tedesco–italiano. Prima di Nic. di Castelli, ma ora esattamente corretto, ed a detta de' Dizionari dell'Accademia della Crusca, e del Signor Abate Franceso de Alberti di Villanuova* (Leipzig, 1782), s.v. 'Lusso'.

[21] Francesco Alberti di Villanuova, *Dizionario compendioso italiano–francese* (Venice, 1774), and his *Nouveau Dictionnaire françois–italien* (Bassano, 1796), s.v. 'Luxe'.

[22] Giuseppe Baretti, *Dizionario inglese–italiano ed italiano–inglese* (Florence, 1816), s.v. 'Lusso' and 'Luxury'.

encountered so far. It is precisely this reluctance to convey a strict and partial judgement of luxury—be it moral or economic—that is characteristic of the Italian approach. Instead, they left as many loose ends as possible in order to accommodate the sense that most fitted the particular intellectual endeavour in which the term was to be employed.

The possible uses of the term 'luxury', its relative vagueness together with a growing convergence of definitions, set the backdrop to the efforts of Italian thinkers to understand the nature of luxury and its realms of influence in the eighteenth century. We should not condemn this apparent conceptual chaos too quickly. When Italian political economists complained that the concept of luxury was too vague to lend itself to easy definition, this must not be taken at face value. The term could indeed express a broad range of meaning. But to keep this range as wide as possible was in the interest of the very authors who polemicized about it. Luxury was not an umbrella term. But it was nevertheless remarkably flexible and could be used both in defence of Christian notions of the good life and in support of theories about the economic value of consumption.

This is what common usage took luxury to mean: a concept more and more appertaining to the economic realm in northern Europe, and a more flexible, ambiguous approach in Italy which left room for old Christian as well as new economic considerations alike. The remainder of this book will be concerned with analysing how this conceptual change could come about, and why the understanding of luxury developed in such different ways in Italy from those in other parts of Europe.

2

Enlightenment Views of Luxury

What's virtue but vice grown fashionable?

(Molière, *Don Juan*)

The ancient legacy of hostility to luxury and the equally critical Christian views endured well into the eighteenth century. In fact, even the German luxury debate at the turn of the twentieth century relied heavily on moralistic notions of luxury which had been developed in antiquity and the Middle Ages.[1] But the first decades of the eighteenth century witnessed a reassessment of luxury which was to channel the luxury debate into an entirely new direction. Like wildfire, the attack on the ancient and Christian traditions spread across Europe. The first spark had been struck in England.

Bernard Mandeville and the English Paradox

Bernard Mandeville, a Dutch physician who had emigrated to England in the 1690s, made his writing debut in English in 1703 with *Some Fables after the Easie and Familiar Method of Monsieur de la Fontaine*. Two years later, and again anonymously, he published *Grumbling Hive, or, Knaves Turne'd Honest*. He later transformed his *Grumbling Hive* into a small book by adding a preface, 'An Enquiry in to the Origin of Moral Virtue', as well as prose remarks which explained and illuminated the meaning of his original verse. The title of his book was *The Fable of the Bees* and it was to become known as a scandalous book. It was not until 1723, however, that Mandeville became a national celebrity after the publication of an enlarged version of his *Fable*. He had added two essays, 'A Search into the Nature of Society' and 'An Essay on Charity and Charity-Schools', and expanded the apparatus of commentary. The work was heavily attacked by the Middlesex grand jury, which claimed that *The Fable* was designed 'to run down Religion and Virtue as prejudicial to Society, and detrimental to the State; and to

[1] Warren G. Breckman, 'Disciplining Consumption: The Debate about Luxury in Wilhelmine Germany, 1890–1914', *Journal of Social History*, 24 (1991), 485–505.

recommend Luxury, Avarice, Pride, and all vices, as being necessary to Public Welfare, and not tending to the Destruction of the Constitution'.[2] What was it that infuriated the members of the jury? Had Mandeville indeed tried to run down religion and virtue as prejudicial to society?

Mandeville's concern was the functioning of modern commercial society. In satirical response to the Society for the Reformation of Manners, and more specifically to Shaftesbury's assumption that man was by nature sociable and benevolent, Mandeville claimed instead that man was driven by passions (in particular that of enriching himself) and that the secret of prospering states lay in the self-regarding interests of their citizens, which he held to have beneficial effects for society at large. His central claim is introduced in the subtitle of the *Fable: Private Vices, Publick Benefits.* What he argued was that vices were necessary for the wealth and well-being of a society. Vices, which Mandeville defined as the indulgence in natural passions, were in fact features of a prosperous and powerful state. Thus, it was counterproductive and hypocritical to demand that a society must live in complete virtue. This, according to Mandeville, would only lead to poverty and unhappiness. Or, as he put it in the moral to his *Fable*,

> Then leave complaints: Fools only strive
> To make a Great an Honest Hive
> T' enjoy the World's Conveniencies,
> Be fame'd in War, yet live in Ease,
> Without great vices is a vain
> EUTOPIA seated in the Brain.[3]

Not surprisingly, such a theory of the necessity of vices met with outrage among Mandeville's readers.[4] In fact, England experienced a widespread and widely accepted denunciation of vice, a fear of luxury and corruption, and an ideology of public and private virtue between the reign of William and Mary and that of George I and beyond. This ideology extended across the political spectrum from Whigs to Tories and was given institutional support by the Society for the Reformation of Manners.[5] The movement was embodied by *The Tatler*, published between 1709 and 1711 by Richard Steele.

[2] Quoted by E. J. Hundert, *The Enlightenment's Fable: Bernard Mandeville and the Discovery of Society* (Cambridge, 1994), 8.

[3] Bernard Mandeville, *The Fable of the Bees, or, Private Vices, Public Benefits*, ed. F. B. Kaye, 2 vols. (Indianapolis, 1988), i. 36.

[4] A useful collection of critical reactions to the *Fable* has been assembled by J. Martin Stafford (ed.), *Private Vices, Public Benefits? The Contemporary Reception of Bernard Mandeville* (Solihull, 1997).

[5] See Maurice M. Goldsmith, *Private Vices, Public Benefits: Bernard Mandeville's Social and Political Thought* (Cambridge, 1985), 21–7.

Contrary to what contemporaries—and even some scholars today—thought, it had never been Mandeville's intention to justify vices morally. In fact, he was at pains to point out that

> When I assert, that Vices are inseparable from great and potent Societies, and that it is impossible their Wealth and Grandeur should subsist without, I do not say that the particular Members of them who are guilty of any should not be continually reprov'd, or not be punish'd for them when they grow into Crimes.[6]

Equally, Mandeville had no doubt that true happiness was only to be found in simple societies.

> [If] I should be ask'd where I thought it was most probable that Men might enjoy true Happiness, I would prefer a small peaceable Society, in which Men, neither envy'd nor esteem'd by Neighbours, should be contented to live upon the Natural Product of the Spot they inhabit, to a vast Multitude abounding in Wealth and Power, . . . and debauching themselves by Foreign Luxury at Home.[7]

If, however, one wanted to enjoy the pleasures brought by modern commercial society, it was hypocritical to expect that refinement and polished manners could be had at no cost. Shaftesbury, against whom Mandeville's argument was directed, had recognized rather than denied the importance of self-interest, especially of the passion for wealth. But, Shaftesbury continued, 'if it grows at length into a real passion, the injury and mischief it does the public is not greater than that which it creates to the person himself'.[8] To this Mandeville retorted that 'To be at once well-bred and sincere, is no less than a Contradiction: and therefore while Man advances in Knowledge, and his Manners are polish'd, we must expect to see at the same time his Desires enlarg'd, his Appetites refin'd, and his Vices increas'd.'[9]

But vices were not only inevitable in modern society. Mandeville went as far as to argue (and this was possibly his most outrageous claim and the one that fuelled the angry response of the grand jury) that moral standards themselves were a social construct.[10] Passions, Mandeville claimed, were natural; vices were the result of the definition of what was virtuous and what was vicious by 'Lawgivers and other wise Men'. He determined (and later thinkers ultimately accepted) that virtue be understood as restraint of the passions, and vice as their indulgence. The 'skilful Politicians' decided

[6] Mandeville, *Fable*, vol. i, Preface, p. 10.

[7] Ibid. 12–13.

[8] Shaftesbury, 'An Inquiry Concerning Virtue and Merit', quoted by Hundert, *The Enlightenment's Fable*, 189.

[9] Mandeville, *Fable*, vol. i, Remark Q, p. 185.

[10] Ibid., 'A Search into the Nature of Society', 330. On the social construction of both human desires and moral standards, see Goldsmith, *Private Vices, Public Benefits*, 142–4.

(and the rest agreed) 'to call every thing, which . . . Man should commit to gratify his Appetites, VICE . . . And to give the Name of VIRTUE to every Performance, by which Man, contrary to the impulse of Nature, should endeavour . . . the Conquest of his own Passions'.[11] In short, 'the Moral Virtues are the Political Offspring which Flattery begot upon Pride' because the skilful politicians had succeeded in convincing man that it was honourable and praiseworthy to restrict his passions.[12] By this simple proposition Mandeville in effect established that the terms in which human behaviour was to be understood were Epicurean–Augustinian (the passions as a vital part of human and societal life), while morality was characterized in Stoic terms. Not surprisingly, he then had no difficulty in exposing the hypocrisy of every normal person, whose natural passions ensured that he or she would fail to live up to the values they professed.

If pride acted as the main incentive for moral behaviour, a similar mechanism was at work in the economic world. In order to achieve opulence, Mandeville argued, the state had to provide an incentive to render prosperity possible. Starting from the assumption that 'Man never exerts himself but when he is rous'd by his Desires,' Mandeville urged the 'dextrous . . . Politician' to 'touch their Passions. Divide the Land . . . Teach them Trades and Handicrafts, and you'll bring Envy and Emulation among them.'[13] The keys to success in the realm of economics, then, were envy and emulation. Fuelling those two was pride, the principal vice that had publicly beneficial consequences. In a truly virtuous age, Mandeville was sure, there would be no pride. But commerce would be crippled accordingly because 'for the Support of Trade there can be nothing equivalent to Pride'. Since man is naturally proud of his appearance, and particularly so among people he does not know, he wants to 'wear clothes above his Rank, especially in large and populous Cities'. Man's (and perhaps even more so woman's) innate desire to emulate thus set in motion an economic chain reaction. The wife of the retailer, Mandeville knew, would soon want to dress like the wife of the wholesale merchant. She, in turn, would look to the court for inspiration. The women at court, finally, unwilling to bear 'the Impudence of the City', would call for new fashion as soon as their dress was being imitated. It 'is this, or at least the consequence of it, that sets the Poor to Work' and adds 'Spurs to Industry'.[14]

11 Mandeville, *Fable*, vol. i, 'An Enquiry into the Origin of Moral Virtue', 41–57, and the quotations on pp. 42 and 47–8. On the origin of vice, see Hundert, *The Enlightenment's Fable*, 89–92.

12 Mandeville, *Fable*, vol. i, 'An Enquiry into the Origin of Moral Virtue', 51.

13 Ibid., Remark Q, p. 184.

14 Ibid., Remark M, pp. 124–30.

Underlying this argument is the conviction that a person's identity in modern society depended on the acquisition of goods.[15] E. J. Hundert has rightly cautioned us not to exaggerate the economic implications of Mandeville's thesis, and has pointed out that the majority of contemporary readers never saw the *Fable* as a work whose significance derived primarily from its economic doctrine.[16] It would be mistaken, however, to ignore the economic dimension of Mandeville's thought by simply characterizing it as partly conventional and partly 'confused, uninformed or simply unimaginative'.[17] In fact, Mandeville had raised the issue of the economic nature of consumption by placing the latter at the centre of his account of the creation of personal identity. Equally, he raised the issue of the economic nature of luxury by justifying it socially. The fact that he failed to answer satisfactorily the economic questions he raised partly explains, I think, why later authors—and the Italians in particular—quarrelled with him and sought to make economic sense of his paradox.

Consumption undoubtedly played a key role in Mandeville's understanding of the workings of a prosperous economy. What is less clear is the extent to which he believed consumption, rather than export, to be the main force behind economic growth. After having taken an anti-mercantilist stance against those who believed a nation would prosper from a cut in imports and an extension of exports by justifying high levels of imports for internal consumption, Mandeville returned to a staunchly mercantilist position in his assessment of the importance of a positive balance of trade. In fact, the 'Good Politician' had to be sure to 'keep a watchful Eye over the Balance of Trade'. As long as that was the case, 'no Nation can ever be impoverished by Foreign Luxury'.[18] Moreover, in order to make sure that private vices translated into public benefit, politicians had to keep wages low, which, by implication, was to argue that mass consumption was insignificant. Echoing views that had come to be criticized even before the *Fable* was published, Mandeville was convinced that the labour force did not need higher purchasing power because their contribution to economic growth through consumption could be neglected. Rather, wages needed to be low in order to provide an incentive for the labourer, for 'When Men shew such an extraordinary proclivity to Idleness and Pleasure, what reason have we to think that they would ever work, unless they are oblig'd to it by immediate Necessity'?[19]

[15] John Brewer and Roy Porter (eds.), *Consumption and the World of Goods* (London, 1993), esp. the editors' introd., pp. 1–15.

[16] Hundert, *The Enlightenment's Fable*, 186.

[17] Ibid. 187.

[18] Mandeville, *Fable*, vol. i, Remark L, pp. 109–11 and 115–16.

[19] Ibid., Remark Q, p. 192. On the pre-Mandevillean criticism of the low-wage theories,

The role of the poor in Mandeville's economic edifice is highly ambiguous. On the one hand, everybody should participate in the economic consequences of pride and emulation—even 'the poorest Labourer's Wife'. On the other hand, it is only the state at large that benefits from such behaviour. For the individual, and in particular for the poor, the effects can be disastrous, and the labourer's wife 'will half starve herself and her Husband to purchase a second-hand Gown and Petticoat, that cannot do her half the Service'.[20] There is no attempt to alleviate the plight of the poor in Mandeville's conclusion that it is 'in the interest of all rich Nations' to keep the majority poor and see to it that they 'continually spend what they get'.[21] The exploitation of the poor (which Mandeville may have overplayed in a polemical response to the Society for the Reformation of Manners) also serves another purpose. Even if hyper-consumption caused effeminacy, as Mandeville was prepared to admit, this would affect only a small part of the population. The 'working slaving People' would always be aplenty to till the ground and be recruited to the army.[22]

It is clear, then, that Mandeville was thinking of the conspicuous consumption only of a moneyed elite and the urban middling rank when he praised the public benefits of consumption and luxury. His view of man as a consuming animal was thus applied to those who had the means to satisfy their boundless appetites, follow fashion, and seek social advance through luxury spending. If luxury is all that which men acquire to satisfy their infinite desires, then it is a relative concept. In fact, luxury is all that which 'is not immediately necessary to make Man subsist', and what is necessary differs among people.[23]

Mandeville made essentially two claims about luxury, namely that luxury and wealth as well as luxury and social progress were inseparable. Both these claims rested on his observation that if we 'look back on old Greece, the Roman Empire, or the great Eastern Nations that flourish'd before them . . . we shall find, that Luxury and Politeness ever grew up together, and were never enjoy'd asunder'.[24] The first claim was directed against

see Charles Wilson, 'The Other Face of Mercantilism', in D. C. Coleman (ed.), *Revisions in Mercantilism* (London, 1969), 118–39. From the middle of the 18th century the better understanding of the relationship between high wages, worker motivation, and prosperity made the low-wage theory appear increasingly out of date; cf. E. J. Hundert, 'The Achievement Motive in Hume's Political Economy', *Journal of the History of Ideas*, 35 (1974), 139–43.

[20] Mandeville, *Fable*, vol. i, Remark M, p. 129.

[21] Ibid., Remark Q, pp. 193–4.

[22] Ibid., Remark L, pp. 119–20.

[23] Ibid. 107–8. See Hundert, *The Enlightenment's Fable*, 197–205, on this and the following paragraphs.

[24] Mandeville, *Fable*, vol. ii, 'The Third Dialogue', p. 147.

moralizing writers such as Shaftesbury who claimed that polished habits and refinement went hand in hand with material growth. Rather than contradicting this claim, Mandeville drew attention to the fact that material growth in opulent societies was driven by excess rather than moderation, and that what appeared to be refinement was in reality carefully concealed extravagance. It was not refinement, then, that great societies rested upon, but 'the Variety of our Wants', and luxury and avarice are portrayed as the 'inseparable Companions' to great wealth.[25]

Following from this was Mandeville's second claim, namely that conspicuous consumption should be seen as the direct consequence of social progress. Not only was luxury historically linked to opulence, it was also necessary to guarantee a state's future prosperity. In fact, the social dynamics of luxury provide the most startling example of public benefits to be derived from private vice. While it is clear to Mandeville that 'the fewer Desires a Man has and the less he covets, the more easy he is to himself', it is equally obvious that the state at large could only profit from the aggregate gain incurred by luxury consumption.[26] It is from this standpoint that Mandeville set out to refute the 'receiv'd Notion that Luxury is as destructive to the Wealth of the whole Body Politic, as it is to that of every individual Person who is guilty of it'.[27] Economically, luxury was necessary because it kept the poor in work and provided an incentive for individuals. For the rich, the incentive function could be so effective as to lead to even further prosperity despite increased spending on luxuries. For the poor, conspicuous consumption almost invariably led to ruin. The luxury spending of both groups, however, could result in continued prosperity for the state as a whole. If, Mandeville argued, England was to cut back on luxury imports (his examples were 'Silk, Mohair, Drugs, etc.' from Turkey) while keeping exports constant, this would in the short term lead to gains due to a more positive balance of trade. In the long run, however, Turkey would no longer be able to afford English products because the income from their luxury exports would fall away. Other countries would fill the gap and take over trade with Turkey, England's export market would break away in turn, and continued prosperity would be jeopardized.[28] No matter what effects conspicuous consumption had on individuals, the state as a whole could not do without it.

[25] Mandeville, *Fable*, vol. ii, 'The Sixth Dialogue', p. 349, and vol. i, Remark Q, p. 185.
[26] Ibid., vol. i, 'A Search into the Nature of Society', p. 355.
[27] Ibid., Remark L, p. 108.
[28] Ibid. 108–15.

The English Paradox on its Way to the Continent: Melon and Voltaire

A French translation of the *Fable of the Bees* appeared in 1740. But the paradox discovered by Mandeville had already been made known to a French audience through Jean-François Melon. A native of Bordeaux, who began his career as a member of the Conseil des Finances in the early Regency in France before becoming secretary to the regent himself, Melon had written his *Essai politique sur le commerce* in 1734.[29] In that work, revised and extended in 1736, he endorsed the views expressed by Mandeville without however explicitly mentioning his source. But Melon's treatment of luxury was more than just an 'enthusiastic summary' of Mandeville's.[30] Whereas Mandeville had made moral claims about communally beneficial hypocrisy in modern commercial society, and had deduced from it the positive economic consequences of private vices and the intimate relationship between luxury, avarice, and great wealth, the Frenchman had no such moral concerns. His treatise in favour of luxury is an unabated defence of the economic role of luxury, which hardly pays any attention to the moral dimension of the issue.

Melon took many of Mandeville's arguments for granted, for example, the claim that it is the passions that govern good behaviour. However, whereas Mandeville had assumed that selfish motives induced a whole range of behaviour, Melon argued that the only dominating and controlling passion was self-interest: 'It is only ambition that makes the soldier brave, and only greed which makes the merchant work.' For Melon it followed that declarations against luxury were futile, for if man were governed by religious faith and purely humanitarian motives, he would no longer need laws. 'But unfortunately the passions are in command and the legislator must try to make them useful for the community.' And luxury, this 'extraordinary sumptuousness which furnishes a government with wealth and security', was an inextricable part of society which had to be accepted.[31] If the legislator decided to banish it, the society would lead a free but also a 'wild life' with 'fierce manners' reminiscent of the American Indians.[32]

[29] Jean-François Melon, *Essai politique sur le commerce* (repr. Amsterdam, 1735; first edn. Bordeaux, 1734). On his treatment of luxury, see Ellen Ross, 'Mandeville, Melon and Voltaire: The Origins of the Luxury Controversy in France', *Studies on Voltaire and the Eighteenth Century*, 155 (1976), 1897–1912.

[30] Characterized as such by Hundert, *The Enlightenment's Fable*, 105.

[31] Melon, *Essai politique*, 121–2.

[32] Ibid. 137–8, where Melon quotes the abbé de Vertot approvingly. Cf. R. A. de Vertot, *Établissement des lois somptuaires en France* (1720), in Vertot, *Œuvres choisies* (Paris, 1819), v. 331–48: 332–3.

For Melon, the tasks of the moralist and the legislator were different. He saw government as the promoter of national wealth and not of virtue. This was not, of course, out of line with Mandeville's reasoning, but it is significant that Melon dropped Mandeville's insistence that luxury was still a vice. It is clear, then, that Melon was much less troubled by the moral paradox than its discoverer had been. Rather, following up the implications of Mandeville's claims, he tried to provide what Mandeville had been weakest at: an account of the economic function of luxury production and consumption. The dual argument he presented was that the availability of luxury goods acted as an incentive to work (the 'incentive argument') and that luxury spending secured the circulation of money (the 'circulation argument').

In a modern state, Melon argued, luxury was necessary because it provided work. If agriculture, defence, and industry are catered for, 'it is useful that the surplus work force is being employed in the luxury trades, because what is left is either this, or idleness'. For those in work, luxury was equally necessary because it served as an incentive to acquire wealth to be spent on conspicuous consumption. Furthermore, and again taking up a theme developed by Mandeville, man will comply much more eagerly with his duties in society, 'the more he is exposed to the regards of envy'.[33]

Next to its function as an incentive, luxury was economically necessary because it accelerated the circulation of money. Mandeville had argued that capital accumulation for the labouring classes was counterproductive to economic development and all income should rather be channelled into consumption.[34] Melon took up this line of argument and extended it to the rich. As Law's secretary, Melon had a clear understanding of the economic value of investment but not of parsimony (a conceptual shift that was to be achieved by Pietro Verri and Adam Smith's stress on savings and capital accumulation), and thus proposed consumption as the surest means of circulation, for if the rich man's money remains 'in his coffers, it will be dead for society'.[35]

Melon's praise of the economic value of luxury, however, should not distract us from the emphasis, often overlooked, which he placed on the primary sector and, as a consequence, on the role of mass consumption for economic development. From the outset he had portrayed the luxury trades as necessary additions to the economy in order to employ excess labour. He later reiterated his conviction when he cautioned that workers

[33] Melon, *Essai politique*, 124 and 126–7.

[34] Mandeville, *Fable*, vol. i, Remark Q, pp. 194–6.

[35] Melon, *Essai politique*, 141.

would not be employed in the luxury trades 'unless there is a sufficient quantity of goods of second necessity; and equally, they will not be employed unless the first necessities are satisfied'. The reason for this is simple but important. The market for luxury goods is restricted and 'the country-dweller does not buy wine or tobacco unless his more pressing needs are satisfied'. The significance of this passage should not be underestimated. Mandeville had been so interested in conspicuous consumption because he believed that the contribution of the poor to economic growth could be neglected. Melon accorded them a much more prominent place. Not only were country-dwellers potential consumers of luxury goods (a fact Mandeville had accepted, but only to draw attention to the ruinous consequences of such consumption). But their consumption of necessary goods could only be neglected at the peril of the economy at large. Their consumption was the necessary basis for the development of a market for more refined products. For the first time, then, mass consumption becomes an important if not the determining factor of economic growth. And because mass consumption was best served through agricultural produce, Melon emphasized the priority of the agricultural sector.[36] That the predominance of the countryside was central to Melon is manifest in the second edition of his *Essai politique*, where he added a chapter in which he described the French economy as predominantly agricultural. It was necessary for France to uphold an 'internal balance' between the capital city and the countryside, in which the latter only rendered the luxury of the former possible, and both were dependent upon each other for mutual benefit.[37]

By drawing attention to the role of internal and mass consumption and by urging the capital cities to sustain, rather than undermine, the countryside, Melon thus distanced himself considerably from Mandeville's enthusiastic defence of capital cities, and of London in particular. It is an exaggeration to claim that Melon gave birth to an economic science in France.[38] However, Melon clearly did much to introduce the concept of luxury into economic discussion. Furthermore, by focusing on the economic implications of luxury and by stressing the importance of the primary sector, Melon performed a task that was to prove vital for subsequent discussions of luxury in Italy. His treatment helped Italian thinkers to insert luxury and its economic consequences into the picture of their own agricultural economy.

[36] Ibid. 138–9.

[37] Jean-François Melon, *Essai politique sur le commerce*, 2nd edn. (Amsterdam, 1736), ch. 22.

[38] M. R. de Labriolle-Rutherford, 'L'Évolution de la notion du luxe depuis Mandeville jusqu'à la révolution', *Studies on Voltaire and the Eighteenth Century*, 26 (1963), 1027.

In subsequent French discussions of luxury, its economic dimension initially receded into the background. Voltaire, for example, even though inspired in his treatments of luxury by both Mandeville and Melon, was mainly interested in the cultural benefits brought by luxury. Nevertheless, his witty verses did much to publicize the case in favour of luxury. In 1736 he composed his poem *Le Mondain*, supplemented in 1737 with his *Défense du Mondain, ou, L'Apologie du luxe*.[39] Voltaire spent no time considering either the moral or at first the economic consequences of luxury.[40] Rather, he sang the Epicurean praise of the light, elegant, and happy life by depicting a pleasurable day in the life of an *honnête homme* in one of Europe's capitals. 'I love luxury,' Voltaire exclaims, before moving on to expose the true reason behind Roman frugality, namely the absence of wealth. Do you admire the ancients, he asked rhetorically? They lacked industry and ease. But was this really a virtue? No, 'it was mere ignorance', for 'which idiot would have slept outside if he could have had a nice and comfortable bed'. Mocking both Christian asceticism and the assumed virtue of the ancients, which in effect masked misery, he described the ancients as 'sadly virtuous' and maintained that 'the earthly paradise is where I am' (namely Paris with its refined life full of luxury).[41]

Voltaire's *Le Mondain* was not simply 'the *Essai politique* in verse' as André Morize has claimed.[42] His aim to expose ancient frugality and to contrast it with his unabashed defence of an Epicurean life was quite different from Melon's economic arguments. Melon himself was quick to point this out. In a letter to the comtesse de Verrue, he acknowledged having read the 'ingenious' apology of luxury which contained 'an excellent lesson of politics presented in an agreeable guise'. But then he immediately shifted attention to his own work and to the economic benefits of luxury (mainly that it created employment), which, it must be deduced, he found underdeveloped in Voltaire's poem. He also cautioned against an unqualified defence of luxury. France, 'as it is the nation in Europe which has most money at present, needs luxury', whereas the Swiss had been well advised to introduce sumptuary laws because 'it must not be that the poor live like the rich'. In the case of Holland, he reiterated Mandeville's argument that

[39] André Morize, *L'Apologie du luxe au XVIIIe siècle et 'Le Mondain' de Voltaire* (Paris, 1909), 7–17, on the publishing history.

[40] *Pace* Hubert C. Johnson, who sees mainly the economic aspect of Voltaire's defence of luxury; 'Spartan Simplicity versus Decadent Luxury', *Proceedings of the Annual Meeting of the Western Society for French History*, 19 (1992), 149–57, esp. pp. 152–6.

[41] François M. Arouet de Voltaire, *Le Mondain*, in Morize, *L'Apologie*, 133–9.

[42] Morize, *L'Apologie*, 30.

Amsterdam had needed extreme frugality in order to succeed in building the Dutch commercial empire.[43]

Nevertheless, Voltaire was deeply indebted to Melon. He himself acknowledged the *Essai politique* as 'the work of a man of spirit, of a citoyen, of a philosopher' and asserted that, Colbert apart, no one in France would have been able to write such a work.[44] And in fact, when Voltaire looked more closely at the moral and economic implications of his previous praise of luxury in the *Défense du Mondain*, he adopted much of Melon's argument.[45] As he explained to Frederick, crown prince of Prussia, when he sent him a copy of the *Défense*, he had written 'a small essay in worldly morality (*morale mondaine*), in which I seek to prove with some humour that luxury, magnificence . . . all the fine arts, all that makes up the splendour of a state also creates its wealth'.[46] The mechanism which transformed luxury spending into public benefits was fuelled by the two passions Melon put at the centre of his analysis of human nature: ambition and greed. In Voltaire's words, 'the rich are born to dispense much, the poor are made to amass much'.[47]

LUXURY AND THE POLITY: MONTESQUIEU'S *DE L'ESPRIT DES LOIS*

With Voltaire's contribution at the latest, the luxury debate had moved to the centre of French intellectual life. While Melon's economic considerations found an increasing number of followers, it was Montesquieu who lifted the discussion about luxury onto a new plane by introducing political-constitutional arguments.[48] In his *De l'esprit des lois* (1748) he set out to consider the social and political implications of commercial society. He did so through a consideration of luxury and its relationship to different forms of government.[49]

[43] Letter, 1736, in *Œuvres complètes de Voltaire*, v (Paris, 1877), letter x, p. 89.

[44] Voltaire, *Observations sur MM. Jean Lass, Melon et Dutot sur le commerce, le luxe, les monnaies, et les impôts* (1738), in *Œuvres complètes de Voltaire* (Paris, 1879), xxii. 359–70: 360.

[45] Voltaire, *Défense du Mondain, ou, L'Apologie du luxe*, in Morize, *L'Apologie*, 153–8.

[46] Letter, Jan. 1737, in *Voltaire's Correspondence*, ed. Theodore Besterman, 98 vols. (Geneva, 1953–64), vi. 14.

[47] Voltaire, *Défense du Mondain*, 155. Voltaire remained faithful to his view of the economic principles underlying luxury consumption which he had found in Melon. It remained virtually unchanged when he later returned to the subject. See e.g. the entry 'Luxe', in his *Dictionnaire philosophique*, ii, in *The Complete Works of Voltaire*, xxxvi (Oxford, 1994), 324–9.

[48] For an early *economic* account of luxury, see Montesquieu, *Lettres persanes* (1721), ed. Paul Vernière (Paris, 1960), letter CVI, pp. 220–3.

[49] I owe much to Istvan Hont's account of this development, which he presented as a working paper at the Warwick Eighteenth Century Centre Reading Group, 16 Mar. 1999.

Montesquieu's treatment of luxury builds on the moral assertion that luxury was related to inequality. In fact, 'luxury is always proportionate to the inequality of fortunes'.[50] Similarly, there is a link between the inequality of fortunes and different forms of government. In a monarchy (the form of government Montesquieu had primarily set out to defend) 'the idea of equality does not even occur' and the system is based on luxury and inequality.[51] This connection is nourished and kept alive by the reward system in monarchical states which procures wealth. Wealth, in turn, leads to ever increasing desires and the development of luxury.

Incidentally, the foundation of monarchies upon inequality had positive *economic* effects because luxury spending returned some of the unequally distributed wealth to the poor. The nobility itself, however, should not take an active role in this economic process because 'it is against the spirit of commerce for nobles to engage in it in a monarchy'.[52]

In a republic things were quite different because republics were founded on equality and frugality. A republic 'under the reign of virtue' depended on the ban of wealth and hence had no role for commerce and no prospect of economic growth and prosperity.[53] Montesquieu's republic thus knew no luxury. The exception to this rule was England. The English example showed that luxury could exist in republics, but that it had to be bought by political concessions and by allowing the nobility to engage in trade. England, for Montesquieu, needed to be considered a republic because the nobility engaged in commerce. In fact, the 'usage that permitted commerce to the nobility in England [was] one of the things that most contributed to weakening monarchical government there'.[54] But contrary to Montesquieu's argument that a republic was based on equality and thus had no place for conspicuous consumption, England was a republic with luxury, a fact that had been sufficiently celebrated by Mandeville. Montesquieu's explanation was that England was the only country that had ever prioritized commercial over political interests.[55] It had paid the price of political decline for a life of luxury. The nobility had lost its function as 'the essence of the monarchy'; they had lost their identity when they had begun to trade.[56] But through the nobility's moderating influence in trade, English luxury proved durable and solid.

[50] Montesquieu, *De l'esprit des lois*, ed. Victor Goldschmidt, 2 vols. (Paris, 1979), bk. VII, ch. i, p. 225. Henceforth, I cite book, chapter, and page reference. Bks. I to XIX are contained in vol. i, bks. XX to XXXI in vol. ii.

[51] Ibid. V. iv, p. 169; V. iv, p. 228; and V. xviii, p. 194.

[52] Ibid. VII. iv, pp. 228–9; the quotation in XX. xxi, p. 22.

[53] Ibid. V. iv, p. 169, and V. xviii, p. 194.

[54] Ibid. XX. xxi, p. 22.

[55] Ibid. XX. vii, p. 14.

[56] Ibid. II. iv, p. 139.

Montesquieu's political approach was clearly known to Italian thinkers.[57] Sometimes they explicitly turned to his arguments to analyse specific issues such as the relationship between nobility and commerce.[58] But different priorities and different intellectual traditions would see to it that Montesquieu's influential lead in the luxury debate was nevertheless rejected by Italian political economists and the Lombards in particular.

The Pendulum Swings Back: Rousseau and the French Critique of Luxury

After the elaborate defences of luxury in the fields of moral, social, economic, and political thought, the task of arguing against what looked set to become a new hegemony fell to Jean-Jacques Rousseau. He reconsidered the moral and social dimensions of luxury, and his critique of modern society and its emphasis on commerce and money was to gain tremendous importance in the European luxury debate. In Italy in particular his thoughts were to be used as a moralist weapon against purely utilitarian arguments in favour of luxury. But before this could happen, Rousseau first had to channel the French discussion into a new direction.[59]

Rousseau first argued about the decline of civilization in 1749 in the prizewinning *Discourse on the Arts and Sciences*, which examined the moral impact of the arts on mankind. Rousseau accepted the Mandevillean dictum that the arts and sciences were born out of vice. But, he cautioned, 'we should be less doubtful of their advantages, if they had sprung from our virtues'.[60] Equally, he acknowledged that the arts and sciences owed their

[57] Christof Dipper, *Politischer Reformismus und begrifflicher Wandel. Eine Untersuchung des historisch-politischen Wortschatzes der Mailänder Aufklärung (1764–1796)* (Tübingen, 1976), 242–5.

[58] Alessandro Verri, 'Alcune riflessioni sulla opinione che il commercio deroghi alla nobiltà', in *Il Caffè, 1764–1766*, ed. Gianni Francioni and Sergio Romagnoli, 2nd edn. (Turin, 1998), i. 256–74.

[59] Of little help in understanding Rousseau's attitude to luxury is the social historical study by Renato Galliani, *Rousseau, le luxe et l'idéologie nobiliaire: Étude socio-historique* (Oxford, 1989). In the context of Italian historiography, Carlo Borghero has drawn attention to the political nature of Rousseau's critique of luxury, which was directed against social inequality, whereas Silvia Hemmeler Benini has presented her contribution as part of a larger moral and pedagogical project aimed at forming the 'virtuous citizen'. Carlo Borghero, 'La polemica sul lusso nella formazione del pensiero politico di J.-J. Rousseau (1750–1753)', *Annali delle Facoltà di Lettere e Filosofia e Magistero dell'Università di Cagliari*, 32 (1969), 1–38; Silvia Hemmeler Benini, 'Ancora su Rousseau e il lusso', *Storia e Politica*, 16 (1977), 1–43.

[60] Jean-Jacques Rousseau, *A Discourse Which Won the Prize at the Academy of Dijon in 1750, on this Question Proposed by the Academy: Has the Restoration of the Arts and Sciences had*

existence to luxury. Implicitly conceding Montesquieu's argument, he was also prepared to admit that luxury, in turn, was the result of vanity. But this did not mean that luxury guaranteed the splendour of a state, as had been argued by Mandeville and Melon, because the 'rectitude of morals is essential to the duration of empires, and . . . luxury is diametrically opposed to such rectitude'.[61]

The force of his argument (which at first sight appears to be little more than a restatement of the ancient emphasis on virtue and frugality) lies in the fact that Rousseau drew attention to what he viewed as the devastating *long-term* consequences of prosperity based on luxury, whereas previous thinkers had either presented the economic short-term effects of luxury as part of a never-ending upward spiral (like Melon), or not bothered with luxury's unintended future consequences at all (like Voltaire). Rousseau now conceded that many of the apparent effects of luxury—such as the multiplication of wealth—might well have been true. But these were beside the point because the challenge of a successful science of government was to ensure the *durability* of a state. This, Rousseau's argument should be taken to mean, the defenders of luxury had failed to grasp, and as 'the conveniences of life increase, as the arts are brought to perfection, and luxury spreads, true courage flags, military virtues disappear'.[62] Ultimately, the state would succumb to its own decadence, corruption, and 'the dissolution of morals, the necessary consequence of luxury'.[63] 'What then is the precise point in dispute about luxury? It is to know which is most advantageous to empires, that their existence should be brilliant and momentary, or virtuous and lasting.'[64]

Rousseau knew that he could not challenge Melon's economic arguments, or rather the economic truth of Mandeville's paradox. Hence he resorted to his praise of poverty, and urged a withdrawal to the country, where life was pure and unaffected by the ills of commercial society: 'Almighty God . . . give us back ignorance, innocence, *and poverty*, which alone can make us happy and precious in Thy sight.'[65]

In his *Discourse on Inequality* (1755) Rousseau refined his argument about luxury and linked it to the central theme of his treatise. He endorsed Montesquieu's contention that luxury and the arts were the product of

a Purifying Effect upon Morals?, in Rousseau, *The Social Contract and Discourses*, trans. G. D. H. Cole, rev. and augm. J. H. Brumfitt and John C. Hall, introd. Alan Ryan (London, 1993), 15.

[61] Ibid. 17. [62] Ibid. 20. [63] Ibid. 19. [64] Ibid. 18.

[65] Ibid. 26–7 (my emphasis). Poverty was thus clearly more desirable than wealth, even though Rousseau opposed *extreme* conditions of wealth and poverty alike; cf. John O'Neal, 'Rousseau's Theory of Wealth', *History of European Ideas*, 7 (1986), 453–67.

inequality, manifest in vanity and the desire of man to appear superior to others. But whereas Montesquieu had stressed the social and economic dynamics of inequality, for Rousseau they were the primary source of evil. From them arose riches that supported both luxury and idleness while at the same time condemning the poor to endless labour and hunger.[66] Rousseau explained his reasoning at greater length in his fragments on luxury, commerce, and the arts, destined perhaps to form part of his projected *Political Institutions*.[67] In the fragments he set out to analyse luxury, commerce, and the arts with respect to the prosperity of a state, and specifically to attack the 'paradox as unheard of until today as it is ridiculous and dangerous'—a clear reference to the teachings of Mandeville and Melon. He attempted to do so by considering the relationship between prosperity and happiness. Employing the post-mercantilist argument that money as such was worthless, its value depending on nothing more than 'tacit convention' (a line of argument later taken up by Adam Smith), he concluded that the moneyed wealth of a state was no valid gauge for its prosperity.[68] In a second step he outlined why prosperity was a relative concept. Building on the assumption that 'the advantages of fortune are felt only according to differences', the poor were only poor because of the existence of the rich. A neighbour's decline had the same effect on relative wealth as one's own financial betterment. Hence, it was in the interest of individuals and nations alike to damage others in the name of private or national interest and sacrifice 'humanity' for the sake of those interests.[69]

There are two issues with Rousseau's argument which later thinkers were to take up. The first is that Rousseau envisaged economic activity as a zero-sum game in which one party's betterment necessarily meant the worsening of the other's situation. This was indeed a serious contention. It emphasized the danger that human nature might more easily be directed towards damaging the interests of others than fostering one's own interests; both had—given the relativity of wealth—the same effects. It was to be one of Adam Smith's great achievements to overcome this argument by presenting the economic game as a positive one, with scope for both rich and poor to improve their situation.[70]

[66] Rousseau, *A Discourse on a Subject Proposed by the Academy of Dijon: What is the Origin of Inequality among Men, and is it Authorised by Natural Law?* (1755), in Rousseau, *The Social Contract and Discourses*, 117–25.

[67] Rousseau, 'Le Luxe, le commerce et les arts', in Rousseau, *Œuvres complètes*, ed. Bernard Gagnebin and Marcel Raymond, iii (Paris, 1966), 516–24.

[68] Ibid. 516–21. [69] Ibid. 521–2.

[70] Donald Winch, *Riches and Poverty: An Intellectual History of Political Economy in Britain, 1750–1834* (Cambridge, 1996), 72.

Secondly, Rousseau's main claim about 'humanity' being sacrificed for the sake of interest introduces a *moral* argument in what Rousseau had presented as a specifically *economic* consideration. This makes it clear once more how difficult it was for Rousseau to dismiss Mandeville's and Melon's arguments altogether. In fact, he had effectively admitted that the 'dangerous doctrines' of Lucretius and Mandeville 'had more than succeeded'.[71] He knew that to lead society back to ancient ignorance and equality would have been impossible, for equality 'is not in the nature of things'.[72] His own prescriptions to remedy the evil consequences of this state of affairs relied heavily on Mandeville. In modern commercial society men were subdued to mutual constraint by the 'knots of self-interest'. In such a society the vicious were required to assume the mask of virtue, 'and persons must cultivate agreeable talents in order to win the approval upon which their worldly success depends'.[73]

If Rousseau failed to defeat the argument that moral corruption was inextricably linked with the progress of civilization, he at least attempted to offer a way that promised economic salvation. In his *Discourse on the Arts and Sciences* Rousseau had argued that luxury and the arts ultimately led to decay and ruin. In the *Discourse on Inequality* he explained how this chain reaction functioned economically. 'From society and the luxury to which it gives birth arise the liberal and mechanical arts, commerce, letters, and all those superfluities which make industry flourish, and enrich and ruin nations.' The fact that such a promising development should lead to ruin lay, Rousseau argued, in the profitability of the arts as opposed to the primary sector. Assuming that the profit to be derived from any economic activity was inversely proportional to its utility (an argument directed against natural law theorists who linked the concept of value to utility), Rousseau concluded that the most necessary activities—agriculture in this case—would be the first to be neglected. Without a sufficient supply of necessaries, decay would ensue, and the peasants would flee to the cities in search of bread rather than providing it. An agricultural economy with self-sufficient agriculturalists, Rousseau concluded, was the only guarantor of population growth and economic survival.[74]

[71] Rousseau, *Narcisse, ou, L'Amant de lui-même*, in Rousseau, *Œuvres complètes*, ed. Bernard Gagnebin and Marcel Raymond, ii (Paris, 1964), 965–6, where he lamented that philosophers did not teach virtue any more.

[72] Rousseau, 'Le Luxe', 522.

[73] Rousseau, *Narcisse*, 967. Cf. Hundert, *The Enlightenment's Fable*, 112–15. On the similarities of Mandeville and Rousseau, cf. Malcolm Jack, 'One State of Nature: Mandeville and Rousseau', *Journal of the History of Ideas*, 39 (1978), 119–24, who argues that the two thinkers differed in their view of the state of nature only in their attitude (negative and positive respectively) towards it. Civilization, for both, depended upon private vice.

[74] Rousseau, *Discourse on the Origin of Inequality*, 122–5.

Again it was Adam Smith who accomplished the task of pointing out the symbiotic relationship between agriculture and manufacture in an economy growing in both sectors. For now, however, Rousseau's contribution gave the discussion about luxury a new direction by rekindling old arguments of frugality, virtue, and equality and by pointing to a model of society and the economy based on the countryside. Both these achievements were to come to prominence in the Italian luxury debate. But so did Rousseau's failure to defeat Mandeville's arguments and the similarity of their prescriptions against the evils of modern society. Rousseau's contribution, apart from offering a renewed defence of ancient virtue, showed that Mandeville had succeeded in transforming the eighteenth-century discourse on modern society. By acknowledging that a return to the state of ignorance and equality was not 'in the nature of things', Rousseau admitted that under modern commercial conditions the classical moral principles no longer sufficed to govern people and that passions other than the zeal for the common good had taken their place.

Making Moral Sense of the English paradox: David Hume

David Hume had reached the same conclusion as Rousseau about the inadequacy of the Christian or antique ethic of self-restraint to govern the behaviour of modern man. He acknowledged that classical moral principles were 'too disinterested and too difficult to support [so that] it is requisite to govern men by other passions, and animate them with a spirit of avarice and industry, art and luxury'.[75] In fact, Hume agreed with Rousseau on various fronts, for example that the development of the arts and sciences and their link to luxury must be seen as a historical *process*. His conclusions, however, were fundamentally different. Not only did Hume advocate a positive view of the ascent of the arts and sciences as a source of refinement and the cause of both public and private happiness, but he also presented an economic argument which contrasted Rousseau's agricultural idyll with a trade-led path to economic development.

Hume's treatment of luxury in the essays *Of Commerce* (1752) and *Of the Refinement in the Arts* (1752) must be understood in relation to his other works, most notably the *Treatise of Human Nature* (1739–40).[76] Following

[75] David Hume, 'Of Commerce', in Hume, *Political Essays*, ed. Knud Haakonssen (Cambridge, 1994), 100.

[76] For a view of Hume's economic thought in the context of his more general philosophical

from Hume's premiss that 'all the sciences have a relation, greater or less, to human nature' and 'are in some measure dependent on the science of Man', his treatment of the development of the arts and sciences, luxury and economic matters in general, starts from a consideration of human nature.[77] The science of man was founded on experience and observation, and observation had convinced Hume that human nature and, to a lesser extent, human behaviour were uniform. Among the constant principles of human nature essential to happiness are 'action, pleasure, and indolence'.[78] Among these, action is the most important because 'no craving [is] more constant than that for exercise and employment'.[79] Hume then applied this reasoning to the economic sphere and concluded that commercial activity and the development of the arts were in accord with human nature and conducive to human happiness because the development of the arts guaranteed employment: 'In times when industry and the arts flourish, men are kept in perpetual occupation, and enjoy, as their reward, the occupation itself.' But occupation is not the only reward of industrial activity. It also generates wealth and permits man to enjoy 'those pleasures which are the fruit of their labour'.[80] Industry thus fulfils another universal passion, namely that of avarice, 'or the desire of gain . . . which operates at all times, in all places, and upon all persons' and which serves a dual function.[81] Riches confer the power to acquire what pleases and to procure the 'pleasures and conveniences of life', but also act as a social reference point because most men are 'desirous of shewing themselves to the world, and of acquiring the love and approbation of mankind'.[82]

This is the background against which Hume discusses the issue of luxury in the two essays *Of Commerce*, where he examines the economic dimension of luxury, and *Of Refinement in the Arts*, which is a predominantly philosophical discussion. It will be useful to consider Hume's economic

edifice, see Eugene Rotwein, *David Hume: Writings on Economics* (Edinburgh, 1955). For Hume's economic thought, see further Andrew S. Skinner, 'David Hume: Principles of Political Economy', in David Fate Norton (ed.), *The Cambridge Companion to Hume* (Cambridge, 1993), 222–54, on which the following account draws. See also Istvan Hont, 'The "Rich Country–Poor Country" Debate in Scottish Classical Political Economy', in Istvan Hont and Michael Ignatieff (eds.), *Wealth and Virtue: The Shaping of Political Economy in the Scottish Enlightenment* (Cambridge, 1983), 271–315.

77 Hume, *A Treatise of Human Nature*, ed. L. A. Selby-Bigge, rev. P. H. Nidditch, 2nd edn. (Oxford, 1978), introd., p. xv.

78 'Of Refinement in the Arts', in Hume, *Political Essays*, 106.

79 'Of Interest', ibid. 130.

80 'Of Refinement in the Arts', 106.

81 'Of the Rise and Progress of the Arts and Sciences', ibid. 59.

82 *Treatise of Human Nature*, II. i. 10, 'Of Property and Riches', 309–16, esp. p. 315; and II. ii. 1, 'Of the Objects and Causes of Love and Hatred', 331–2.

arguments first because many of his reasons for defending luxury *philosophically* depend on the fact that he considered it economically beneficial.

The leading question of the essay *Of Commerce* is the one that had also occupied centre-stage in Mandeville's *Fable of the Bees*, namely the relationship between trade, commerce, and industry, and both the greatness of a state and the happiness of its subjects. For Hume, this theme had particular urgency because Scotland had traded political freedom for the hope of economic development in the Union of 1707, and one of Hume's central concerns was to understand the mechanisms through which prosperity—not only in Scotland but in modern states in general—could be achieved.[83] In line with his conviction that the functioning of modern society was best understood through historical analysis, Hume approached his subject by giving an account of the development of modern commercial society. In 'their savage state' men were hunters and fishers, but upon quitting this stage they became peasants and manufacturers. Though 'the arts of agriculture employ *at first* the most numerous part of the society', productivity gains meant that excess labour would soon become available to be employed in the finer arts, and full employment and high wages 'add to the happiness of the state; since they afford to many the opportunity of receiving enjoyments, with which they would otherwise have been unacquainted'. Hume was convinced that most of Europe lived under conditions that warranted such an account. Arguing against Melon, who had claimed that 80 per cent of the French were peasants, he asserted that in Europe half of the population lived in cities, and a third of those living in the countryside were artisans.[84] This was an ill-founded criticism—Melon's estimate came much closer to a reality where nine out of ten Europeans lived in small towns and villages and most engaged in farming—but it enabled Hume to make a passionate case for a trade-led path to economic development.[85]

Hume agreed with Rousseau that without industry and manufacture, and the applied arts in particular, the economy of any state would be predominantly agricultural. But at the same time Hume took up Melon's incentive argument and argued that indolence would prevail at the expense of action as there was no incentive for peasants to improve agriculture and produce a surplus, because 'they cannot exchange that superfluity for any

[83] On the Union, the hopes attached to it, and the debates surrounding it, see John Robertson (ed.), *A Union for Empire: Political Thought and the Union of 1707* (Cambridge, 1995).

[84] 'Of Commerce', 94–5.

[85] On population distribution, see Robert S. Duplessis, *Transitions to Capitalism in Early Modern Europe* (Cambridge, 1997), 3, and, in more detail, E. A. Wrigley, *People, Cities and Wealth: The Transformation of Traditional Society* (Oxford, 1987).

commodities, which may serve either to their pleasure or vanity'. The balance of action, pleasure, and indolence will be disturbed at the cost of individual happiness. If the arts and manufacture thrive, on the contrary, this has a positive effect on agriculture as well, because now landowners 'study agriculture as a science, and redouble their industry and attention'. The surplus generated through increased efforts is not lost, but exchanged 'for those commodities, which men's luxury now makes them covet'.[86]

The fact that the excess labour is employed 'beyond mere necessaries' in the refined arts therefore has a beneficial effect on the happiness of the subjects. It also led, Hume argued, to the greatness of the state—again assuming that there was indeed an excess labour force in need of employment (a widespread assumption in the eighteenth century). Hume suggested that those working in the luxury trades constituted a 'stock of labour' which in times of crisis could easily be turned to public use, for example to supply armies. Foreign commerce equally provided such a versatile pool of labour. Beyond that, however, it was the engine of economic growth in that it led to refinement and luxury at home: through it men became acquainted with 'the pleasures of luxury and the profits of commerce, and their delicacy and industry, being once awakened, carry them on to farther improvement'. Foreign commerce set this upward spiral of economic activity and refinement in motion, but once it had gained momentum, foreign commerce might well cease, the engine then being fuelled by home consumption. China constituted an apt example of such a state of affairs.[87]

Mandeville would not have disagreed with Hume's account of the functioning of commerce and the role of the arts and of luxury to improve agriculture and boost economic growth. Hume's final justification of the beneficial nature of the process he had outlined, however, reveals a fundamental difference between him and Mandeville. The latter had thought it necessary to keep wages low in order to provide a continuous incentive for the poor to work. He had also relied on 'the working, slaving People' to do the dirty work and support a class of well-off citizens. Hume, on the contrary, was convinced that the beneficial economic spiral made high wages possible, and that all would profit from economic growth. It is against Mandeville in particular that he asserted that 'Every person . . . ought to enjoy the fruits of his labour, in a full possession of all the necessaries, and many of the conveniences of life.'[88] The conviction that commercial society was capable of achieving this idea underlies all of Hume's economic writings.

[86] 'Of Commerce', 98–9. [87] Ibid. 100–2. [88] Ibid. 102.

In the essay *Of Refinement in the Arts* Hume used some of the concepts developed in the preceding essay, but tied them into the general frame of a philosophical discussion of luxury. It is this essay, entitled *Of Luxury* until 1758, that serves as the major vehicle for Hume to engage—mostly implicitly—with the contributions of Mandeville, Montesquieu, and Rousseau.[89] '. . . Delicacy in meat, drink or apparel', (Hume here used the standard eighteenth-century definition for luxury, which he extended to mean the 'great refinement in the gratification of the senses') was not a vice per se. Innocent luxury could, however, become vicious if it was pursued at the expense of virtues such as liberality and charity. With this distinction between virtuous and vicious luxury, Hume set up his essay against both 'men of severe morals' who 'blame even the most innocent luxury' as a source of corruption and disorder and whom Rousseau had come to represent, and 'men of libertine principles' who 'bestow praise even on vicious luxury' (whose mouthpiece Mandeville had become).

In order to argue against the position of Rousseau, Hume proceeded to show that there was a connection between luxury and virtue and that in fact the 'ages of refinement are both the happiest and most virtuous'. They witnessed individual happiness, Hume argued, because luxury guaranteed employment and hence action as one of the cornerstones of human happiness. Again, this argument was based on Hume's assumption that the arts were indeed needed to employ excess labour. As we shall see, it was an assumption that Italian thinkers in particular found hard to understand and relate to their own experience. But luxury also led to increased sociability in the cities where manners improve and men become moderate and sociable. Indeed, 'they must feel an encrease in humanity', and hence industry, knowledge, and humanity are linked by an 'indissoluble chain'. But Hume asserted that luxury had a beneficial influence on the public as well. Employing the same reasoning he had developed in the essay *Of Commerce* he presented those working in the luxury industry as a storehouse of labour which could easily be drawn on in times of crisis. Furthermore, Hume believed that the laws and police could only be perfected if the more vulgar arts of commerce and manufacture were practised. To the degree that societies grew more refined, superstition vanished; this in turn

[89] The essay thus has a broader ambition than being 'designedly organised as a response to Mandeville', as Christopher Berry has claimed. His decision to explain Hume's arguments about luxury from the perspective of his treatment of Sparta runs, I think, the risk of ignoring some of the more specific attacks against positions introduced by Montesquieu and Rousseau. Berry, *Idea of Luxury*, 142–3.

had a positive public effect because superstition 'throws the government off its bias'.[90]

All the effects of luxury outlined so far were beneficial both to the individual and to the state at large. Hence, Hume argued, luxury could not be a vice. In fact, it seemed to him 'little less than a contradiction in terms, to talk of a vice, which is in general beneficial to society'. There was a limit, however, beyond which the indulgence in luxury both became vicious and ceased to be beneficial. In order to argue against those who bestowed praise on vicious luxury, Hume set out to show that Mandeville had been wrong in assuming that out of private vices grew public benefits because 'wherever luxury ceases to be innocent, it also ceases to be beneficial'.[91] This was the case when man became such a slave to luxury that he forgot his charitable duties. Even then, however, it may not be useful to ban even vicious luxury altogether. Tackling Rousseau's argument that the poor should not be poor in the first place so that luxury spending would not be needed to alleviate their lot, Hume answered that it was the duty of good government not to change the situation it found itself in but to make the best of it.[92] Accordingly, it was best to allow luxury in order to provide a remedy for defects in human nature such as selfishness in the same way 'as one poison may be an antidote to another'. In other words, and against Rousseau's claim, luxury was an antidote better than the evil it was meant to cure. The moral distinction, however, remained intact, and even when vicious luxury had to be allowed as an antidote, it did not thereby become virtuous. '. . . virtue, like wholesome food, is better than poison, however corrected.'[93]

Whereas Hume disagreed with Rousseau over the value of luxury and its potential beneficial effects in general, his attitude towards Mandeville's arguments was more complex. He endorsed the latter's view that luxury was beneficial for society as well as for individuals. But this was a political phenomenon, and luxury's beneficial effects had thus to be judged in a context of political and economic utility. Morally, however, the issue of luxury had to be treated on a different level. Here it was indeed possible to distinguish between vicious and virtuous luxury regardless of their public effects. His critique that it was inconsistent of Mandeville 'to assert in one page, that moral distinctions are inventions of politicians for public interest, and in the next page maintain, that vice is advantageous to the public' therefore did not question the advantageous link of luxury and public benefit, nor

[90] 'Of Refinement in the Arts', 105–7.
[91] Ibid. 113–14. [92] 'Of Commerce', 98.
[93] 'Of Refinement in the Arts', 108–14.

even the beneficial effects of vicious luxury. Rather, he criticized Mandeville for mixing two levels of analysis, namely the philosophical and the political, without making it clear that his perspective was political.

With Montesquieu, Hume engaged in argument over the impact of luxury on liberty. Whereas Montesquieu had allowed for a connection between the two only in the exceptional case of England, Hume advanced a more general argument which ran counter to Montesquieu's thesis of frugal republics and prosperous monarchies. In fact, 'a progress in the arts is rather favourable to liberty, and has a general tendency to preserve, if not produce a free government'. He agreed with Montesquieu, however, on the moderating effects of commerce and its tendency to blur social distinctions. Whereas Montesquieu had stressed the fact that commerce diminished the role of the nobility, Hume argued from the opposite end. When luxury nourishes commerce and industry, he observed, 'the peasants, by a proper cultivation of the land, become rich and independent'. And the increasingly wealthy merchants 'draw authority and consideration to that middling rank of men, who are the best and firmest basis of public liberty'. Elaborating on Montesquieu's observations (and drawing on his better understanding of the British constitution and polity), Hume had swiftly transformed Montesquieu's qualified argument about English commercial society into a general case for the stabilizing effects of commercial society on public liberty.[94]

After Rousseau, and after Hume's essays at the latest, the luxury problem came to be seen within the context of a historical process whose long-term prospects had to be assessed (today's 'sustainable development'). Hume had based his reasoning on the assumption of a country dominated by industry and manufacture. As will become clear, Italian thinkers could follow Hume's case for a process analysis, but reach different conclusions as a result of assuming the agricultural nature of the Italian society: an agriculture-led path to development within the context of a predominantly rural society. Before that, however, the centre of the debate returned once more to France.[95]

[94] Ibid. 111–12.

[95] For Hume's continuing influence in Scotland, see Anthony Brewer, 'An Eighteenth-Century View of Economic Development: Hume and Steuart', *European Journal of the History of Economic Thought*, 4 (1997), 1–22, and, more generally, Andrew S. Skinner, 'The Shaping of Political Economy in the Enlightenment', *Scottish Journal of Political Economy*, 37 (1990), 145–65, which summarizes much of Skinner's previous findings.

THE *ENCYCLOPÉDIE*: SAINT-LAMBERT'S ARTICLE *LUXE*

The article entitled 'Luxe' appeared in the ninth volume of the *Encyclopédie* in 1765. Its central contentions—that luxury needed to be considered not in general but in the specific political and economic contexts in which it occurred, and that the political system, not luxury, determined the greatness and ruin of nations—marked a decisive step in the development of the debate. The wide circulation of the *Encyclopédie* in the peninsula guaranteed that this development did not go unnoticed in Italy.[96] Written by Jean-François de Saint-Lambert—and not by Diderot as has often been thought—the article drew a new conclusion from the arguments put forth in the preceding decades by refusing to take a clear position either in favour of or against luxury.[97] It has been the cause of some puzzle that Saint-Lambert merely summarized the various positive and negative arguments without coming down on either side of the argument.[98] The reason lies in the fact that he believed the whole debate to be misplaced. Previous contributions had shown that the language in which the issue of luxury had been discussed was too ambiguous to offer any hope of a possible solution.[99] Consequently, Saint-Lambert began his treatment of luxury with the dry contention that history showed that both the defenders and the critics of luxury had contradicted themselves.

Saint-Lambert's critique of the course of the debate entailed essentially two elements which were closely connected. The first was his conviction that luxury needed to be judged against the specific political and economic background in which it occurred. The second, following from the first, was that the reasons for economic development and decline were political rather than rooted in luxury itself.

If the language used to discuss luxury was indeed—and could only be—ambiguous, then every attempt at generalization was doomed to fail. In fact, Saint-Lambert complained that the opinion according to which luxury was a necessary condition for wealth and power which advanced the development of states up to a point beyond which decline and destruction would

[96] See below, Chs. 6 and 8.

[97] The article is not signed, but it was attributed to Saint-Lambert as early as 1764 in a review by Melchior Grimm: Grimm, *Correspondance littéraire, philosophique et critique* (Paris, 1881), v. 465–70. It was later attributed to Diderot and inserted into the collection of his works. Saint-Lambert's authorship has finally been confirmed by Herbert Dieckmann, 'The Sixth Volume of Saint-Lambert's Works', *Romantic Review*, 42 (1951), 109–21.

[98] Berry, *Idea of Luxury*, 136–7.

[99] This point was made by Istvan Hont in a working paper presented at the Warwick Eighteenth Century Centre Reading Group, 16 Mar. 1999.

follow was 'rather general, and even Mr Hume does not depart from it'.[100] Rather, Saint-Lambert argued, it was necessary to consider luxury in relation to the specific situation and the economic system of the country in question. Whereas Holland needed to remain frugal in order to guarantee its ability to undersell foreign competition and hence keep her exports and the Swiss should only allow luxury once their industry had made up for the scarcity of their land, luxury was permissible in Portugal and Spain, where a constant supply of precious metals would always provide money for exchange. Equally France would continue to prosper through commerce even if agriculture was neglected, and be able to sustain luxury with her fashion, which was still imitated across Europe. Precisely because luxury was relative to the riches of nations and their specific situation, it was not adequate as an explanatory tool to account for the greatness and happiness of a state. In fact, 'luxury could not well have been the cause of either the fall or the prosperity of empires and of the character of certain nations'.[101]

Following from this sceptical judgement of the explanatory force of luxury was Saint-Lambert's contention that the reasons for greatness were to be found in the realm of politics. While Mandeville had explained that the negative effects of luxury were due to 'bad Politicks' and 'Mismanagement of the Rulers',[102] Saint-Lambert extended the argument to its positive effects as well, which were due to good administration. When states got rich, their luxury increased; this, however, was a natural development and the increase of wealth was not the effect of luxury. Equally, the decline of Persia and ancient Rome was due to the seeds of anarchy and despotism rather than the spread of luxury, and that of Athens was caused by the debasement of the senate rather than the luxury of its citizens.

Once the primacy of politics was asserted, Saint-Lambert went on to emphasize the positive effects of luxury (mainly that it provided an incentive which led to employment and wealth) under the precondition of a good and vigorous government. Importantly, the availability of luxury goods would lead to an increase in agricultural productivity (an argument taken directly from David Hume) and would thus allow for an 'honest' and 'slow' rise to wealth without the excesses associated with luxury in a corrupt state.[103]

The achievement of the *Encyclopédie* article is that it took up and extended Montesquieu's political treatment of luxury. Saint-Lambert accepted Montesquieu's point that the luxury debate must be aimed at

[100] Jean-François de Saint-Lambert, 'Luxe', in *Encyclopédie, ou, Dictionnaire raisonné des sciences, des arts et des métiers*, ix (Neufchastel, 1765), 764.

[101] Ibid. 765.

[102] Mandeville, *Fable*, vol. i, Remark L, p. 117.

[103] Saint-Lambert, 'Luxe', 768–71.

finding a political order that would bring out the positive effects of luxury without its harmful excesses. Going one step further still, he distanced himself from Montesquieu's claim that this was possible only in monarchies and in the special case of England. He presented instead a general case for a vigorous government paying due attention to agriculture and considering the countryside as the starting point for the desirable taming of luxury's excesses and their channelling into public benefits.[104] Tuscan agriculturalists in particular could relate to this assessment.[105]

Physiocracy and its Critics

The most powerful reaction against the new tendency to consider luxury as a consequence or corollary of specific political systems and vigorous or corrupt government came from the physiocrats. Like no other group, they were to polarize discussion in Italy, where positions ranged from enthusiastic endorsement in Tuscany to outright rejection among Milanese thinkers. The physiocratic contribution lifted the discussion back to the economic plane, which, they felt, previous contributors to the debate had unduly neglected. In 1758 the surgeon-physician and medical adviser to Mme de Pompadour and founder of the physiocratic 'sect', François Quesnay, had attacked the 'luxury of decoration' as detrimental to an increase in agricultural productivity because it drained money away from the countryside.[106] In his plea for unified taxation, he argued that landlord *income* should be taxed because otherwise it would be consumed on unproductive

[104] The social order, it should be noted, was to remain unaffected in Saint-Lambert's conception. Whereas for Hume the whole point of the exercise had been to increase public liberty through universal wealth, for Saint-Lambert this was morally and socially objectionable: 'Il est moralement nécessaire que l'usage des richesses soit contraire au bon ordre & aux mœurs.' If industry, commerce, and luxury create 'new kinds of wealth' which are open to all and hence conducive to transcending old social distinctions, this was bad because those distinctions were needed to keep the population 'attached to the general order' (ibid. 767).

[105] See below, Ch. 6.

[106] In a supplement to, and political commentary on, his *Tableau économique*: François Quesnay, *Maximes du gouvernement économique d'un royaume agricole* (1758), in Quesnay, *Œuvres économiques et philosophiques*, ed. August Oncken (Paris, 1888), 329–58. For a first introduction on Quesnay and the physiocrats, see Henri Denis, *Histoire de la pensée économique*, 10th edn. (Paris, 1993), 156–80, and, for a Marxist perspective, Ronald L. Meek, *The Economics of Physiocracy* (London, 1962). Physiocracy has been placed in its social and political context (rather than being treated as an exclusively economic doctrine) by Elizabeth Fox-Genovese, *The Origins of Physiocracy: Economic Revolution and Social Order in Eighteenth-Century France* (Ithaca, NY, 1976). On the intimate connection between physiocracy and absolutism, see also Ulrich Muhlack, 'Physiokratie und Absolutismus in Frankreich und Deutschland', *Zeitschrift für historische Forschung*, 9 (1982), 15–46.

expenditure such as luxury goods and servants. Since landlord income was the only portion of the revenue which could be taxed without damage to agricultural production, it was vital not to waste it on luxuries. Thus, Quesnay argued, 'a high level of expenditure on luxury in the way of ornamentation and conspicuous consumption is ruinous'.[107] Mirabeau, the most independent-minded member of the Quesnay circle, had made a case for social conservatism in which he argued against Melon and Hume in favour of pomp as 'gradual magnificence' respecting class distinctions, but against luxury, which was destructive of the social order.[108] But it was Nicolas Baudeau who gave 'the most complete formulation of the physiocratic doctrine on luxury . . . which has ever been written by the Quesnay school'.[109]

Born in 1730, Baudeau lived a life of shifting alliances and convictions. A canon and professor of theology, he abandoned the ecclesiastical state and settled in Paris, where in 1765 he founded the *Éphémérides du citoyen, ou, Chronique de l'esprit national*, originally designed to combat the ideas of the physiocrats. Converted by Quesnay just a year later, he devoted his energies to popularizing Quesnay's doctrine. An efficient editor, his *Éphémérides du citoyen* subsequently became the leading journal of physiocracy, and it was here that his thoughts on luxury first appeared in 1767.[110]

Baudeau's starting point was the conviction that the sign of a nation's greatness—'the thermometer of empires'—lay in the effects of its investments, which in turn are understood as any spending directed towards an increase in national revenue. Since the money needed to invest is a mere substitute for *in natura* exchange and thus necessarily originates in agricultural production, a flourishing agriculture is needed to enrich a state. From this assumption grew the physiocrats' conviction that it was necessary to return to the land both what was needed for production and what helped to increase productivity. In 'productive consumption' of this kind lay the secret of wealth and continuing prosperity.

Within this context Baudeau considered luxury and offered a neutral

[107] On Quesnay's theory of taxation, see Lefteris Tsoulfidis, 'The Physiocratic Theory of Tax Incidence', *Scottish Journal of Political Economy*, 36 (1989), 301–10: 303.

[108] Victor de Riqueti Mirabeau, *L'Ami des hommes, ou, Traité de la population* (1756), new edn. (Avignon, 1758), vol. ii, ch. 5, pp. 139–93, on 'magnificence graduelle', p. 157.

[109] A. Dubois, 'Notice', in Nicolas Baudeau, *Principes de la science morale et politique sur le luxe et les lois somptuaires* (1767), ed. Dubois (Paris, 1912), pp. v–vi.

[110] Baudeau, 'Du luxe et des lois somptuaires', *Éphémérides du citoyen, ou, Bibliothèque raisonnée des sciences morales et politiques* (Paris, 1767), i. 171–234. I quote from Dubois's edition. On the closed world of the *Éphémérides du citoyen* (which mainly praised works close to the physiocratic school, and heavily attacked those against it), see Chiara Cusanno, 'Fisiocrati e stampa: la strategia giornalistica delle "*Éphémérides du citoyen*"', *Rivista storica italiana*, 103 (1991), 557–98, esp. pp. 585–6 on the luxury controversy.

definition that tried to overcome the difficulties caused by the ambiguous language of needs and necessities. Luxury, for Baudeau, is everything 'which increases the amount of non-productive expenditure at the expense of that expenditure which serves towards production, and, at the same time, at the expense of production itself'.[111] What seemed at first to be no more than a restatement of the primacy of agriculture over luxury as the pleasures of the city is in effect a complex and qualified argument. By separating the notion of luxury from specific objects of conspicuous consumption and by stripping it of its moral connotation, conspicuous consumption as such could be justified provided it was kept within limits which did not threaten agricultural development.

Baudeau thus gave a different reason from Montesquieu in his explanation why England could afford luxury by advancing the purely economic argument that England had a sufficiently productive agriculture to allow for excess spending to go into the consumption of luxury goods. Equally, the results of his analysis could easily be reconciled with Saint-Lambert's conclusion that countries such as France and Spain did not have to fear luxury whereas the scarcity of the Swiss countryside made conspicuous consumption there detrimental to prosperity. As we shall see, Tuscan thinkers could adopt precisely this kind of reasoning—that luxury expenditure was permissible as long as agricultural production was guaranteed—in their argument against luxury because the necessary condition was not met.

Successful though the physiocrats' attempt at providing a neutral definition of luxury was, Baudeau found it difficult to force an entirely new meaning onto the concept of luxury. By arguing that conspicuous consumption had nothing to do with luxury as long as agriculture received its fair share of the net product, he resorted to the paradox that luxury could be had without luxury. Alleviating the countryside and increasing production, Baudeau argued, would lead to an increase in disposable revenue which could be used 'without luxury for the very objects that luxury today provides'.[112]

The tensions within the physiocratic concept of luxury made it prey to attacks soon after it was voiced. But the critics of Quesnay, Mirabeau, and Baudeau directed their criticism not so much against the new attempt at

[111] Baudeau, *Principes*, 4–14.

[112] Ibid. 23. Equally paradoxical was his contention that sumptuary laws were a luxury because of the high cost of their enforcement (ibid. 23–4). Incidentally, this was a line of reasoning that Ferdinando Galiani, the great critic of physiocracy, endorsed when he equated luxury with 'an excess of imposts' in the *Dialogues sur le commerce des bleds* (1770), ed. Fausto Nicolini (Milan, 1959), 122.

definition but rather against the economic assumptions underlying the model. If Baudeau's intervention did not gain universal acceptance, then he had at least successfully redirected the debate onto the economic plane, which it had left after the intervention of Melon.

Of the critics of the physiocratic doctrine and their view of luxury George-Marie Butel-Dumont is most representative. Born in Paris in 1725, the diplomat and member of the French financial administration was a student of Forbonnais and belonged to the school of Gournay. His *Théorie du luxe* of 1771, written in the climate of almost universal condemnation of luxury in French intellectual circles,[113] was rejected by Baudeau in his *Éphémérides* but defended in a pamphlet which launched a stark attack against the 'congregation of Quesnayites'.[114]

Butel-Dumont's analysis of the ultimate scope of economic progress is decidedly Humean in character. The main task of government consisted in securing that the worker obtain 'the full enjoyment of the fruits of his ideas and his labour'. To secure this it was essential to make people work through incentives, and the best incentive was the availability of luxury goods. Rehearsing old incentive arguments, Butel-Dumont maintained that 'Man works only in order to be able to enjoy', and such a stimulus could only be derived from the arts. His justification of the importance of the arts places him squarely against the physiocrats. If the economic system was built on total liberty and 'the fantasy of the consumer', this would lead to an upward spiral of demand and economic production; he remarked that 'the concatenation of these effects generates opulence, power, in one word the lasting happiness of an empire'.[115]

Butel-Dumont's critique of the physiocratic contribution to the debate came at a price, however. His challenging of Baudeau on economic grounds had led to a partial reintroduction of the moral side of the argument: he had to abandon the notion that luxury could be defined neutrally with reference to spending and investment alone. His case for luxury as an incentive for men to produce more than they 'naturally needed' fell back on the ambiguous

[113] For the context of condemnation in and against which Butel-Dumont wrote in 1770–1, cf. Renato Galliani, 'Le Débat en France sur le luxe: Voltaire ou Rousseau?', *Studies on Voltaire and the Eighteenth Century*, 161 (1976), 205–17.

[114] The *Théorie du luxe, ou, Traité dans lequel on entreprend d'établir que le luxe est un ressort non-seulement utile, mais même indispensablement nécessaire à la prosperité des États* appeared without place of publishing in 1771. It must have been available before, however, because the critical review by Baudeau appeared in the *Éphémérides du citoyen* in 1770, pt. II, art. IV, pp. 181–206. The anonymous pamphlet *Lettre sur la 'Théorie du luxe'* appeared in 1771. Cf. Borghero, *La polemica sul lusso nel Settecento francese*, 107.

[115] Butel-Dumont, *Théorie du luxe*, pt. I, ch. 2, pp. 31–44.

language of the moral authority of needs which, from their different perspectives, Saint-Lambert and the physiocrats had previously tried to overcome. Accordingly, Butel-Dumont was forced to consider the moral effects of luxury once more.[116] In an attempt to show that the voluntary reduction of needs was not in the public interest, Butel-Dumont again employed an argument derived from Hume. Whereas the latter had praised the public advantages of the arts as a 'storehouse of labour', Butel-Dumont argued that the prosperous consumer of luxury goods was used to spending much, so giving some money in times of need would only be a light privation. The well-off artisan could thus discharge his civic duties through the contribution towards military equipment. It is the same argument as Hume's, only that in Butel-Dumont's model the citizen could pay his way out of conscription.[117]

From the physiocratic contributions onwards, the debate oscillated between the poles of economic treatment and political and moral consideration. Most exposed among the latter was Claude-Adrien Helvétius, who after a career in the financial administration retired to the countryside at the age of 36 in 1751 and became an agriculturalist and shoe manufacturer. His own contribution to the French debate is of limited importance, but his work was avidly read by Italian political economists.[118] Helvétius was thus one of the channels through which French thinking reached the peninsula. After the great success of his anonymous tract *De l'esprit* of 1758, *De l'Homme* appeared posthumously in 1772.[119] Helvétius agreed with the defenders of luxury that as man was lazy by nature he needed an incentive to work and that luxury was hence necessary. But in figurative language that explicitly evoked Mandeville's *Fable* he argued that 'in the beehive that is human society' it was necessary that all vice and corruption be eliminated and that all work towards the common good.[120] Thus challenging

[116] Butel-Dumont, *Théorie du luxe*, pt. II, ch. 7, pp. 132–54.

[117] Butel-Dumont is a typical example of a critic of physiocracy who combined his criticism with a defence of luxury. This was not necessarily the case. Condillac, for example, maintained against the physiocrats that industry 'adds value to a range of production which they would not have without it' and was indeed a source of wealth, while maintaining that the French 'in our misery' must realize that only the simple life can make a nation rich and powerful. Étienne Bonnot de Condillac, *Œuvres philosophiques*, ed. G. Le Roy (Paris, 1948), ii. 258 and 308–11. Condillac, a friend of Quesnay, endorsed many of physiocracy's key propositions, but ultimately refused to follow its lead (and his work was rejected by Baudeau and other physiocrats in turn); cf. Walter Eltis, 'L'Abbé de Condillac and the Physiocrats', *History of Political Economy*, 27 (1995), 217–36.

[118] The influence of Helvétius on the Milanese Enlightenment has been stressed by Franco Venturi, *Settecento riformatore*, i. 677, 686, 706–7, 729.

[119] Claude-Adrien Helvétius, *De l'Homme, de ses facultés intellectuelles et de son éducation* (London, 1772).

[120] Ibid., sect. VI, ch. 5.

Mandeville's central assumption, he went on to argue that it was not luxury as such that had led to decadence and the loss of virtue but the causes that had given rise to luxury in the first place. Recalling Montesquieu's association of luxury with the government of one, he described the rise of luxury as a corollary of despotic tendencies. They were, Helvétius was convinced, the unavoidable consequence of government by representation (itself necessitated by an expanding and otherwise ungovernable nation), which eventually led to the separation of interest between the rulers and those represented. The alienation of the rulers from the ruled, Helvétius warned, had always been the beginning of the end of empires because it had given rise to favouritism and the excessively unequal distribution of wealth.[121] Following the standard argument that luxury was the result of inequality, he conceded that the necessary process of alienation would lead to luxury. But whereas the unequal distribution of wealth was an evil, luxury was 'in some respect a remedy of this evil' because it facilitated redistribution.[122] We shall encounter this argument again in the Milanese Enlightenment, where Pietro Verri repeated it almost literally in the context of his early defence of luxury.

Helvétius's conclusion, however, remained deeply sceptical. Deploring the unequal accumulation of wealth in a few hands through the introduction of money, which eventually led to the separation of private from public interest, he sighed that 'Maybe, under the current form of government, such an evil is inevitable for empires.' He thus resigned himself to the power and apparent force of commercial society as Rousseau had before him, but he never endorsed Butel-Dumont's enthusiastic optimism, which claimed to have found in luxury the secret for a never-ending success story of prosperity and happiness.[123] But at least he was sure that any attack against luxury was misplaced, and that luxury as such could not be condemned because it alleviated the evil effects of corrupt government. It was the effect of despotism, and hence the enemies of luxury should direct their attack against despotic government.[124]

[121] Ibid., chs. 7 and 8.

[122] Ibid., ch. 13.

[123] Helvétius's pessimism was in turn subjected to criticism. Diderot, in an explicit refutation of Helvétius, argued that as long as inequality was based on industry rather than privilege, nations would continue to flourish and enjoy 'all those fascinating vices which make for the happiness of man in this world and his damnation in the next'. Morals might decline, but at least one did not have to suffer those vices produced by misery. Denis Diderot, *Mémoires pour Cathérine II: Du luxe*, written in St Petersburg in 1773–4, but only first published in 1899; it was subsequently edited by Paul Vernière (Paris, 1964), 145–60. Diderot only converted from the position of an agriculturalist to one favouring industry around 1770; see Anthony Strugnell, 'Diderot on Luxury, Commerce and the Merchant', *Studies on Voltaire and the Eighteenth Century*, 217 (1983), 83–93.

[124] Helvétius, *De l'Homme*, sect. VI, ch. 9.

THE CONTRIBUTION OF ADAM SMITH

My account of the European luxury debate ends with Adam Smith. This is not because the debate itself ended with his contribution (in fact, there was continued interest in the question of luxury well into the third quarter of the eighteenth century),[125] but because Smith's work in many ways marks the culmination of the eighteenth-century debate by both addressing, and offering solutions to, its central concerns.[126] Despite early references to Smith's *Wealth of Nations* in Italy, real interest in his work did not take off until the last decade of the eighteenth century. Adam Smith is important to an understanding of the European luxury debate because he drew its various threads together. His influence on the Italian debate, however, was less pronounced than may have been expected.[127]

Adam Smith had examined the philosophical issues raised by luxury in his *Theory of Moral Sentiments* of 1759. Elaborating on Hume's criticism that Mandeville was a poor moral philosopher, Smith showed that the sophisticated ways in which man in modern commercial society reached moral judgements could not be explained adequately by Mandeville's blunt assertion that man's actions, even if done from a sense of propriety, derive purely from vanity. It was, Smith insisted, 'the great fallacy of Dr. Mandeville's book to present every passion as wholly vicious, which is so in any degree and in any direction', from which he derived his conclusion that private vices were public benefits. But Smith acknowledged that Mandeville was right in attacking the 'popular ascetic doctrines which had been current before his time, and which placed virtue in the entire extirpation and

[125] Influenced by Rousseau and to some extent by the physiocratic critique of luxury, the French debate in particular was revived in the 1770s and 1780s and assumed an increasingly critical tone. All contributions for a prize essay about luxury in 1782, for example, were critical of luxury; see Giuseppe Barbini, '"Le Luxe détruit-il les mœurs et les empires?" Concorso indetto nel 1782 dall'accademia di Besançon', *Studi francesi*, 40 (1996), 319–26.

[126] There is a range of good literature on Smith's contribution to the luxury debate, and my account does not pretend to add significantly to previous findings. I have particularly benefited from Donald Winch's account in his *Riches and Poverty: An Intellectual History of Political Economy in Britain, 1750–1834* (Cambridge, 1996), 57–89. See also Berry, *Idea of Luxury*, 152–73, who tackles Smith's stance on luxury from the perspective of the relation between opulence and freedom in his thought, and Anthony Brewer, 'Luxury and Economic Development: David Hume and Adam Smith', *Scottish Journal of Political Economy*, 45 (1998), 78–98.

[127] For early references in Italy, see Oslavia Vercillo, 'Della conoscenza di Adamo Smith in Italia nel sec. XVIII', *Economia e storia*, 10 (1963), 413–24. For the relaying of Smith through Francesco Mengotti (1749–1830) in the 1790s, see Leone Iraci Fedeli, 'Letture di economisti italiani dei secoli XVIII e XIX: Francesco Mengotti e il "Colbertismo"', *Annali dell'Istituto Giangiacomo Feltrinelli*, 2 (1959), 560–76, and more generally Gabriella Gioli, 'Gli albori dello smithianesimo in Italia', *Rivista di politica economica*, 62 (1972), 917–62.

annihilation of all our passions'. Mandeville may have gone over the top in calling the indulgence in any passion vice, but his theory 'in some respects bordered upon the truth'.[128] It was the truth of the English paradox that Smith set out to scrutinize in the *Wealth of Nations*.

It has often been argued that Smith paid mere lip-service to the role of consumption in fostering economic growth. Perhaps most notoriously, Joseph Alois Schumpeter dismissed Smith's own contention that 'Consumption is the sole end and purpose of all production' as 'no more than a platitude and entirely stripped of any connotation hostile to saving'.[129] It is increasingly becoming clear, however, how important a role consumption played in Smith's thought.[130] It is in the context of consumption that Smith begins his treatment of luxury. Defining necessaries as 'not only the commodities which are indispensably necessary for the support of life, but whatever the custom of the country renders it indecent for creditable people, even of the lowest order, to be without', the definition of luxury followed by default: 'All other things, I call luxuries, without meaning by this appellation, to throw the smallest degree of reproach upon the temperate use of them.'[131] The qualifying remark about temperate use enabled Smith to bypass the moral discussion of luxury (because no one would argue in favour of potentially self-destructive intemperance) and concentrate on its economic effects instead. Smith could assert that unproductive expenditure continued to serve the function of generating employment and facilitating the circulation of money. But it was not here that the secret to economic growth lay. Rather, and in direct contrast to Mandeville, Smith argued that only parsimony and the resulting accumulation of capital could put productive labour to work and increase our stock for future consumption.[132] In the words of Donald Winch, it was precisely the 'productive use of the results of private frugality [which] provided Smith with the capstone

[128] Adam Smith, *The Theory of Moral Sentiments*, ed. D. D. Raphael and A. L. Macfie (Oxford, 1976; repr. Indianapolis, 1982), 308–13. I follow and supplement John Robertson's account of Smith's 'philosophical' treatment of luxury presented at the Warwick Eighteenth Century Centre's workshop on the Luxury Debates of the Eighteenth Century, Jan. 1998.

[129] Adam Smith, *An Inquiry into the Nature and Causes of the Wealth of Nations* (1776), ed. R. H. Campbell and A. S. Skinner (Oxford, 1976; repr. Indianapolis, 1982), bk. IV, ch. viii, para. 49, and Joseph Alois Schumpeter, *History of Economic Analysis* (London, 1997), 324 n. 3.

[130] See most recently Neil de Marchi, 'Adam Smith's Accommodation of "Altogether Endless" Desires', in Maxine Berg and Helen Clifford (eds.), *Consumers and Luxury: Consumer Culture in Europe 1650–1850* (Manchester, 1999), 18–36.

[131] Smith, *Wealth of Nations*, bk. V, ch. ii.k. para. 3.

[132] Ibid., bk. II, ch. ii, esp. paras. 14–15. It is in this sense that Neil de Marchi speaks of savings as 'postponed consumption', challenging the old view that parsimony was antithetical to consumption; see de Marchi, 'Accommodation', 26.

of his answer to jeremiads on luxury'.[133] In line with his conviction that there was a 'natural' order of growth which made it necessary first to invest in agriculture, then in manufactures, and finally in foreign commerce, Smith could also assign a new role to the capital cities. Rather than stimulating economic development, the cities which were the residence of a court were detrimental to general industriousness because they made the lower ranks 'idle, dissolute, and poor'. Real contributions to opulence, Smith argued, could only be expected from cities which boasted of manufactures and industry and which were supported by their agricultural hinterland.[134]

Smith had thus attempted to answer the main economic questions raised by the luxury debate, and he had come up with a solution that made luxury appear in a new light. By allowing for the 'temperate use' of luxury (and thus lifting the treatment of luxury out of the context of moral concerns about excess and intemperance), but at the same time tying it closely to his concept of individual parsimony (which was meant to 'augment the stock which may be reserved for immediate consumption'), he managed to rescue luxury's public benefits but subordinated it to what made wealth grow: frugality and capital accumulation, which increase the possibilities of future consumption.[135]

[133] Winch, *Riches and Poverty*, 80.

[134] Smith, *Wealth of Nations*, bk. II, ch. iii, para. 12.

[135] Ibid., bk. II, ch. i, para. 26.

3

The Origins of Political Economy in Italy

The Catholic Enlightenment: Muratori and the Introduction of Melon into Italy

Ludovico Antonio Muratori was a man of the *ancien régime*. Born in 1672 near Modena, he became a priest and in his early twenties was made librarian of the Biblioteca Ambrosiana in Milan. Called back to Modena by the Este family, he was appointed their archivist, a position which allowed him to pursue a vast intellectual activity spanning literature and history, moral philosophy, and economy. A conservative and a defender of tradition for some, a philosopher of the rank of Montesquieu and Vico for others, he should be understood as one of the most important and influential members of the early Italian Enlightenment.[1] His thought must be placed in the context of enlightened Catholicism, which he was indebted to and which he, in turn, shaped.

The origins of what contemporaries called *cristianesimo illuminato* or *pietà illuminata* are difficult to locate with precision.[2] It is clear, however, that a heated debate about philosophy and Cartesian and atomist science in Naples in the 1680s laid the grounds for an ever-increasing anticurialism.[3] From around 1710 onwards, Lockean and Newtonian philosophy spread across Italy.[4] Journals like the *Raccolta di opuscoli scientifici e filologici* tried

[1] Franco Venturi has characterized him as a *preilluminista*. The subtitle of the first volume of his *Settecento riformatore: da Muratori a Beccaria*, clearly brings out Venturi's conviction of the importance of Muratori for the Italian Enlightenment, while at the same time indicating the distance that separated his *preilluminismo* from the high point of the Italian Enlightenment at the time of Beccaria and *Il Caffè*. On Muratori, see Venturi, *Settecento riformatore*, vol. i. (Turin, 1998), 162–86.

[2] On the proliferation of these terms mainly in France as *chrétiens éclairés* but also among Italian writers, see Daniele Menozzi, '"Aufklärung" delle Chiese cristiane e "chrétiens éclairés": in margine ai lavori della terza sezione del Congresso C.I.H.E.C. di Varsavia', *Critica storica*, 16 (1979), 150–61.

[3] See e.g. Vittor Ivo Comparato, 'Ragione e fede nelle discussioni istoriche, teologiche e filosofiche di Costantino Grimaldi', in *Saggi e ricerche sul Settecento* (Naples, 1968), 48–93.

[4] Vincenzo Ferrone, *Scienza natura religione: mondo newtoniano e cultura italiana nel primo Settecento* (Naples, 1982), 171–233.

to unite the new scientific culture with historical erudition. These 'new efforts to analyse reality' did not leave the Church unaffected.[5] Partly in response to the new trends, the Church aimed to adapt on two levels. At first, it united behind the common project of improving the training of the clergy, of strengthening the role of the parish priests and their task of teaching religion to the common people (for example, through catechisms for children), as well as of stressing the practical duties of the secular clergy. The immediate results of this development were a moderate diffusion of practical knowledge to educate peasants and to increase the awareness of landlords by teaching botany, mineralogy, plant sciences, and the like. There was as yet no underlying enlightened vision behind such efforts. Nevertheless, new viewpoints, a new open-mindedness, and a European perspective did begin to penetrate the Church—and this would ultimately lead to the rise of practically minded, cosmopolitan reform priests such as Ferdinando Paoletti and Ubaldo Montelatici, founder of the Tuscan agrarian academy the Accademia dei Georgofili in the second half of the century.

There was a second element of enlightened Catholicism, however, which created the passage from erudition and the new philosophical–scientific interest to the notion of public happiness, a passage that was to lead to the symbiosis of culture and politics with a civil and humanitarian vision. The new movement affected large parts of Italy (Florence, Pisa, Rome, and Naples among others), but the outstanding intellectual figure to negotiate this passage was Ludovico Antonio Muratori from Modena. What had brought about the new approach, it has been argued by Mario Rosa, was the failure in the 1740s to create a new metaphysics on rationalistic and empirical grounds, a failure identified with the name of Antonio Genovesi, who gave up on the project in 1747.[6] His failure caused Catholics to turn their attention elsewhere. Priests like Casto Innocente Ansaldi began to defend the social function of religion against pure philosophical reasoning—the *benefici del cristianesimo*.[7] Enlightened Catholics placed their emphasis more and more on the humanity of religion, its practical value, and its attainability rather than on revelation and transcendence. Catholic thinkers, in other words, directed their attention to the science of society.

Muratori's most influential contribution to the science of society is to be

[5] Mario Rosa, 'Introduzione all'*Aufklärung* cattolica in Italia', in Rosa (ed.), *Cattolicesimo e lumi nel Settecento italiano* (Rome, 1981), 1–47: 7.

[6] Ibid. 16–21.

[7] See Mario Rosa, 'Ansaldi, Casto Innocente', in *Dizionario biografico degli italiani*, iii (Rome, 1961), 362–5.

found in his mature political work *Della pubblica felicità*, which appeared in 1749.[8] While it is true that many of the themes of the book can be traced back to his early works on moral philosophy, *Della pubblica felicità* should be seen as a new synthesis and the culmination of his thought.[9] The central parameters of Muratori's thought are, on the one hand, the insertion of his political thought into the realm of the Catholic religion, and hence the defence of the 'good costumes' against the passions; on the other, a paternalistic concept of political authority, and hence his conviction that political and economic reform had to originate from the prince. It is within this framework that Muratori turned his attention to luxury.

Mandeville had celebrated luxury in all its aspects, and Melon had decided to exclude the moral value of luxury from his treatment in order to underline the economic effects of luxury more convincingly. Muratori responded to both these positions. He made the arguments of Melon known to Italian readers by summing up the ninth chapter of the *Essai politique sur le commerce* in his treatment of luxury, and he presented arguments in favour of luxury spending by the rich.[10] His main arguments were that the circulation of money was facilitated by spending on luxury goods, that production would increase, and that money could be spread from a few hands to many. As we shall see, these arguments were taken up by most political economists who argued in favour of luxury. As far as foreign trade was concerned, Muratori remained clearly in the mercantilist tradition that placed great emphasis on a positive balance of trade. Imported luxury was considered harmful because it reduced that balance. He was equally sceptical about the frequent change of fashion and the decline in monetary value it brought about. Hence he preferred lasting luxury goods such as gold and silverware, 'because this does not mean to throw money away, but simply to change its face'.[11]

Muratori was not interested in the economic aspect of luxury alone. Even though his principal source on luxury was Melon's economic defence, he took great care to answer Mandeville's theory of private vices becoming public benefits: Muratori maintained the categorical distinction between

[8] Ludovico Antonio Muratori, *Della pubblica felicità oggetto de' buoni principi*, ed. Cesare Mozzarelli (Rome, 1996).

[9] The continuities in the development of Muratori's thought, and in particular the similarities between *Della pubblica felicità* and the *Rudimenti di filosofia morale per il Principe* from 1713–14, have been stressed by Sergio Bertelli, *Erudizione e storia in Ludovico Antonio Muratori* (Naples, 1960), 173. Cesare Mozzarelli has insisted on the differences between the old-fashioned *Rudimenti*, which were written in the mirror for princes tradition, and the *Pubblica Felicità* (Mozzarelli, 'Introduzione', in Muratori, *Della Pubblica Felicità*, pp. xii–xxi).

[10] Muratori, *Della pubblica felicità*, ch. xix, 'Sul lusso', p. 168.

[11] Ibid. 171.

private and public good.[12] The two were different—even if they could at times coincide—and one did not follow necessarily from the other. The only way in which private interest could ever be reconciled with public happiness was through reason, which led men to help one another (and hence to be concerned about the common good), because such behaviour promised help from others in return.[13] The argument in favour of luxury could thus not be that luxury as private vice was transformed into public benefit. Rather, he adopted the purely Augustinian argument that the passions governed human behaviour, and that among them was the passion for luxury. In the words of Muratori, luxury is 'a practically indispensable consequence of those most rigorous passions which are born together with man'.[14] The Augustinians considered a life of abundance vicious, if not sinful, and this sentiment is still present in Muratori, even though expressed in somewhat less categorical fashion. Given, however, that the passion for luxury could not be eradicated—sumptuary laws, Muratori tells us, have never worked—it was necessary to tolerate it (a conclusion not dissimilar from Mandeville's) but direct it towards durable goods produced at home.

Another aspect which would become vital for subsequent discussions in Italy was Muratori's understanding of luxury as the desire to emulate those of superior rank.[15] The connection between luxury and social status had been absent from Melon's understanding. Muratori reintroduced it into the discussion, and it was to prove central to attempts (by Ferdinando Paoletti in Tuscany among others) to link luxury with ruinous expenditure beyond one's economic capacities, which were in turn determined by social status. Such use of Muratori's arguments was still a while in the coming, however. The more immediate significance of *Della pubblica felicità* was that it absorbed some of the new ideas that had originated in enlightened Europe into mainstream Catholicism. The discussion of luxury is a particularly illuminating case in point. Muratori had shown that some of the technical aspects of Melon's arguments in favour of luxury could be justified as long as the issue at large remained closely tied into the edifice of enlightened Catholicism, and in this instance it meant that economic activity remained linked to morality. The long-term result of this move was different, however. Melon's new ideas were introduced in Italy by one of the most respected intellectuals. Once they were known, they could later be employed outside Muratori's context of enlightened Catholicism.

One region where such a development can be observed is Naples.

[12] Muratori, *Della pubblica felicità*, ch. xix, 'Sul lusso', 8.
[13] Ibid. 40.
[14] Ibid. 167.
[15] Ibid. 173–4.

Antonio Genovesi and the Foundation of Political Economy in Naples

Melon's *Essai politique sur le commerce* had travelled to the northern part of the Italian peninsula with the help of Muratori, but it was also known in Naples. It helped shape the thinking of Antonio Genovesi, a priest and one of the great hopes of Italian intellectuals, about luxury and about the economy in general.[16] In fact, when Genovesi was appointed to Italy's (and indeed Europe's) first chair of political economy, he could draw on the teachings of Melon and Muratori. At the same time, he engaged with an older strand of the humanist critique of luxury developed in Naples by Paolo Mattia Doria and Carlo Antonio Broggia and with the most recent moral considerations developed by Jean-Jacques Rousseau.

An important context for the development of Genovesi's thought is the private academy set up by Bartolomeo Intieri to teach commerce to the youth of the kingdom.[17] Intieri, a Tuscan who had moved to Naples in 1699, had first earned a living by publishing books on mathematics before he turned into a very successful administrator of land. Intieri did not publish much during his lifetime, but he was an avid reader of the latest developments in economic thinking. In 1738 he got hold of Melon's *Essai politique*, which he regarded as a 'never quite sufficiently praised booklet'. Melon's treatment of luxury in particular appealed to Intieri, and he wanted to send a copy of it to his friend Celestino Galiani as early as December 1738. It seemed to confirm Intieri in his judgement that 'man runs to where the money is'.[18] More and more interested in political economy and morality rather than mere erudition, he set up a private study and gathered promising young intellectuals around him. It was here, in fact, that Ferdinando Galiani wrote his tract *Della moneta* in 1751, and that Antonio Genovesi turned his attention towards economics. The explanatory remarks which Genovesi attached to his edition of Ubaldo Montelatici's programme for agricultural reform have been characterized by Franco Venturi as the 'manifesto of the new school' around Intieri.[19] They are fuelled by an

[16] On Genovesi, see Eluggero Pii, *Antonio Genovesi: dalla politica economica alla 'politica civile'* (Florence, 1984), with further references. On the Neapolitan luxury debate, see Paolo Frascani, 'Il dibattito sul lusso nella cultura napoletana del '700', *Critica storica*, 11 (1971), 397–424.

[17] See Venturi, *Settecento riformatore*, i. 552–63.

[18] Letters from Intieri to Celestino Galiani, Oct. and Dec. 1738, Jan. 1739; quoted in Ferrone, *Scienza natura religione*, 559, 565, and 563.

[19] The Tuscan agriculturalist Ubaldo Montelatici was the founder of the first agricultural academy in Europe, the Accademia dei Georgofili. His *Ragionamento sopra i mezzi più necessari*

optimism that economic progress in Naples was possible. What was needed, Genovesi urged, was a philosophy that was 'all real and directed at the true advantages of man'. Among the most advantageous was the cultivation of the land, and hence Genovesi demanded an agricultural academy based on the Tuscan model. Education and agriculture, more than metaphysical speculation and erudition, must be the starting point to break out of Neapolitan misery and economic backwardness. Genovesi's mentor Intieri saw to it that his pupil could carry through his ambitious programme. He endowed a chair of political economy in Naples upon the condition that Genovesi be the first incumbent. He delivered his inaugural lecture in November 1754 amid great public interest. And in the next decade Genovesi's thinking (as well as his attitude towards luxury) grew out of his university lectures.[20]

Genovesi's emphasis in thinking about luxury changed significantly over the course of the ten years from the beginning of the 1750s to the 1760s, and he oscillated between a purely economic approach in his first writings and a moral approach later. In the *Lezioni di commercio o sia d'economia politica* of 1765–7 (but first drafted in the late 1750s) he found a way to reconcile an economic with a moral view of luxury.[21]

Before he began to publish on economic subjects, Genovesi had become an avid reader of late mercantilist and early free-trade literature in French, and English writers in French translation. In particular François Véron de Forbonnais's articles in the *Encyclopédie* exerted a great influence on Genovesi, and Forbonnais's example persuaded him to leave aside the 'mechanics' (one part of his newly endowed chair in 'mechanics and political economy') and concentrate on economics as a science.[22] The underlying motivation of Genovesi's thought is best understood in the context of the 'rich country–poor country debate'. How advanced countries could remain (and

per far rifiorire l'agricoltura . . . con un discorso di Antonio Genovesi (Naples, 1753) is based on the original edition published in Florence in 1752. On Genovesi's *Discorso*, see Venturi, *Settecento riformatore*, i. 560–2: 560.

[20] On the institutional context of the development of political economy as a science, see Gabriella Gioli, 'La nascita e l'affermazione dell'insegnamento dell'economia politica in Italia: continuità e discontinuità (1750–1900)', in M. Augello (ed.), *Le cattedre di economia politica in Italia: la diffusione di una disciplina 'sospetta' (1750–1900)* (Milan, 1988), 385–410; brief remarks on Genovesi are also in Gioli, 'Il concorso di economia pubblica del 1844 all'università di Napoli ed il dibattito sul lusso e lo sviluppo delle manifatture', *Ricerche storiche*, 12 (1982), 409–44.

[21] *Pace* Eluggero Pii, who has argued that 'from the *Lettere accademiche* onwards, Genovesi abandoned the moral approach to the question' of luxury (Pii, *Antonio Genovesi*, 199).

[22] Forbonnais's articles were later collectively published as *Elemens du commerce* in 2 vols. in 1754.

poor ones become) rich was a question that engaged the minds of those concerned with economic progress across Europe.[23] But whereas English thinkers were concerned with the problem of how to maintain the competitive advantages of the rich country, Genovesi viewed the issue from the opposite perspective. Naples was clearly not as powerful and wealthy as England. But was it desirable to follow in the footsteps of English mercantilism? After all, Genovesi remarked that 'England cannot aspire to more greatness, but makes her arts actually decline.'[24] Thinking of the Spanish model and the reform programmes there, Genovesi was convinced that it was time for the 'latecomers' (the expression Genovesi actually used was *quei che vengono dopo*, or *coloro che vengono fatte già le messe*) such as Naples to move in. Spain and England were thus two poles between which Genovesi's economic thought oscillated, and both had vital lessons to teach. England was the object of admiration because of her efficiency, her sciences, and her power. Spain, in contrast, showed the endless possibilities for a poor country which became competitive by way of an extended reform programme. Naples lacked both the power of the one and the reform spirit of the other nation. By underselling the rich nations, however, Naples might be able to enter the market and build up a strong position in commerce.[25] But England and Spain were not the only countries from which Genovesi sought instruction. Like most thinkers in Italy, the 'Anglophile ... in French dress' was aware of the most recent thinking emanating from France.[26] Not only was France important as the basic model of an agricultural economy, its thinkers had also paved the way for Genovesi's own economic programme. In the writings of the Gournay circle, for example, he found his conviction that the grain trade should be liberated.[27] *Lascerà fare* was the principle to adopt in the running of the economy. But agriculture was not everything. In the long term, he was convinced, even an agricultural economy such as Naples could not prosper without the development of manufacture.

[23] Cf. Istvan Hont, 'The "Rich Country–Poor Country" Debate in Scottish Classical Political Economy', in Istvan Hont and Michael Ignatieff (eds.), *Wealth and Virtue: The Shaping of Political Economy in the Scottish Enlightenment* (Cambridge, 1983), 271–315.

[24] John Cary, *Storia del commercio della Gran Bretagna ... con un ragionamento sul commercio in universale e alcune annotazioni riguardanti l'economia del nostro Regno di Antonio Genovesi*, trans. Antonio Genovesi, 3 vols. (Naples, 1757 [1758]), iii. 390 n. 26.

[25] For the role of the Spanish and English models in Genovesi's thought, cf. Venturi, *Settecento riformatore*, i. 572–7, his reference to the 'late-comers' on p. 573.

[26] John Robertson, 'The Enlightenment above National Context: Political Economy in Eighteenth-Century Scotland and Naples', *Historical Journal*, 40 (1997), 687–92: 689.

[27] *Riflessioni sull'economia generale dei grani, tradotte dal Francese, con un discorso preliminare del Signor Abate Genovesi* (Naples, 1765), a translation of Claude Herbert, *Essai sur la police générale des grains* of 1754.

Guided by those general principles, Genovesi wrote his first major work on economic thought, the 'Elementi del commercio', in 1753. It is an explanation of the functioning of modern, commercial society, formed the basis for his lectures on political economy, and circulated in Naples in manuscript form. In the 'Elementi' Genovesi followed Mandeville and distanced himself from Rousseau in that he considered it mistaken to long for a primitive egalitarian world: it was the complex functioning of modern refined nations that needed explaining. Admitting that needs had given rise to the first arts, Genovesi saw no paradox in maintaining that—in the advanced state of the civil world—this process had been reversed and the arts produced needs. This observation translated into his treatment of luxury. Distinguishing between foreign luxury (which was bad) and home luxury (which was good), he listed the by now common benefits good luxury could bring: the spread of money down the layers of society, its increased circulation, and hence an effective increase of the money supply, its boost to economic activity through the perfection of the arts. Genovesi's predominantly economic defence of luxury can be explained by the influence Melon's *Essai politique* had exerted among the Intieri circle. Both Melon and Muratori had decided to exclude the moral side of the argument, and Genovesi followed this lead in his early economic writings. In an almost literal translation of Melon he contended that moral concerns were not the 'the principal concern of the politician'.[28] This was still a time when Genovesi was optimistic that a programme of economic reform alone could solve the region's most pressing problems.

Ten years later, however, Genovesi returned to the question of luxury, and he had become much less convinced that its moral value could be ignored. In the *Lettere accademiche* of 1764 (a dialogue between a defender of religious morals and the simple life and a priest—Genovesi—defending the arts and refinement in modern society), Genovesi had outlined the two functions of luxury: that it acted as an incentive to work and that it facilitated the redistribution of wealth. Though born out of inequality, luxury was a 'remedy against poverty'.[29] In his *Dialoghi morali* (a commentary to the *Lettere accademiche*) Genovesi distanced himself from this all too enthusiastic endorsement by characterizing exaggerated luxury as 'a theft' which could lead to ruin.[30] Now, Genovesi was faced with a dilemma. On

[28] Genovesi, 'Elementi del commercio', Biblioteca Nationale, Naples, MS XIII-B-92; quoted by Pii, *Antonio Genovesi*, 198.

[29] Genovesi, *Lettere accademiche*, in *Illuministi italiani*, vol. ii/1, letter x, pp. 257 and 255.

[30] Genovesi, *Dialoghi morali inediti*, Biblioteca Nationale, Naples, MS XIV-B-39; repr. in Lucio Villari, *Il pensiero economico di Antonio Genovesi* (Florence, 1958), 138–86. Villari has

the one hand, he was still convinced of the economic need for luxury—he had said so in the 'Elementi' at the beginning of the 1750s, and he had just repeated it in the *Lettere accademiche*. On the other, he had realized that the moral question could not as easily be brushed aside as he had done in the 'Elementi' with its endorsement of the position of Melon. There was in fact a strong strand of Neapolitan thinking which was extremely critical of Melon, and which had treated luxury as a predominantly moral phenomenon. It was difficult to ignore this position because of the influence it had exerted in Naples for over a generation. It had been presented by members of one of Naples's most important academies, the Accademia degli Oziosi, in the 1730s and 1740s, and in particular by its members Paolo Mattia Doria and Carlo Antonio Broggia.

Doria, a humanist of Genoese origin who had moved to Naples in the 1760s, had become a critic of Newtonian philosophy and of the new economic theories as embodied by Melon.[31] He did not single out Melon explicitly, but his attack on the *civile epicurea società* was clear enough.[32] In fact, even Muratori was criticized as too lenient in his denunciation of Epicureanism and the repudiation of the passions.[33] Doria's economic thought consequently placed special emphasis on the eminently social character of economic activity.[34] The essence of the economy was 'the mutual support' lent each other by 'the people who are united in civil society'. This view left no room for luxury, which 'by nature is a vice and poison for republics'.[35] Doria's contemporary Carlo Antonio Broggia, a merchant turned political economist writing in the tradition of a Christian economy, had argued against 'the sophisticated sceptical Epicureans who are so fashionable nowadays' that luxury led to 'moral disorder'. The arguments of Melon were dismissed as 'a branch of errors'.[36]

published five of the twenty-four dialogues. The one quoted here is dialogue XVI, printed by Villari as no. 1; the reference to luxury on pp. 139–40.

[31] On the Accademia degli Oziosi and on Doria's active role in it, see Ferrone, *Scienza natura religione*, 525–30.

[32] Doria, *Difesa della metafisica*, quoted by Ferrone, *Scienza natura religione*, 592.

[33] The criticism of Muratori in his *Ragionamenti e poesie varie* is printed in Enrico Vidal, *Il pensiero civile di Paolo Mattia Doria negli scritti inediti: con il testo del manoscritto 'Del commercio del Regno di Napoli'* (Milan, 1953), 70–2.

[34] On Doria's economic thought, Vidal, *Il pensiero civile*, 81–101, is still of some use.

[35] Paolo Mattia Doria, *Del commercio del Regno di Napoli* (1740), in Vidal, *Il pensiero civile*, 162–5 and 209.

[36] Carlo Antonio Broggia, *Memoria ad oggetto di varie politiche ed economiche ragioni* (Naples, 1754), in Raffaele Ajello, Marino Berengo, *et al.* (eds.), *Dal Muratori al Cesarotti*, v (Milan, 1978), 1041–59: 1041–2 and 1050–1. Broggia noted that he was aware of the spread of Epicurean ideas through the work of Thomas Stanley, *The History of Philosophy* (London,

If Genovesi wanted to rescue Melon and defend the economic benefits of luxury, he had to show that it was not morally reproachable and did not lead to moral disorder. He did so in his *Lezioni di commercio o sia d'economia civile* by adapting arguments about refinement from David Hume, and by making a Christian case for distributive justice born out of luxury. When Genovesi published his *Lezioni di commercio* in 1765 and 1767, he rehearsed the economic benefits of luxury (such as the circulation and distribution arguments, and its positive effects on consumption and the perfection of the arts).[37] He also dropped his previous critique of foreign luxury (which he had repeated in the first version of the *Lezioni di commercio*) in the final form which appeared in print. In the first version of 1757–8 he had basically followed Muratori in his attack on foreign luxury, which was 'pernicious . . . because [it] drains money out of the country'.[38] When Genovesi gave his lectures to the press, he recognized the positive effects of international competition: the presence of imported luxury goods of high quality awakened the competitive spirit and the ambition of the artisan at home and thus led to the improvement of the arts.[39] On top of those changes, he added two new arguments to his economic defence of luxury. First, he argued that luxury led to cultural refinement. Luxury signified 'the refinement of the mode of living'.[40] It was 'necessary for the culture, diligence, and politeness of nations'.[41] Luxury as a catalyst for the refinement of nations significantly changed its moral value. No longer a vice, it could even within certain limits be understood as virtue. This argument takes up David Hume, who had argued against Mandeville that it was 'little less than a contradiction in terms, to talk of a vice, which is in general beneficial to society'.[42] Hume himself had not drawn the conclusion that it should thus be seen as virtue, but Genovesi did. It was the first element of his moral justification of luxury.

The second element is his consideration of the role of luxury in the downfall of individuals. Muratori had observed that luxury may well lead

1655–62), which he probably knew in its Latin version, which had come out in Venice in 1731; Broggia, *Memoria*, 1049 and n.

[37] Genovesi, *Delle lezioni di commercio o sia d'economia civile*, 2 vols. (Naples, 1765, 1767). I quote from the selection in *Illuministi italiani*, ii/2. 177–251.

[38] The first manuscript version is given by Venturi in his notes to the *Lezioni di commercio*, 191 n. 2. On the different versions, cf. Franco Venturi, 'Le *Lezioni di Commercio* di Antonio Genovesi: manoscritti, edizioni e traduzioni', *Rivista storica italiana*, 72 (1960), 511–30.

[39] Genovesi, *Lezioni di commercio*, 193. [40] Ibid. 184. [41] Ibid. 179.

[42] Hume, 'Of Refinement in the Arts', in Hume, *Political Essays*, ed. Knud Haakonssen (Cambridge, 1994), 114. On Genovesi's knowledge and use of Hume in general, see Pii, *Antonio Genovesi*, 203–5.

families into ruin, and that this was an individual disaster mitigated only by the fact that it did not harm society at large.[43] Genovesi turned the example into a case of distributive justice in which luxury became instrumental. It was true, Genovesi conceded, that luxury 'ruins the grand old families, and lifts up new ones'. But, he continued, this was instrumental in ensuring that 'the rich reimburse to the poor what they have taken from the public patrimony . . . so that the slaves are freed, and the free enslaved'.[44] Similar to the *Lettere accademiche*, which had been a critical engagement with Jean-Jacques Rousseau,[45] this argument also takes issue with one of Rousseau's central contentions. Rousseau had argued that luxury led to poverty in the long term because of the downfall of families once they had fallen prey to luxury. Genovesi admitted this, but the incentive function of luxury would see to it that poor families would rise and perpetuate national wealth. This economic principle served as a moral argument *for* luxury to counter Rousseau's moral argument against it: distributive justice against the claim of the decline of morals.

Genovesi's moral defence of luxury came at a price, however. It had made a case for distributive justice which was directed against those who held luxury responsible for the ruin of individuals. It was an attempt to beat Doria and Broggia with their own weapons. It employed their language in order to rescue their adversary Melon. But the very reasoning rests on the old Christian fear of the corrupting influence of wealth which had characterized the Accademia degli Oziosi. The argument that luxury spending turned the rich into slaves of the material world and set the poor free was nothing but a new formulation of the old contention that conspicuous consumption was against the will of God and led to ruin—both material and spiritual. Ultimately, Genovesi refused to abandon the Christian notion that God would punish the greedy.

But Genovesi had found a way out of the dilemma he had created: the tension between the positive economic effects of luxury on the one hand, and the early characterization as 'theft' which led to the downfall of individuals on the other. Moving attention away from its effects on the rich individual and introducing his case for distributive justice, the *mercatante* in

[43] The issue had been dismissed by Mandeville, who had aptly stated that such ruin was the fault not of luxury but of folly since whoever lived above his income was a fool (Mandeville, *The Fable of the Bees, or, Private Vices, Public Benefits*, ed. F. B. Kaye, 2 vols. (Indianapolis, 1988), i. 249. Muratori had taken the problem more seriously but had justified it with reference to the public benefit of luxury.

[44] Genovesi, *Lezioni di commercio*, 190.

[45] Paola Zambelli, *La formazione filosofica di Antonio Genovesi* (Naples, 1972), esp. pp. 421–37.

him could stand by his conviction that luxury was needed for economic development. Against the background of the economic concerns of the Intieri circle, which was his intellectual home, against the background of his professional concern for political economy from the 1750s onwards, and against the truly eye-opening crop disaster of 1764, Genovesi ultimately accepted luxury as an economic force notwithstanding its moral ambiguity.

Luxury in Naples: Galiani, Money, and Melon

If Antonio Genovesi remained ambiguous towards luxury and oscillated between metaphysics and the new science of economics, Ferdinando Galiani was a man more at home in the intellectual world of Newtonianism. A close associate of Diderot and one of the most outspoken critics of physiocracy, Galiani championed rational, empirical methods to explain society.[46] Whereas the older generation of Neapolitans such as Paolo Mattia Doria had expressed a deep concern with Christian morality, and had tried to place economic development within the general context of social justice, Galiani (as well as his teacher Intieri) viewed morality and justice as entirely economic in orientation.[47] Not dissimilar to Mandeville's thesis, and well in line with Augustinian and Epicurean thinking, the two understood human nature to be determined by passions which society needed in order to prosper. Passions constituted public benefits. Galiani expressed this thought and its relation to the prevailing Newtonian ideology very clearly when he stated that the 'desire for gain; or to live happily' was equivalent in the moral sciences to gravity in the physical. Since 'man is a complex of passions, which move him with unequal force' these can be studied and made to yield benefits for society at large.[48]

Galiani tackled the question of luxury at the early age of 22 in his influential work *Della moneta*, which appeared in 1751. In his explanation of why prices had been low in the Middle Ages and had been rising since the fifteenth century, he accepted the common theory that scarcity of precious metals and government manipulation had caused a rise in prices even before the discovery of America. But it was the introduction of American gold

[46] Marco Minerbi, 'Diderot, Galiani e la polemica sulla fisiocrazia', *Studi storici*, 14 (1973), 147–84, esp. pp. 159–84. The critique of physiocracy (which led Diderot to reconsider his own position) is Ferdinando Galiani, *Dialogues sur le commerce des bleds* (1770), ed. Fausto Nicolini (Milan, 1959).

[47] Cf. Raffaele Ajello, 'La critica del regime in Doria, Intieri e Broggia', in Ajello, *Arcana iuris: diritto e politica nel Settecento italiano* (Naples, 1976), 389–427.

[48] Ferdinando Galiani, *Della moneta libri cinque* (Naples, 1750 [1751]), 279.

and silver in particular which had given a boost to economic life in Europe. It had brought not only commerce and industry but also 'peace and humanity, perfection of the arts, luxury and magnificence', and Europe was 'wondrously filled with wealth and happiness'.[49] The positive tone underlying his treatment of luxury was thus set, and it is quite possible that it was inspired in no small part by his reading of Melon, whom he praised as a 'man superior to all by a long way because of the acuteness of his mind and his experience in human things'.[50] But in his *Digressione intorno al lusso*, which form part of *Della moneta*, Galiani offered a more balanced account, which was partly directed against Melon. He pointed out the corrupting influence of luxury, and in this respect Melon was wrong to argue that luxury was the source of all good. It was the effect, not the cause, of good government, an argument which was to become the central contention of the *Encyclopédie* article on luxury.[51] It is tempting to think that Galiani, who was acquainted with the members of the *Encyclopédie* circle, was the intellectual father of the influential argument that appeared in France more than a decade later. But unlike the later French treatment, Galiani argued that luxury was the *unavoidable* fruit of prosperity. To ban luxury would be like forbidding the fruit to ripen in the hope that they would thus remain forever green. The metaphor employed by Galiani, and which invoked a cyclical course of history, is reminiscent of Vico.[52] But whereas the latter had been most sceptical about this development, Galiani's optimism again gained the upper hand. Was it not fortunate to live in an age where the fruits of previous hardship could finally be harvested? To rail against luxury was simply to exalt 'military barbarism by calling it virtue and to declare the mercantile industry ignoble'. Economics was a zero-sum game for Galiani just as it was for Rousseau, who wrote his first discourse at the very same time. 'It is clear that in a world with today's population one cannot get richer without another one getting poorer.' But this had to be accepted, and the only question was whether to increase wealth through commerce or conquest. How could

[49] Galiani, *Digressione intorno al lusso, considerato generalmente*, in *Della moneta*, 17. The money debate in Naples has received growing attention in recent years. See e.g. Alessandro Roncaglia (ed.), *Alle origini del pensiero economico in Italia*, i: *Moneta e sviluppo negli economisti napoletani dei secoli* XVII–XVIII (Bologna, 1995). On the importance of Galiani's book in the Italian debate on money and on its implicit opposition to Carlo Antonio Broggia's *Trattato dei tributi*, see Venturi, *Settecento riformatore*, i. 490–508. See also Luigi Einaudi, 'Galiani economista', in Einaudi, *Saggi bibliografici e storici intorno alle dottrine economiche* (Rome, 1953), 269–305.

[50] Galiani, *Della moneta*, 233.

[51] See above, Ch. 2.

[52] On Vichean influence on Galiani, see Terence Hutchison, *Before Adam Smith: The Emergence of Political Economy, 1662–1776* (Oxford, 1988), 255–70.

commerce not be preferred given that it 'sucks the blood even from more distant [peoples], less gloriously perhaps, but with more commodity.'[53]

Economic and social thought had gone a long way in Naples in the course of the eighteenth century. At the beginning luxury was considered as part of a Christian economy, which stressed the eminently social character of economic activity. The theories of Doria and Broggia were by no means in line with official Church doctrine (a fact aptly illustrated by the persecution of Doria, which led to the burning of his last book posthumously in 1753), but they reflect a deep concern with Christian morality.[54] The influence of Newtonian science more and more affected the social sciences as well.[55] Ferdinando Galiani made this clear when he compared the laws governing human behaviour with those of gravity. And as early as 1738 Bartolomeo Intieri spoke of economics as a science, a *scienza del commercio*.[56] With the rational approach came practical concerns, and they lay at the heart of Antonio Genovesi's economic works. On one level, this translated into concrete proposals how to foster economic development in Naples, the institution of academies to generate useful knowledge, census projects, and the like. On a more intellectual level, the new approach led to a rigorous analysis of the moving forces of human behaviour and how they related to the well-being of society at large. This explains why Melon's teaching was so favourably received by the Intieri circle, and why (in Broggia's frustrated phrase) the Epicureans had become so fashionable. Luxury was part of this reassessment, even though the Neapolitans (and Genovesi in particular) never quite abandoned the Neapolitan tradition and the sceptical positions of enlightened Catholicism. At first, the new approach was encouraged by the administration. The hopes that came with independence in 1734 were great, and the new reform spirit brought a host of thinkers to occupy themselves seriously with the future of their land. But the reforms stalled in the 1740s, and enthusiasm gave way to increasing scepticism. Bernardo Tanucci, the former professor from Tuscany and important political leader in Naples who had held key positions in politics since the early days of the new regime, remained if not hostile to, then largely ignorant of, enlightened projects. In 1764 he is reported to have asked Galiani what exactly the *Encyclopédie* was.[57] The age of Genovesi was not one of enlightened

[53] Galiani, *Della moneta*, 287–91.

[54] Paola Zambelli, 'Il rogo postumo di Paolo Mattia Doria', in Zambelli (ed.), *Ricerche sulla cultura dell'Italia moderna* (Laterza, 1973), 147–98, esp. pp. 183–92.

[55] For the interplay between Newtonian science and enlightened Catholicism, see Ferrone, *Scienza natura religione*, chs. 5 and 6.

[56] In frequent letters to Celestino Galiani in 1738–9; cf. ibid. 575.

[57] Venturi, *Settecento riformatore*, v/1. 275.

hegemony, and the distance was growing between Tanucci's reforms and what Genovesi and his pupils were writing. When Genovesi's chair became vacant after his death in 1769, it was abolished. But Genovesi had left his mark. In the words of the Venetian man of letters Griselini, he had brought about 'a revolution in the way of thinking' by placing the economy at the centre of his thought.[58] And Cesare Beccaria spoke for future generations of political economists when he called Genovesi 'the founder of this science in Italy'.[59]

[58] *Giornale d'Italia spettante alla scienza naturale e principalmente all'agricoltura, alle arti ed al commercio*, 23 (1768), 177.

[59] Cesare Beccaria, *Prolusione letta il giorno 9 Gennaio 1769 nell'apertura della nuova cattedra di scienze camerali nelle scuole palatine di Milano*, in Beccaria, *Opere*, ed. Sergio Romagnoli (Florence, 1958), 376.

II

Public Culture and the Transmission of Ideas

4

Tuscany: The Politics of Reform in an Agricultural Land

Old Problems and a New Beginning under the House of Lorraine

The final years of the Medici regime in Tuscany witnessed a state of political decline.[1] Incapable of securing decent living conditions through a prospering economy, the grand duchy saw its population diminish continuously over the decades, with only marginal increases in Florence and declines in other cities such as Siena.[2] Political and economic power lay in the hands of Florentine patricians, who had managed to keep their dominant role through the centuries by maintaining positions at court and by means of office, which, in turn, served to promote their own mercantile interests.

The political balance changed once the Medici dynasty gave way to the Lorraine regency, and later Peter Leopold. Soon after taking up office, Francis Stephen, the new grand duke, attempted to limit noble hegemony by curbing spheres of noble influence. All consuls of city guilds, who had hitherto been drawn exclusively from the patriciate, were dismissed in 1739 and replaced by qualified experts, who were put in charge of carrying out new economic and fiscal policies. Subsequent attempts to redefine the role of the nobility were guided not so much by the desire to further weaken the once dominating class, but to control them. The restriction of the eligibility to apply for *fidecommessi* in 1749, for example, effectively secured continuing noble influence, and the new definition of the legal status of the nobility in 1750 served the same purpose.

[1] The best recent general account of the Medici regime is Furio Diaz, *I Medici* (Turin, 1976). On the political and social history of 18th-century Tuscany, see Diaz, 'La Reggenza', in Diaz, Luigi Mascilli Migliorini, and Carlo Mangio, *Il Granducato di Toscana: i Lorena dalla Reggenza agli anni rivoluzionari* (Turin, 1997), 3–245. For the time from the 1760s up to the revolution, see Luigi Mascilli Migliorini, 'L'età delle riforme', ibid. 249–421.

[2] Cf. Giulio Beloch, 'La popolazione d'Italia nei secoli sedicesimo, diciasettesimo, diciottesimo', in Carlo Cipolla (ed.), *Storia dell'economia italiana* (Turin, 1965), 449–500. See also Giuseppe Parenti, *La popolazione della Toscana sotto la Reggenza lorense* (Florence, 1937), and Lorenzo del Panta, *Una traccia di storia demografica della Toscana nei secoli* XVI–XVIII (Florence, 1974).

When Francis Stephen took over as grand duke in 1737, he was confronted with a malfunctioning administration that needed reform. Most of the work was not carried out by him, however, but by the several plenipotentiaries whom he installed during his reign. Invariably, the new administration had to take stock at first and commissioned an investigation into the situation of the region before they could even begin to implement reforms. Hostility of the old leading classes towards the new rulers made matters even more difficult. In fact, the term *lorense* carried a derogatory meaning in Tuscany for a long time after the ascent of Francis Stephen.[3] Government activity was therefore directed at setting up an efficient working administration. In this, the new regime proved successful. It should not be surprising, however, that it took time to align all forces behind the new rulers. As a consequence, social and economic issues were not tackled at first and the Lorraine regency left the existing social structure relatively intact. Measures which paved the way towards subsequent economic liberalization and social change, such as the lifting of export restrictions on grain in 1738, were exceptions to this rule, as was the restructuring of the guild system. Nevertheless, the importance of the initial period of the new regime should not be undervalued. Not only did it prepare the ground for future reform policies by creating an administrative environment in which they could be carried out. Perhaps more importantly, it instilled in the educated younger generation the conviction that the fresh start offered them possibilities which would have seemed unthinkable under Medici rule. Allegiance, it is true, had to be owed to the central power, and this helped overcome the fragmented nature of pre-Lorraine Tuscan society. However, the very existence of an external power increased the possibility of offering the expert advice without which the Habsburg rulers could not act.

Pompeo Neri, a Florentine who rose to become an influential administrator in Tuscany, is a case in point. Though not a *homo novus* himself, he nevertheless benefited from the new regime. In the late 1740s he was commissioned to reflect on the proper role and status of the nobility. His thoughts, which appeared in print under the title *Trattato della nobiltà* in 1776, provided the basis for the new legislation on the nobility which demanded proof of descent.[4]

Neri's text is not only an example of Tuscan influence in the preparation of Habsburg legislation. It also serves to show that the installation of a new

[3] Eric Cochrane, *Florence in the Forgotten Centuries, 1527–1800* (Chicago, 1973), 346.

[4] The text is now in Franco Venturi's edition of the *Illuministi italiani*: Pompeo Neri, *Discorso sopra lo stato antico e moderno della nobiltà di Toscana* (1748), in *Illuministi italiani*, i/2. 951–7.

regime went hand in hand with a shift in emphasis away from legal preoccupations towards enquiries with a focus on social and economic issues.[5] Neri's basic assumption was that a purely legal frame of enquiry was inadequate to comprehend the character of the nobility in Tuscany. Rather, a distinction between natural and civil nobility should be adopted, the former being universal and unchangeable, the latter being created by, and subject to the needs of, government. His central claim was that privilege had no place in the definition of nobility. Nobility was identical with the social and political role of the ruling class. What Neri envisaged here is a sort of *noblesse de robe avant la lettre*, and in turning away from legal concepts, Neri effectively followed the example set by Muratori in his *Dei difetti della giurisprudenza* (1742). His new interest in things social and economic was later to be taken up by the Milanese circle around Pietro Verri, who was fighting his own struggle against the legal minds of the generation of his father.[6]

New Ways of Thinking and the Forums for Education and Debate: Universities and Academies

In Tuscany, however, the new line of thinking—partly encouraged by the new government—gained momentum and spread through the grand duchy. Breeding grounds for new ideas were the universities, where most administrators were educated. The University of Pisa in particular played a decisive role in shaping the intellectual outlook of the Tuscan administrative elite. A large part of the ruling class of eighteenth-century Tuscany passed through its law school. For the most part sons of Florentine patricians and middling landowners, they were convinced of the need for reform based on a thorough and empirical understanding of Tuscan problems. Their pragmatism and the conviction that the observation of nature should be the starting point of any enquiry was congenially expressed in the teachings of professors in Pisa such as Giuseppe Averani. His legal school educated generations of new leaders and passed on to them a veneration for Galileo and his scientific method which was transposed into the realm of political and economic enquiry.[7]

[5] This is not, of course, an entirely new enterprise. Bandini's purely economic work from the 1730s precedes Neri's treatise by more than a decade. What is new here is that themes that would hitherto have been treated as legal matters were now being considered in their social and economic dimension.

[6] On Neri and his *Trattato della nobiltà*, cf. Franco Venturi, *Settecento riformatore*, i (Turin, 1998), 325–30.

[7] Nicola Carranza, 'L'università di Pisa e la formazione culturale del ceto dirigente toscano

If universities were responsible for the education of the promising youth of the region, academies provided the forum for those already in office. The academies had long been an important part of Tuscan intellectual life. Founded mostly in the sixteenth century to replace the humanist academies of the Renaissance, institutions like the Accademia della Crusca and the Accademia Fiorentina (to name but the two most famous Florentine academies) soon became gathering places for the intellectual elite in Tuscany.[8] Many of the old academies continued to prosper in the eighteenth century, and proudly acknowledged their heritage from the times of Tuscan grandeur—with the result that both their constitutions and their activities remained virtually unchanged from the times of Medician rule.[9] Translation from Latin and Greek into Tuscan, erudition, and history were the domains of the early academies well into the eighteenth century, and the ambitious dictionary of the Tuscan language published in various editions by the Accademia della Crusca is a typical and perhaps the most accomplished example of the academies' concerns. In the age of reform, however, this rapidly began to change with the formation of new academies in almost every Tuscan community—and three in Florence alone.[10] To be sure, membership of old and new academies alike continued to comprise almost everyone of any intellectual or social prominence, but their association with the highest layers of government became ever more pronounced. Nearly all the royal ministers under Peter Leopold, for example, were active in the famous Accademia dei Georgofili, founded in 1753 as one of the first agricultural academies in Europe.[11]

The functions of the academies were manifold. First and foremost, they created an intellectual community which other institutions could not offer. Tuscan universities had achieved their professional and intellectual standing at the cost of interdisciplinary exchange by forming highly independent

nel Settecento: studi di storia pisana e toscana in onore del professore Ottorino Bertolini', *Bolletino storico pisano*, 33–5 (1964–6), 469–537.

[8] On the early academies, see the exhaustive work by Michel Maylender, *Storia delle accademie d'Italia*, 5 vols. (Bologna, 1926–30), esp. vol. iv, and August Buck, 'Die humanistischen Akademien in Italien', in Fritz Hartmann and Rudolf Vierhaus (eds.), *Der Akademiegedanke im 17. und 18. Jahrhundert* (Bremen, 1977), 11–25, on the decline of the humanistic academies at the beginning of the 16th century.

[9] On the academies in the 18th century, see the pioneering and still valuable study by Eric Cochrane, *Tradition and Enlightenment in the Tuscan Academies, 1690–1800* (Chicago, 1961), esp. pp. 1–34 on the development of the academies from the 16th to the 18th century.

[10] On the academies' changing range of activities, see ibid. 35–65.

[11] On the Accademia dei Georgofili, see most recently Renato Pasta, 'L'Accademia dei Georgofili e la riforma dell'agricoltura', *Rivista storica italiana*, 105 (1993), 484–501.

chairs and lectureships in distinct and isolated subjects such as law. Tuscan *salotti* never achieved the prominence of their Parisian counterparts partly because women played a considerably less important role in Tuscan society than in Paris.[12] Freemasonry, finally, never gained the strength and importance in the grand duchy that it did in, say, Naples, and the earliest Tuscan lodges seem to have been dissolved at the first signs of official disapproval.[13] If it fell to the academies to provide a home for the intellectual community and encourage debate, they played an important role in the dissemination of ideas, too. Even though Tuscan academies were proud of their Tuscan origins, they nevertheless saw themselves as part of a cosmopolitan republic of letters, and it was in the academies more than anywhere else that new ideas from across Europe were first received and discussed before they found a wider audience through Tuscan journals. As a channel for ideas, the importance of the academies can hardly be undervalued, and subsequent chapters will analyse their pivotal role in shaping public opinion.[14]

Finally, the academies were a place where individual research could be abandoned in favour of teamwork, which the academicians increasingly saw as the only form of enquiry which could solve the political and economic problems of their age. It was this aspect of a team of highly qualified, intellectually rigorous, politically interested individuals that made some academies the precursors of today's think-tanks. The Accademia dei Georgofili in particular played an important role in the preparation of legislation. From 1753 onwards the head of the regency walked in on meetings to use the academy as a 'pool of intellect' to draw upon for assistance.[15] The reform of 'colonial' contracts between landowners and tenants, for example, was prepared by academicians: the government had asked the Accademia dei Georgofili to voice its opinion, and its verdict was later incorporated into the legislation.[16]

[12] See Dena Goodman, *The Republic of Letters: A Cultural History of the French Enlightenment* (Ithaca, NY, 1994), on Parisian salons.

[13] See Vincenzo Ferrone, *I profeti dell'illuminismo: metamorfosi della ragione nel tardo Settecento italiano* (Rome, 1989), on freemasonry in late 18th-century Italy, and Giuseppe Giarizzo, *Massoneria e illuminismo nell'Europa del Settecento* (Venice, 1994), which also treats the German and Austrian world.

[14] Eric Cochrane, 'Le relazioni delle accademie toscane del Settecento con la cultura europea', *Archivio storico italiano*, 111 (1953), 78–108. See below, Chs. 5 and 6.

[15] Cochrane, *Tradition and Enlightenment*, 54.

[16] Mario Mirri, 'Un'inchiesta toscana sui tributi pagati dai mezzadri e sui patti colonici nella seconda metà del Settecento: le memorie di Pelli-Bencivenni, Pagnini, Tramontani e Paoletti', *Annali dell'Istituto Giangiacomo Feltrinelli*, 2 (1959), 483–559.

The Desire for Reform: New Political Momentum under Peter Leopold

Both universities and academies helped shape the formulation of government policies, either directly as in the case of colonial contracts, or indirectly as in the case of the universities, which educated future administrators. The ready participation of the Tuscan intellectuals in the administration was in fact one of the most striking characteristics of the grand duchy, which contrasted sharply with, for example, Germany's *gebildete Stände*, whose political participation was often (as in the case of Hamburg) marred by perpetual struggles with magistrates.[17] If Naples was characterized by 'a divorce between the intellectuals and the crown', in Tuscany the marriage remained intact.[18] Reform, however, ultimately depended on the grand duke and his plenipotentiaries. Under Count Richecourt (the plenipotentiary from 1737 jointly with the prince of Craon, and alone from 1747 to 1757) administrative reform made noticeable leeway, whereas under the marchese Antonio Botta Adorno (1757 to 1765) the pace of reform slackened considerably. But again, among their most prominent contributions to reform was precisely that they made intellectuals unusually welcome to contribute to government activity through both public discussion and direct involvement in the administration.

In this respect, even the slowing down of reform activity in the decade before the ascent of Peter Leopold (which was partly due to the lack of interest and ability of the Genoese Botta Adorno) was fruitful in that it allowed reform programmes to mature and enabled the formation of a group of intellectuals capable of lending their voice to the government's newly found optimism.

When Peter Leopold arrived in Florence in 1765, Tuscan politics took a turn for the better. Not only did the second son of Maria Theresa personally reside in the grand duchy—a novelty since the days of the Medici. He was also open to wide-ranging reform programmes. From the very beginning Peter Leopold took a keen personal interest in the welfare of his lands, and in ways of improving the desolate economic situation. The basis for such endeavours was the 'Great Enquiry' of 1766, which relied largely on local input. The enquiry was to provide an account of the present state of the arts and commerce, of the balance of trade, and of agricultural

[17] Joachim Whaley, *Religious Toleration and Social Change in Hamburg* (Cambridge, 1985), and, more generally, Mack Walker, *German Home Towns: Community, State, General Estates, 1648–1871* (Ithaca, NY, 1971).

[18] On Naples, see Ferrone, *I profeti dell'illuminismo*, 196–9: 198.

production. Carried out by Tuscans (Francesco Maria Gianni, who was to become one of Peter Leopold's most trusted advisers, was part of the commission), it is an important example of the ways in which the Tuscan intellectual elite could influence the course of Habsburg legislation. In fact, Peter Leopold seems to have valued local support even more than his predecessor, a tendency reinforced by the higher degree of independence from Vienna that he enjoyed after the death of his father, and which allowed him to focus more on Tuscan issues. Transcending purely empirical goals, the enquiry prepared the grounds for some of Peter Leopold's subsequent legislation. The concern with which the enquiry treated the issue of transport routes, and the assessment of the importance of different means of transport, for example, translated directly into Peter Leopold's transport legislation.[19]

The role played by external advisers in the formulation of legislation should also remind us of the fact that Peter Leopold, an enlightened absolutist ruler though he was, was uniquely inclined to rethink the nature of his authority. Even though his plans for a written constitution did not in the end come to fruition, he was nevertheless the 'first monarch convinced of the need of constitutional monarchy to have resided in Europe'.[20] Peter Leopold, the self-styled 'philosopher' on the throne, a man of shrewd intelligence and intellectual perceptiveness, managed to incorporate almost the entire Tuscan intellectual class in the drawing up and sometimes in the execution of reforms.[21] The active participation in government—much more pronounced than in any other Italian, or indeed European, state—led to two significant results. First, by being given the chance to bring about actual change, the elite directed its efforts towards practical goals rather than theoretical elaboration. The Great Enquiry is a case in point. This is not to say, of course, that theoretical works with a wider-ranging critical perspective were absent during the period under consideration, and much of the following chapters will be concerned with identifying and analysing these. However, the prevalence of empirical works with practical applicability can

[19] Cf. Luigi Dal Pane, 'I lavori preparatori per la grande inchiesta del 1766 sull'economia toscana', in *Studi in onore di Gioacchino Volpe per il suo ottantesimo compleanno* (Florence, 1958), i. 261–313, esp. pp. 263–4 and 312.

[20] Heinz Holldack, 'Die Reformpolitik Leopolds von Toskana', *Historische Zeitschrift*, 165 (1942), 23–46, the quotation on p. 46. Much has been written about the constitution project. The classic account is Johann Zimmermann, *Das Verfassungsprojekt des Grossherzogs Peter Leopold von Toskana* (Heidelberg, 1901). See, more recently, Giulio M. Manetti, *La Costituzione inattuata: Pietro Leopoldo granduca di Toscana: dalla riforma comunitativa al progetto di costituzione* (Florence, 1991).

[21] Adam Wandruszka, 'Die Persönlichkeit Kaiser Leopold II.', *Historische Zeitschrift*, 192 (1961), 295–317.

be explained by the positive use that was made of them. When Dino Carpanetto observes that the Tuscan intellectuals all but ignored the influence of the *lumières* and were 'unwilling to abandon [the] experimental and pragmatic tradition', and suggests that this was because they were 'incapable of understanding the radical implications of many books which were arriving from outside', this only tells half the story.[22] What is more important is that they were in the fortunate situation of seeing their works adapted and used for legislative activity. Theirs was an opportunity that was hard to miss. Secondly, the warm welcome of the intellectual class into the centre of power helped overcome the initial resentment and hostility towards the new regime. It was one of the main reasons for the nearly unanimous acceptance of enlightened absolutism that characterized Tuscan thought throughout the eighteenth century and that allowed other concerns—most notably the economic fate of the country—to come to the fore and dominate intellectual debate.

Through a publishing industry that gained in prestige and importance in the course of the century, intellectual debate spread from the inner circles of the administration, from the universities and from the academies, to a much wider—albeit still very limited—public. If we can speak of a closed ministerial culture in the first half of the century (the clearest sign of which is the fact that most contributions to political economy which will be discussed in Chapter 5 took the form of administrative memorandums), the 1750s witnessed a remarkable change towards a public culture. Convinced that a much wider audience had to participate in matters of state and the economy, the ministerial papers were increasingly substituted by journal contributions and widely available political treatises. In such an environment the growing Florentine publishing industry benefited from, and contributed to, this new mode of political discourse.

The Spread of Ideas: Tuscan Journals and the Publishing Industry

It has long been thought that in Florence books were a rather insignificant local product for a local market. In the words of Eric Cochrane, 'Far from broadening the horizon of Florentine readers, they tended to increase their isolation from the rest of the world.'[23] This overly sceptical judgement of

[22] Dino Carpanetto and Giuseppe Ricuperati, *Italy in the Age of Reason, 1685–1789* (London, 1987), 210–11.

[23] Cochrane, *Florence in the Forgotten Centuries*, 319.

the Tuscan publishing industry has been corrected by recent scholarship. Even if the expansion of the Florentine publishing industry into foreign markets was limited, the commercialization of the book (often carried out by writers themselves) was an important factor in urban life.[24] Particularly from the 1760s onwards the profession recovered and boasted almost as many publishing houses as Milan, namely ten (which admittedly came nowhere near the 45 *stampatori* in Naples). Also the subject matter of the published books changed in the course of the century. Devotional literature, though still a major segment, yielded ground against the fine arts and journals, which, in the period between 1743 and 1767, made up more than 40 per cent of all published material, followed by legal and religious texts.[25]

Attracted by the freedom of the press, journalists flocked into the grand duchy from the 1760s, and periodicals flourished. Florence became one of the capitals of Italian journalism, and periodicals like the *Gazetta universale* reached a distribution of some 2,500 copies. Agricultural subjects in particular benefited from the new enthusiasm. Always practical in their approach, agricultural journals often took the lead in the coverage of Italian debates. The *Magazzino georgico* and the *Giornale fiorentino d'agricoltura, di arti, di economia politica e di commercio* were added to the venerable early fruits of Tuscan journalism and turned Florence into one of the centres of discussion for agricultural matters.

Those early fruits had established the fame of Tuscan journalism, and regular journals on economic subjects began to circulate much earlier than, for example, in France. The uncontested leader of this journalism from the period of the Lorraine regency to the first years of the government of Peter Leopold was Giovanni Lami. His *Novelle letterarie* effectively ended Venetian hegemony in the field of learned journals.[26] As I shall show in a subsequent chapter, its review section in particular is one of the most important examples of the transmission of ideas into the grand duchy.[27] Through personal connections rather than a sophisticated commercial network, Lami acquired between 150 and 300 subscribers (a third of them in Tuscany, the rest mainly in Lombardy), and his journal was read by the

[24] Françoise Waquet, 'I letterati-editori: produzione, finanziamento e commercio del libro erudito in Italia e in Europa (XVII–XVIII secolo)', *Quaderni storici*, 72 (1989), 821–38.

[25] Renato Pasta, 'Editoria e stampa nella Firenze del Settecento', *Roma moderna e contemporanea*, 2 (1994), 379–418.

[26] For the development of Tuscan journalism from the regency to the 1760s, cf. Giuseppe Ricuperati, 'Giornali e società nell'Italia dell' "Ancien Regime" (1668–1789)', in Valerio Castronovo and Nicola Tranfaglia (eds.), *La stampa italiana dal '500 all'800* (Rome, 1980), esp. pp. 165–91.

[27] See below, Ch. 5.

clergy, the nobility, and important administrators such as Pallavicini and Neri.[28] Begun in 1740 as a literary journal, the *Novelle letterarie* shifted its attention to economic matters in the 1750s with reviews of the works of Galiani and Hume. The review of the translation of Hume's *Political Discourses* in 1755, in particular, marked the beginning of a systematic interest in economic matters. Lami used the occasion to make the authors referred to by the translator, namely Melon, Ustariz, and Ulloa, known to his Tuscan readers.[29] The *Novelle letterarie* continued to be the flagship of learned journalism until the 1760s, the last decade of their publication, when they became increasingly anachronistic and out of line with recent developments in political economy.

Following in their wake was a series of smaller journals such as the *Giornale de' letterati* (1742–8, 1771–96), the *Magazzino Italiano* (1752), and the *Magazzino Toscano d'istruzione e di piacere* (1755–6). It was in these journals, which covered a broad range of subjects on the model of the *Spectator*, that economic debate was carried out or made public in eighteenth-century Tuscany.[30]

With the exception of Cesare Beccaria's mathematical work in the Milanese *Il Caffè*, articles in Italian learned journals were seldom of a purely theoretical nature. The reading public to which the predominantly regional journals were addressed was rarely interested in political economy as such but rather in political orientation, technical information, pedagogical message, or moral prescription, and journals devoted to a particular school as in France developed only gradually in the course of the nineteenth century.[31] It is from those vantage points that questions of political economy are often treated, and this explains why much of the debate was carried out in generalist journals and why the practical aspects were never lost from sight. They disseminated 'a science for the landowning class' with an overwhelming focus on specific, practical issues. But despite the restraints set by the demands of the reading public, the journals did encompass the big themes of political economy and featured its main authors. The review and

[28] Françoise and Jean-Claude Waquet, 'Presse et société: Le Public des "Novelle letterarie" de Florence (1749–1769)', *Revue française d'histoire du livre*, 22 (1979), 39–60.

[29] *Novelle letterarie*, 16/3 (1755), 42–6.

[30] On the character of Italian learned journals in the 18th century, cf. Massimo Augello and Marco Guidi, 'The Emergence of Economic Periodical Literature in Italy (1750–1900)', *History of Economic Ideas*, 4/3 (1996), 15–62, esp. pp. 19–35.

[31] Cf. Vieri Becagli, 'L'economia nei periodici del granducato di Toscana: la prima reggenza lorenese (1737–1765)', in Massimo Augello, Marco Bianchini, *et al.* (eds.), *Le riviste di economia in Italia (1700–1900): dai giornali scientifico–letterari ai periodici specialistici* (Milan, 1996), 69–88, esp. pp. 71–2.

survey section in particular served as 'access routes' for the more theoretical incarnations of the emerging science.[32]

The Economic System: A Model

The economic prospect of Italy in the eighteenth century was still overshadowed by the decline that had hit the peninsula in the previous century. The 'crisis' left virtually no sectors unaffected.[33] Particularly devastating effects, however, can be observed in the textile industry and the major cities. The seventeenth century effectively marked the end of Italian dominance, and indeed even competitiveness, in the fields of manufacture and industry. Much has been written about the origins of the decline. It seems certain now that it was caused by a multiplicity of trends both in Italy and abroad. Within Italian cities, rigid guild controls have been blamed for a reluctance to adapt to changing international markets and changing tastes. High labour costs and growing competition from abroad led to dwindling exports, which, in turn, affected the internal economy as a whole.[34] Mercantilist policies in Europe only served to magnify the problem since they accelerated the decline of foreign demand.

Italian industry reacted to the changing competitive environment. The reaction, however, was a predominantly conservative one. In the face of shrinking markets and cheap imitations from abroad, Italian industry decided to keep quality high. This made some economic sense as long as there was a market, however small, for high-price goods.[35] And there are in fact signs that the industries that survived and prospered were those 'that depended on exquisite and still unsurpassed workmanship for producing luxury or artistic objects in which quality counted more than costs'.[36]

Despite these occasional rays of hope, the diminishing role of the standard products that had characterized the economy in the seventeenth

[32] Augello, 'The Emergence', 28 and 35.

[33] Ruggiero Romano, 'L'Italia nella crisi del secolo XVII', *Studi storici*, 9 (1968), 723–41. The expression has since been commonly used to describe the state of the Italian economy in the 17th century; cf. e.g. Enrico Stumpo, 'La crisi del Seicento in Italia', in Nicola Tranfaglia and Massimo Firpo (eds.), *La storia: i grandi problemi dal Medioevo all'Età contemporanea*, v. (Turin, 1987), 313–37.

[34] Cf. Carlo M. Cipolla, 'The Economic Decline of Italy' (1952), in Brian Pullan (ed.), *Crisis and Change in the Venetian Economy in the Sixteenth and Seventeenth Centuries* (Methuen, 1968), 127–45.

[35] Paolo Malanima, *La decadenza di un'economia cittadina: l'industria a Firenze nei secoli XVI–XVIII* (Bologna, 1982), 166–70.

[36] Domenico Sella, *Italy in the Seventeenth Century* (London, 1997), 41.

century led to a shift in the range of successful goods. First of all, the centres of production moved away from the cities into the countryside. To the degree that the predominantly urban economy lost its competitive edge, the economic structure shifted towards a less urbanized society and a ruralization of industry. It is in the rural industries that lay outside guild jurisdiction that we find the strongest evidence of resilience and growth. In Tuscany a law of 1739 allowed the production of cloth outside the city walls, something the corporations had hitherto successfully opposed. The law caused an increase of textile production in rural Tuscany, albeit of lower quality than in Florence. As in other European countries, silk was best produced in towns and hence remained within the confines of Florence, whereas the production of cotton and linen increasingly moved away from the centre. The inferior quality resulted in prices about half those of Florentine cloth.[37]

The countryside also profited from what has been called the 'regionalization' of trade. The big cities lost their monopoly of commerce as various regions started to exchange their produce regardless of state boundaries and without the mediation of the capital cities.[38]

When the economy recovered towards the end of the seventeenth century (and finally, after slumps in the 1730s, from the 1740s onwards), its profile had changed dramatically. The countryside had taken the place hitherto occupied by the capital cities, and agriculture had become the only hope of development. As Domenico Sella has shown, the tradition-bound, over-regulated, and sheltered urban economy, incapable of innovation, was opposed by a resilient and even prospering agriculture in most of northern Italy.[39] It is not surprising, then, that agriculture soon offered the highest returns on investment in Tuscany and that resources were increasingly channelled to the countryside. At the same time as recession made peasants seek opportunities in the cities, wealth was increasingly transferred from the mercantile sector to investment in the land. The accumulation of capital did not, however, lead to a significant process of modernization. The term 'refeudalization' is justly being criticized today, but it serves well to describe the 'obstructionist and backward-looking tendencies' that went hand in hand with the influx of capital into the countryside (often without a corresponding influx of proprietors, so that absenteeism continued to

[37] Malanima, *Decadenza*, 166.

[38] Renzo Paolo Corritore, 'Il processo di "ruralizzazione" in Italia nei secoli XVII–XVIII: verso una regionalizzazione', *Rivista di storia economica*, 10 (1993), 353–86.

[39] Domenico Sella, *Crisis and Continuity: The Economy of Spanish Lombardy in the Seventeenth Century* (Cambridge, Mass., 1979).

upset the power structures in the countryside). Commercial ventures resulting from this situation, for example, generally failed to create wealth for further investment and served to entrench the social status quo.[40]

No matter whether the further development of agriculture was seen as the necessary condition for the subsequent revival of industry and commerce (as was argued by a member of the financial administration, Angiolo Tavanti) or whether it was hailed as the only sensible means of production (as was claimed by the secretary of the Accademia dei Georgofili, Giuseppe Sarchiani), one thing had become clear to contemporaries: agriculture was now the invariable starting point for any economic endeavour, and for any programme of economic reform.[41]

Most of Italy had become predominantly agricultural in response to the crisis, but different regions need to be characterized by different economic models: the feudal south with its large estates; central Italy, dominated by sharecropping, or *mezzadria*; and the flat areas in the north, where the management and the organization of agriculture proved open to the changes of a more capitalist mode of production such as long-term investment and systematic irrigation.

Sharecropping had been the dominant mode of agricultural production in Tuscany as well as major parts of central and northern Italy since the high Middle Ages.[42] Standard sharecropping contracts would last for a year, with the *mezzadro* working the land and half of the produce being handed over to the landlord. The latter, in turn, took charge of any investments in the land (such as drainage and the planting of mulberry trees for the production of silk), furnished buildings, tools, livestock, seed, and capital. Sharecropping did, it is true, give the poor access to the land. Not much, however, was done to improve cultivation, and the consequences of the system were frustrating on two accounts, especially as increased competition from abroad put increasing pressure on the economy. From the perspective of the peasant, it made little sense to invest any effort in long-term improvement of the land.

[40] Carpanetto and Ricuperati, *Italy in the Age of Reason*, 23.

[41] Lorenzo Pignotti, *Elogio storico di Angiolo Tavanti* (Florence, 1782), and Giuseppe Sarchiani, *Regolamento sul commercio, arti e manifatture della Toscana* (Florence, 1781), 107. Cf., on both authors, Luigi Mascilli Migliorini, 'L'età delle riforme', in Diaz *et al.*, *Il Granducato di Toscana*, 333–6 and 362–3.

[42] S. R. Epstein, 'Cities, Regions and the Late Medieval Crisis: Sicily and Tuscany Compared', *Past and Present*, 130 (1991), 3–50. Epstein argues that the transformation of agrarian structures into sharecropping farms based on the idea of self-sufficiency hindered long-term economic development but promised short-term gains for the leading *mezzadria* landlords. This needs to be understood in the context of his central argument that economic stagnation in the high Middle Ages was due not to institutional but to technical constraints. For ample bibliographical references on sharecropping, see ibid. 39 n. 82.

Since the duration of tenure could rarely be foreseen, the tenant would in all likelihood plant seeds the fruits of which he would not live to see. As a consequence, his marginal returns on any but the most needed investments was so low that he had no incentive to undertake them. Even when tenants stayed on longer than expected, the uncertainty of their contracts served to deter them from producing more than they needed for their subsistence.[43] This was further enhanced by the knowledge that so much of their income would be skimmed off that it proved economical to produce as little surplus as possible. If, then, far-sighted improvement of the land could not reasonably be expected from the tenant, it was equally little beneficial for the landlord. Given that he had to bear the whole cost of any investment in the land, but gained only half the profit it generated, his marginal returns, too, proved too low to be a sufficient incentive. The money that did flow into the countryside was employed there, but it was employed to lease out family-sized holdings to tenants, which guaranteed a steady—if modest—income. In Tuscany (contrary to other European regions with a strong and innovative agriculture such as the Low Countries) it was not used to pump capital into large properties with the hope of intensifying, rather than simply extending, production.[44] European competition made this road of simple extension increasingly difficult to take.

Nevertheless, land reform did take place, and in some cases it changed the structure of landownership for the better. The 1760s saw the beginning of a new economic policy which leased large plots of land to farmers, effectively distinguishing between formal ownership and working ownership as the system envisaged a perpetual lease with nominal rent. The advantage of the system, called *a livello*, was that it made tenancy more secure and fashioned long-term contracts which, in turn, made it economically sensible for the farmer to invest in his land. Once the new system had firmly taken root, agriculture improved.[45]

It has long been thought that Tuscany was transformed into the land of small property holders in the course of the eighteenth century. Mario Mirri has shown, however, that quite on the contrary the period of reform under Peter Leopold was in fact one which made big landowners the dominant

[43] Cf. Carlo Poni, *Gli aratri e l'economia agraria nel Bolognese dal XVII al XIX secolo* (Bologna, 1963), for a detailed analysis of this process.

[44] Jan de Vries and Ad van der Wonde, *The First Modern Economy: Success, Failure, and Perseverance of the Dutch Economy, 1500–1815* (Cambridge, 1997), 220–7. The Tuscan *mezzadria* has recently been placed in a wider European context by Robert S. Duplessis, *Transitions to Capitalism in Early Modern Europe* (Cambridge, 1997), esp. pp. 145–89.

[45] Giorgio Giorgetti, 'Per uno studio delle allivellazioni leopoldine', *Studi storici*, 2 (1966), 245–90.

class in Tuscany. He goes so far as to speak of a 'revival of the sharecropping system' in eighteenth-century Tuscany.[46] Much of the faith historians had placed in a change towards small property holdings stems from the land reform in the second half of the century. Peter Leopold had indeed disentailed 20–5 per cent of the entire land of the grand duchy from 1769 onwards. Crown and communal lands, Church property, and the grounds owned by hospitals were all brought to the market. It is now clear, however, that—contrary to the original aim of selling the land to peasants—it was bought up by rich landowners, whose interest it was to preserve sharecropping as the dominant form of agriculture. We know of the case of a Tuscan vicar who had given his disentailed land to peasants at their request. He was brought back into line by the grand duke, the land was seized, and most workers expelled from the former Church lands. Ultimately, most of the land was bought by rich landowners.[47] Considerations of justice apart, increasing farm sizes eventually gave way to large-scale investment in the land, which was geared towards long-term gain rather than subsistence. But again, as in the case of the *a livello* system, this took time. Until then, economic progress was doomed to languish.

The situation was not made better by the existence of an organ that acted as a mediator between the city and the countryside and which effectively regulated the grain market and set prices. The *annona* had been set up in the sixteenth century to provide bread for the towns and to control prices in the urban market. Soon considered indispensable, its growing importance in the seventeenth century was an outcome of the economic crisis which had led to a rural exodus. The urban ruling classes, keen to defend themselves against famine and revolt, responded with a strengthening of the powers of the *annona*, which became centres of networks of officials, merchants, major producers, bankers, and speculators.[48] In Rome, the city about whose *annona* we know most, it became a financial power of great influence. Not only did it provide bread and regulate prices, it also intervened in commercial dealings and the system of production through the retailing of grain and by giving credits to producers.[49] Paradoxically, the power to control prices

[46] Mario Mirri, 'Proprietari e contadini nelle riforme leopoldine', *Movimento operaio*, 7 (1955), 173–229: 227. The point is reiterated by Enzo Piscitelli, 'Il pensiero degli economisti italiani del '700 sull'agricoltura, la proprietà terriera e la condizione dei contadini', *Clio*, 15 (1979), 245–92, esp. pp. 286–7.

[47] Marina Laguzzi, 'L'alienazione dei beni ecclesiastici in Tocana sotto Pietro Leopoldo: un sondaggio in Valdinievole', *Archivio storico italiano*, 153 (1995), 335–67.

[48] Cf. Carpanetto and Ricuperati, *Italy in the Age of Reason*, 24–5.

[49] Volker Reinhardt, *Überleben in der frühneuzeitlichen Stadt. Annona und Getreideversorgung in Rom, 1563–1797* (Tübingen, 1991), 37–95, 361–411, and Jacques Revel, 'Le Grain

generally played into the hands of landowners and major producers. The level of the fixed prices guaranteed landowners the best price when grain was sold and secured their absolute monopoly with minimal risk. Price controls also allowed for a rapid turnover of grain without any speculative hoarding which, in turn, accelerated the return of the producer's capital and hence increased his profit.[50] Under this system no improvement in agricultural production was in sight. And if contemporaries recognized free trade and competition as the main instrument to achieve economic growth, then the *annona* effectively stood in the way of such development because it held a tight grip on the grain market.

The System and its Consequences

The implications of this system for the economy of Tuscany were manifold. They comprised living standards, prices, and exports. Where grain consumption was stable and seeds were provided by the landlord, living standards were directly proportional to the variable portion of the produce used to acquire goods and services. Under the sharecropping system, economic logic demanded that this portion was kept low because the peasant could only reap half the profit of an increase in production. It is notable, however, that the economic recovery of the 1740s affected peasant lifestyles. In England it has been observed that rising living standards and demands for luxury goods in the 1750s led to a heated and lengthy series of letters from members of the provincial gentry against the forces of luxury.[51] In Italy we can observe an increase in demands and expectations of the local population. Recent research has confirmed that Tuscan dietary habits changed significantly from the 1740s onwards. Contemporary opinion supports this assessment. As one observer remarked, the peasant who had long been content with bread and *aquarello* now demanded meat and wine on the table. And as for clothing, contemporaries noted that peasants were no longer happy to wear the simple linen clothes tailored by their wives.

de Rome et la crise de l'annone dans la seconde moitié du XVIIIe siècle', *Mélanges de l'École Française de Rome* (s. Moyen Age–Temps Modernes), 84 (1972), 201–81. The power of the Tuscan *annona* was less direct because it did not fix prices openly but levelled peaks by releasing grain from public stores in times of need.

[50] The role of the *annona* in safeguarding landed interest has been analysed for Bologna by Alberto Guenzi, 'Il "calmiero del formento": controllo del prezzo del pane e difesa della rendita terriera a Bologna nei secoli XVII e XVIII', *Annali della Fondazione Luigi Einaudi*, 11 (1977), 143–201.

[51] John Sekora, *Luxury: The Concept in Western Thought, Eden to Smollett* (Baltimore, 1977), 64–5.

Pistoia witnessed a strong rise in demand for foreign embroidery and luxurious clothing. The situation in Galluzzo was even more extreme, and contemporaries claimed that the economy was in decline because it had become too easy for peasants to purchase expensive foreign cloth.[52]

Greater availability of goods and changing fashion only helped increase the discrepancy between expectations and actual living standards, however. On the whole, the latter remained very low indeed, as contemporary memoirs and letters suggest.[53] For the most part the new attitude had been confined to the hinterland and did not extend to the remoter places of rural Tuscany. And when it reached the countryside it could rarely be satisfied: by the end of the century there was hardly one *mezzadro* in ten who owed nothing to his landlord.[54] The case of the Tuscan estate of Altopascio is typical. Peasant indebtedness had increased more than sixteenfold during the seventeenth century until 1718, and the situation grew even worse until the estate was sold in 1783. At that point the great majority of the peasants were left with no property whatsoever.[55] It does not seem, then, that the material reality of the peasant improved significantly in the course of the century. On the contrary, the change of attitude towards luxury goods in the rural population could have made the subjective perception of the peasant's own economic status even more negative. Luxury goods were within reach and yet not attainable.

The economic system prevalent in eighteenth-century Tuscany affected the development of prices, which, in turn, had repercussions on living standards. A large part of the grain, to be sure, did not go to the market but was tied up in home consumption. The price of the grain that did reach the market places—Florence, Pisa, Prato, and Siena in the case of Tuscany—determined the living standards of artisans and the city poor. Bread was the essential part of the diet, and the bread price was determined by the price of grain.[56] As we shall see, prices also affected the peasants even when they sold little or no surplus grain.

[52] Paolo Malanima, *Il lusso dei contadini: consumo e industrie nelle campagne toscane del Sei e Settecento* (Bologna, 1990), 137–41.

[53] See Mirri, 'Proprietari', 188. Even though this was true for most of Italy at the time, it seems appropriate to view the situation in Lombardy, 'the jewel of Italian agriculture' (Carpanetto and Ricuperati, *Italy in the Age of Reason*, 49), in more positive terms.

[54] Mirri, 'Proprietari', 217.

[55] Frank McArdle, *Altopascio: A Study in Tuscan Rural Society* (Cambridge, 1974).

[56] To be precise, the price of bread was always constant, but the weight of the bread depended on the grain price. Furthermore, the grain authorities had the power to sell grain below or above market price to bakers in order to ensure a relatively even price level over time. Cf. Orsola Gori, 'Mercato e prezzi del grano a Firenze nel secolo XVIII', *Archivio storico italiano*, 147 (1989), 525–623, esp. pp. 551–2. The following account on prices and price development concentrates on Florence because price development was strikingly similar in the major Tuscan cities; for a comparison see ibid., table 1, pp. 608–9.

Tuscany was no exception to the pan-European trend of stagnating prices from the middle of the seventeenth century. Equally, when prices began to rise across Europe from the 1730s onwards, Tuscany again followed suit. As in other countries, the rise persisted until the end of the century. Within this general framework, however, we encounter features that were specific to economic systems such as Tuscany's and a price development partly out of line with European developments. In an economy not fully mercantilized, in which a large part of the produce is kept for home consumption, in which transport is tiresome and sometimes (especially during the winter months) impossible, and finally in an economy regulated by trade restrictions, prices reflect a local, rather than regional or national, economic reality. Local conditions also explain the large oscillations we find in the Tuscan grain price development. Very frequently in the eighteenth century prices rose by 50 to 60 per cent in the course of one year, especially during times of poor harvests. Peasants and *mezzadri* suffered doubly from oscillating prices. First, their existence close to the level of subsistence meant that they could not determine when to sell their surplus grain. Rather, they were forced to sell immediately once it became available, and often even before the actual harvest (*in erba*). This was, of course, the time when prices were lowest. Secondly, bad harvests often led to peasant indebtedness, as we have seen. The landlords had an interest in giving credit in times of need so that the labour force could be maintained and future harvests guaranteed. Credit was usually given in the form of grain, which was expensive in times of bad harvests. It could only be paid back in good years with consequentially low grain prices. The difference in value had to be covered by the debtor.[57]

Paradoxically from today's point of view, the very fluctuation of prices that was partly caused by market restrictions often served as an argument for the maintenance of powerful controls over prices and grain distribution, and hence secured the influential position of the grain authorities. Their role was dramatically called into question in the middle of the 1760s when one of the fiercest famines of the century afflicted the grand duchy.[58] The Florentine poor were reduced to eating wild herbs and, as the English

[57] Giorgio Giorgetti, 'Note sul grande affitto in Toscana nel secolo XVIII', *Quaderni storici*, 14 (1970), 453–506.

[58] Franco Venturi, 'Quattro anni di carestia in Toscana (1764–1767)', *Rivista storica italiana*, 88 (1976), 649–707, for an account of the relationship between the famines and the development of economic thought. The most detailed analysis is Orsola Gori, 'La carestia del 1763–1767 e i suoi riflessi nel dibattito economico e politico nel Granducato di Toscana', MA thesis, University of Florence, 1977.

envoy to Tuscany Horace Mann noted, 'many people in the country have literally died of hunger'.[59] Economic policy changed after the famine had shown the weaknesses of the current system. Before that date the export ban on grain had been a central concern of economic policy which led to the introduction of protective zones within three miles of the border into which no grain was to be introduced. In September 1767 the ban was lifted and a general law allowed the import and export of grain for a maximum price based on the medium of Tuscan market prices. In August 1775 even that restriction was lifted and free trade of agricultural produce introduced.[60]

The immediate result of the new laws was an overall rise in prices. In the decade after the introduction of free trade, prices were 52 per cent higher than in the decade preceding the shift in economic policy. The economy benefited from the newly gained freedom, and when the famines ended in 1767, more prosperous times ensued. It is true that a new period of severe shortages afflicted Tuscany from 1772 to 1774, and that the high price level indicates even worse harvests than in the previous decade, if prices and harvests are assumed to be inversely proportional. The relative lack of pauperism, the absence of epidemic diseases, and the lower mortality rate all seem to suggest, however, that the famine of the 1760s had been much worse than the shortages after the partial liberalization of the grain trade. The high price level, in other words, is mostly to be explained by the effects of the open market, not by low grain supply.[61]

The export of grain only became legal in the 1760s. But even before, of course, the export of primary materials had played an important role in the Tuscan economy, which had been export- and trade-oriented for most of the early modern period. In the commercial sectors of the Renaissance economy, for example, Italians dominated the trade of luxury goods imported from the Near East and exported throughout northern Europe. Growing demand for luxury goods in northern Europe and the need to balance payments for goods received from the Near East accelerated the development of both the manufacturing and agricultural sectors to satisfy demand. From the eleventh century through to the sixteenth, the Italian system had been oriented towards the export of goods and services, and this had made Italy, and Tuscany in particular, the leader of economic growth

[59] Horace Mann in a letter to Walpole in February 1767; quoted by Gori, 'Mercato e prezzi', 577.

[60] Cf. Mario Mirri, *La lotta politica in Toscana intorno alle 'riforme annonarie' (1764–1775)* (Pisa, 1972), 28–66.

[61] Gori, 'Mercato e prezzi', 600 and 616–18.

in the West.[62] By the beginning of the eighteenth century all this had long ceased to exist. The economic network (which had extended across the peninsula in the previous centuries) had by then acquired a decidedly regional, if not local, character. The decline in the amount of European trade went hand in hand with the breaking up of the Italian economy into smaller centres. By the 1660s, for example, only negligible amounts of cloth were exported abroad, the main markets having become the internal market in Florence and the neighbouring papal states. Even though the continuing export of silk compensated for some of the losses in other export sectors, the Tuscan export of secondary materials had clearly lost its driving force.[63]

The Economy and Economic Thought

It is in this context that attention focused increasingly on the export of agricultural produce. Even though the need for commerce was still clearly perceived (the *Magazzino toscano*, for example, launched a defence of trade in the 1750s), the goods with which trade was now deemed profitable were agricultural.[64] Thinkers like Giuseppe Sarchiani had made agricultural produce the main focus of their economic interest.[65] Gianrinaldo Carli, the influential political economist from Istria working in Milan, underpinned this view with an account of export figures. It was true, he asserted, that manufactured goods ('cloth and straw hats') still accounted for a little more than 60 per cent of Tuscan exports. But the wool industry in the whole of Tuscany was now twenty times less productive than it had been four centuries ago in Florence alone. The 'main posts' of Tuscan export material were now oil, wine, victuals, and vegetables.[66] If there was any hope of regaining the pole position lost since the Renaissance, contemporaries were convinced, it no longer lay in the export of goods and services, but in the products of the land. It is clear, then, that agriculture had taken the lead role

[62] Richard A. Goldthwaite, *Wealth and the Demand for Art in Italy, 1300–1600*, pbk. edn. (Baltimore, 1995), 12–63, esp. pp. 13–14.

[63] Malanima, *Decadenza*, 253–70, esp. pp. 259–61.

[64] Anon., 'Brevi e generali riflessioni di un Inglese sopra il commercio della sua nazione', *Magazzino toscano d'istruzione e di piacere*, 1 (1754), 424–32, which provided a short history of the development and importance of commerce with the aim of making Tuscan readers realize that trade was good for them.

[65] Sarchiani, *Regolamento sul commercio*.

[66] Gianrinaldo Carli, *Saggio politico ed economico sopra la Toscana fatto nell'anno 1757*, in Carli, *Opere*, 19 vols. (Milan, 1784), i. 336–8, 348, 365–7. The export figures are confirmed by Malanima, *Decadenza*, 271.

in the Tuscan economy. Contemporary judgements to this effect were well in line with the economic reality as it reveals itself to present-day economic historians. What is equally beyond doubt, however, is that the system left much to be desired. The 'refeudalization' had channelled wealth from the mercantile sector to the countryside in the seventeenth century, albeit without the expectation of profit. Manufacture was declining in a dwindling European market, against competition whose higher quality and lower prices Tuscany found difficult to match. Many of the shortcomings were noted by political economists and agriculturalists in the eighteenth century; many others have only been uncovered by recent research. But in addressing vital flaws of the economic system, intellectuals and administrators alike had made one valuable discovery, namely that well-substantiated criticism could lead to reform in the grand duchy. And reform, they soon learned, could bring results. It is for this reason that we find such an eager preoccupation with agricultural reform in the economic thinking of the period.

Tuscan writers accepted the new reality, but they tried to turn it into a virtue. How could the money that flowed into the countryside be put to good use? How could those who invested in the land be made interested in profit? How could the prices for agricultural goods be made to suit the interests of those who produced them? The answers to these questions paved the way towards the development of the Tuscan economic system in the direction of what would later be known as agricultural capitalism. Such a line of development left industry in a precarious state. Nevertheless, manufacture did play an important, if secondary, role in the development of economic thought. If the export of manufactured goods had lost most of its glamour, it was perhaps time to concentrate on home consumption and the development of the internal market. This had consequences for the products manufactured, and since the move of some of the textile industry to the countryside had favoured low- to medium-quality cloth already, the way was open to further development in this direction. Luxury goods, the pride of Tuscany's past, were, of course, not left unaffected by this account. They were to enjoy an important yet ambiguous role in the development of Tuscan thought. Finally, as far as devastatingly fluctuating prices in a closed economy were concerned, free trade was to offer a possible solution to the price problem.

It is not surprising in such a context that Tuscan intellectuals should have looked abroad in their desire to reframe the profile of their economy. It is equally understandable that they should have directed their attention to a region that was perceived to share similar conditions and premisses. In the analysis of the development of Tuscan economic thought, then, we should not be surprised to find that the received opinion of an almost random Tuscan eclecticism does not hold true. Instead, it will become clear that most of the attention was quite justifiably directed towards both Tuscan precedent and French agricultural thought, which was perceived to address Tuscan problems most adequately.

5

Tuscan Economic Thought: Ministerial Memorandums and Public Discourse

> . . . I have done nothing but adapt the teachings of a celebrated French author to our Maremma region.
>
> (Sallustio Bandini to a professor at Siena University, 1735?)
>
> Boisguilbert is . . . the true and only precursor of the physiocrats.
>
> (Victor Mirabeau to Alfonso Longo, 1775)

The Tuscan luxury debate entered its most heated phase towards the end of the 1760s before it culminated with the contributions of the priest and agriculturalist Ferdinando Paoletti in the 1770s. But neither the debate of the 1760s nor Paoletti's intervention can be understood without the development of economic thought in eighteenth-century Tuscany that began with Sallustio Bandini in the 1730s. Bandini did not devote much space to luxury in his teachings. But his example, I wish to argue, was the foundation of all subsequent economic thought in the grand duchy. Bandini served as a matrix and a filter for subsequent discourse, and this holds true alike for administrators (who wrote ministerial memorandums or circulated manuscripts in order to improve the economic situation of their homeland) and academicians and contributors to journals (who published their views in an increasingly public culture). This chapter first attempts to show Bandini's formative influence on Tuscan thinkers and establish his own debts to French thought in particular. The second half of the chapter focuses on the luxury debate proper. Luxury, as I wish to show, is a particularly good example for an analysis of the transmission of French ideas into Tuscany, as well as of the formation of an increasingly public culture in the second half of the century. At the same time I will explain the specific turn of the Tuscan luxury debate with the 'French connection' first established by Bandini.

Sallustio Bandini and the Foundation of Tuscan Economic Thought

Arguably, Tuscan economic thought starts with Sallustio Bandini. From the writing of his defence of free trade, the *Discorso sopra la Maremma di Siena*, in 1737, and even more so after its publication in 1775, Tuscan intellectuals found inspiration in the Sienese writer. They took his characterization of Tuscany's agricultural economy for granted, they used him to explain their arguments in favour of free trade, and they quarrelled with him over the value of low or high grain prices. In fact, earlier than anybody else, Bandini had laid out his programme for reform and economic progress in Tuscany, and had developed a theory of foreign trade, as well as a monetary and fiscal theory.

Sallustio Bandini was born to a Sienese patrician family in 1677.[1] Educated at a Jesuit school and later at Siena University, he graduated in philosophy in 1700. After having spent some time as a lecturer in canon law he was ordained as a priest in 1705. As the third son, he was faced with the choice of either a military or ecclesiastical career, and he soon found that the Church would offer him more room for his own pursuits than life as a soldier. Bandini made a decent though by no means spectacular career in the Church, and became archdeacon of the cathedral in Siena in 1723. His interests were manifold and covered practical as well as theoretical matters. By 1711 he had shown that chalk could be used as a disinfectant for grain seeds. In 1718–19 he wrote about the circulation of money in Siena. His main ambition during this period, however, seems to have been to improve the intellectual situation of his native Siena by inducing the rich to donate scholarships and by setting up a library, which eventually grew into the university library.[2]

He returned to economic matters in 1737 when he drafted his *Discorso sopra la Maremma di Siena*. The work contains an economic model which Bandini had tailored to the situation of his homeland, and which was to enjoy belated recognition with the implementation of many of its maxims under the reign of Peter Leopold. Bandini is concerned with the Maremma, i.e. that part of coastal southern Tuscany which had been neglected for many years and which had been the victim of numerous famines. The region, today one of Tuscany's most famous holiday resorts,

[1] On the details of Bandini's life, see Renato Mori, 'Presupposti politici del riformismo di Sallustio Bandini', *Storia e politica*, 23 (1984), 301–29.

[2] Mario de Gregorio, 'Prima di Bandini: tentativi di biblioteca universitaria a Siena nel Settecento', *Societa e Storia*, 19 (1996), 253–81.

had become known for its foul air and agricultural and industrial backwardness. 'The State of Siena cannot prosper, because the Maremma is a burden' was the swift phrase of a minister in charge of overseeing the region.[3] Bandini denied this fatalistic charge and claimed that the problems were man-made. The Maremma could well contribute to the prosperity of the whole state if only it was governed in the right fashion.

Bandini argued that the Maremma's only chance lay in developing its agricultural economy. Contrary to the orthodoxy of his times, Bandini claimed that export restrictions and fixed grain prices were not the necessary response to the continuous threat of famine. Rather, it was precisely this sort of government intervention that caused famines in the first place.

The emphasis Bandini placed on the free trade of agricultural produce sold at market prices was inspired by the French political economist Pierre de Boisguilbert. Bandini kept an edition of the work of Boisguilbert in his library, and (as he himself acknowledged in a letter) he drew on the French thinker liberally.[4] In fact, as I shall argue, it was through Boisguilbert's influence on Bandini, and the influence Bandini in turn exerted on Tuscan thought, that physiocratic ideas could become so fashionable in Tuscany several decades later: the physiocrats themselves had drawn much inspiration from their compatriot.[5] Against the mercantilists, Boisguilbert had argued that the way towards economic growth lay purely in the development of the agricultural economy. In order to provide an incentive to production, agricultural produce had to be traded freely.[6]

The pinnacle of Bandini's defence of free trade, as well as the central category of his economic thought, was money. In a society not based on barter, only money fostered the arts by making facilitating the demand for their

[3] Sallustio Bandini, *Discorso sopra la Maremma di Siena*, ed. Lucia Conenna Bonelli, in George R. F. Baker, *Sallustio Bandini: con una nuova edizione del Discorso sopra la Maremma di Siena a cura di L. Conenna Bonelli* (Florence, 1978), 201–96; the quotation on p. 254.

[4] For the holdings of Bandini's library, cf. Baker, *Bandini*, 49. The letter in which Bandini acknowledged his debt to 'a famous French thinker' is printed in Jean-Claude Waquet, 'La Composition du *Discorso sopra la Maremma di Siena*: pensée française et politique locale dans la Toscane des Médicis', *Studies on Voltaire and the Eighteenth Century*, 242 (1986), 233–42, here pp. 239–42. The similarities between Bandini and Boisguilbert have first been observed by Ulisse Gobbi, *La concorrenza estera e gli antichi economisti italiani* (Milan, 1884), 114–18. See also Glauco Tozzi, 'Sallustio Bandini: economista senese', *Atti della R. Accademia dei Lincei: memorie della classe di scienze morali, storiche e filologiche*, 6/5 (1933–6), 61–141, for an unconvincing attempt to defend the originality of Bandini's thought against Boisguilbert.

[5] Louis Salleron, 'Boisguilbert précurseur des physiocrates', in *Pierre de Boisguilbert, ou, La Naissance de l'économie politique*, 2 vols. (Paris, 1966), i. 41–52.

[6] Catherine Larrère, *L'Invention de l'économie politique au* XVIIIe *siècle: du droit naturel à la physiocracy* (Paris, 1992), 99 and 177.

produce without which they could not flourish.[7] An increased money supply was thus the precondition for economic development, and it could be achieved either via increased circulation or via the encouragement of the supply side. To illustrate the first means of increasing the money supply, Bandini used an analogy. Money behaved like a little torch in the hand of a child. If spun around fast enough, it will appear to be a circle of fire rather than the little source of light it really is.[8] Bandini's treatment of money builds on Boisguilbert's theory according to which the fundamental importance of money lies in its function as a means of circulation.[9] But he extended Boisguilbert's notion by emphasizing that the circulation of money can counterbalance the scarcity of the money supply. Now, the poor are much more likely to spend money quickly than the rich, whose capital was usually tied up in long-term investments.[10] It is therefore vital to ensure that the poor have enough money at their disposal to buy not only the necessaries, but superfluous goods, too. This line of argument takes great care to emphasize the role of the poor peasant and his purchasing power in demand-driven economic growth—again building on Boisguilbert, who had emphasized the vital role of what would today be called mass consumption in fostering economic development.[11]

The second way to increase the amount of money in circulation involves the encouragement of the supply side: the best way to get money was to produce and sell goods. Given that Bandini quite rightly assumed that the products Tuscany had to offer were predominantly agricultural, this meant selling grain.[12] The problem faced by the Maremma was, according to Bandini, that neither peasants nor landowners had an incentive to produce grain because of export restrictions and government-set maximum prices. In fact, it was not until September 1738 that Tuscany allowed two-thirds of the harvest to be exported out of the Maremma, and only in 1775 did Peter Leopold finally lift all export restrictions on agricultural produce.[13] To

[7] Bandini, *Discorso*, 226. [8] Ibid. 233.

[9] Pierre de Boisguilbert, *Dissertation de la nature des richesses, de l'argent et des tributes, où l'on découvre la fausse idée qui règne dans le monde à l'égard de ces trois articles* (1704), in *Pierre de Boisguilbert*, ii. 976. [10] Bandini, *Discorso*, 240–1.

[11] Pierre de Boisguilbert, *Le Détail de la France: La Cause de la diminution de ses biens, et la facilité du remède, en fournissant en un mois tout l'argent dont le Roi a besoin, et enrichissant tout le monde* (1696–1707 edn.), in *Pierre de Boisguilbert*, ii. 619–20. For an interpretation of Boisguilbert's thought that calls attention to his emphasis on mass consumption, see Hazel van Dyke Roberts, *Boisguilbert: Economist of the Reign of Louis XIV* (New York, 1935).

[12] Renzo Paolo Corritore, 'Il processo di "ruralizzazione" in Italia nei secoli XVII–XVIII: verso una regionalizzazione', *Rivista di storia economica*, 10 (1993), 353–86.

[13] Mario Mirri, *La lotta politica in Toscana intorno alle 'riforme annonarie' (1764–1775)* (Pisa, 1972).

create such an incentive, export must be allowed, and the market must be left to establish a 'just price' which 'compensates the producer for his expenses, yet does not hurt buyers excessively'.[14]

It is at this point that Bandini's monetary theory merges with his defence of free trade and high prices. For Bandini's primary goal had been to increase the amount of money in circulation. One possibility would have been to lower the grain price, thereby effectively increasing the value of money in circulation. Simply reducing the grain price would have solved one problem (the scarcity of money) but at the expense of his main objective, the increase of consumption and production. Writing at a time when prices were only just beginning to rise after a century of decline or stagnation, his remedy was thus to propose high prices, and solve the scarcity issue by focusing on the speed of circulation.[15] He could do so by introducing one central assumption, which at the same time linked his two ways for increasing the money supply. High grain prices, far from devaluing money and limiting the population's purchasing power, in fact had the opposite effect. Not only did landowners profit from high prices, but so did the peasant population at large. Since their income almost exclusively depended on selling grain, grain prices and their earnings would be proportional. Hence, not only would high prices provide an incentive for production, they would at the same time increase the disposable income of the greatest part of the population, the peasants. That this was to be achieved at the expense of city-dwellers, who would have to pay dearly for their grain, was a fact that Bandini accepted. In fact, he urged those who normally had so much compassion for the poor citizen to think about poor peasants for once, for they were 'ten times as numerous'.[16]

Bandini was faced with a dilemma. On the one hand, he argued in favour of high grain prices as an incentive to production. On the other hand, he was well aware that long-term growth could only be achieved if the market for agricultural produce was extended beyond the borders of the Maremma. This, however, made competitive prices necessary, and since grain prices in Europe had stagnated in the seventeenth century, and did not start to rise again considerably until the middle of the eighteenth century, the price would have to be low. If, he reasoned, Tuscan agricultural

[14] Bandini, *Discorso*, 236. This is in fact the equilibrium price that Boisguilbert had called for, but given a moralistic twist by Bandini's notion of the 'just price', cf. Gilbert Faccarello, *Aux origines de l'économie politique libérale: Pierre de Boisguilbert* (Paris, 1986), 217–23.

[15] Cf. Orsola Gori, 'Mercato e prezzi del grano a Firenze nel secolo XVIII', *Archivio storico italiano*, 147 (1989), 525–623, esp. pp. 525–6.

[16] Bandini, *Discorso*, 229.

products were more expensive than foreign ones, grain would be bought from abroad. The effect would be doubly disastrous. Arguing from a mercantilist point of view, money would be drained off the impoverished region. But also the incentive to cultivate would no longer exist, agriculture would be abandoned, and famines ensue. Bandini's proposal was to reduce the tax burden which pushed prices up and to simplify the tax system.[17] In this respect, his fiscal theory was a direct consequence of his belief in the need for free export, and the former was developed as a means of safeguarding the latter.

Bandini acknowledged the need for a certain tax income to pay for administration, infrastructure, and the army. Hence, a simple reduction in tax revenue was difficult to justify. In a proposal that prefigured the tax farm of 1740, the *appalto generale*, he called for a reduction of the administrative costs of tax collection, which were high owing to the multitude of taxes levied in Tuscany.[18] Even if the total revenue of the state remained constant, the tax burden weighing down on producers could thus be significantly reduced. Furthermore, the tax collected had to have no negative influence on consumption. The salt tax in particular aroused Bandini's critique, as he viewed it as a pernicious indirect consumption tax. The only effect of the tax was, according to Bandini, that people consumed less salt. When salt was used as a preservative, for example for cheese, the tax was additionally damaging because less salt in cheese meant that the produce went off more quickly and was thus less suitable for export.[19]

No consumption taxes, but direct taxation; not many taxes, but few, possibly only one—this was Bandini's recipe for low prices. The tax Bandini was looking for had to be 'easily collectable and difficult to evade, cheap to collect, not a burden on the poor, and not a hindrance to agricultural production'. Above all, it had to be a tax on profit, rather than on land or revenue. The similarities with Boisguilbert's proposal for a tax reform in France are again striking. In his *Factum de la France* Boisguilbert had proposed a single tax on revenue to be paid in money. In a similar vein, Bandini envisaged that a percentage of the grain harvest be paid in money by landowners only.[20] Bandini is unclear here how this proposed tax differs from a tax on revenue. However, his socially and economically progressive

[17] Bandini, *Discorso*, 270.

[18] On the tax farm, see Adam Wandruszka, *Österreich und Italien im 18. Jahrhundert* (Munich, 1963), 51–3.

[19] Bandini, *Discorso*, 274.

[20] Jean Féry, 'Le Système fiscal et monétaire de Boisguilbert', in *Pierre de Boisguilbert*, 53–69; on fiscal reform, pp. 64–5.

thrust is clearly discernible in his refusal to tax those who make no profit or indeed who make a loss. Equally, tenant farmers as well as all hired workers were to be exempt.[21] Bandini's proposal rests on the assumption that the unified tax would not hinder agricultural production. With the increase of agricultural produce, the tax revenue would increase as well, whereas ordinary consumption taxes, which hindered consumption, would cause a decline in tax revenue.[22]

Agriculture, export, and taxation of landowners are the dominant themes in Bandini's *Discorso sopra la Maremma*. References to industrial production or moral arguments in favour of the agricultural economy Bandini favoured are conspicuously absent from his treatise, as they are from Boisguilbert's work, too. There are, however, some instances where Bandini does attempt moral or religious justifications for his economic arguments. His defence of export is a case in point, where he finds a clever link between the Christian obligation to give away what you do not need, and free trade. Just as the rich who do not give freely to the poor will be eternally damned, Bandini argues, so that country which does not export in order to fulfil other people's needs—making a profit along the way, of course—can never be truly happy.[23] Bandini thus gives a theological twist to Boisguilbert's claim not only that exchange is vital for a functioning economy, but that it is also a natural consequence of specific endowments of different countries, which result in complementary economies and hence make free trade advantageous for all parties involved.[24] As a Christian defence of free trade, Bandini's analogy may not go a long way. It is important to note, however, that moral justification is at least attempted. It should remind us of the need that Bandini felt to justify his economic programme with arguments taken from outside the economic sphere. What is possibly even more important is how rarely he attempts moral or religious justifications. No doubt this was determined by Boisguilbert's choice not to blur his economic reasoning with too many moral considerations, and by Bandini's attempt to solve the economic problems of the Maremma with economic tools alone—and this is what I call the 'pragmatic school' of Tuscan economic thinking. As Bandini's thought was taken up by later generations, however, the moral side of his argument was missing. When people like Ferdinando Paoletti looked for a moral justification of the programmes developed out of Bandini's thought, they had to look elsewhere. It is ironic that they should have turned to Ludovico Antonio Muratori, who

[21] Bandini, *Discorso*, 280–1. [22] Ibid. 286. [23] Ibid. 247.

[24] e.g. Pierre de Boisguilbert, *Mémoire sur les blés et les liqueurs*, in *Pierre de Boisguilbert*, i. 411.

introduced a different stream of French economic reasoning on luxury to the Italian literary public, a stream which was completely alien to everything Bandini and Boisguilbert stood for.

Bandini's *Discorso sopra la Maremma* was only published in 1775. It did, however, circulate widely in manuscript form and was well known to Tuscan writers and administrators.[25] In fact, Bandini's audience was wide, but confined to a narrow region. It appears that no Tuscan intellectual could afford to ignore the grand old man of Tuscan economic thought, whereas Bandini's fate outside the grand duchy was much less happy. Not only was he of no interest to political economists in the north, but outside Tuscany the publication of his work was only acknowledged once, in a journal from Modena.[26] The consequences of this regional divide in reception were far-reaching. Much of the development of Tuscan thought in the course of the eighteenth century can only be understood as a reply to Bandini. Subsequent theorists struggled to incorporate recent ideas about commerce and industry into his economic framework, and tried to add a moral component that had been lacking in his thought. The rest of Italy, and Lombardy in particular, was not similarly constrained by any such single basic text.

Bandini's thought began to exert influence immediately after he had finished his manuscript. Quite unlike his previous work it aroused the interest of writers and administrators alike, ultimately leading both to the implementation of his proposal for free trade under Peter Leopold,[27] and to his leading role in setting the intellectual agenda for economic debate among Tuscan political economists.

By the time Bandini had finished his manuscript, the economic predicament of Siena called for action. In March 1738 the army commander of Siena complained that there was not enough grain to feed his men.[28] This was despite the fact that all grain harvested in the Maremma region was not to be exported but to be used for internal consumption. Something was wrong, and Bandini had the answer. His elder brother, Alfonso, was a member of the Balìa di Siena, and this very body had urged the government in Florence to improve the economic situation of the Siena region in the

[25] For manuscripts in circulation, see Lucia Conenna Bonelli, 'Premessa', in Bandini, *Discorso*, 205–10. Manuscripts often circulated widely in the 18th century; cf. François Moureau (ed.), *De bonne main: La Communication manuscrite au XVIIIe siècle* (Paris, 1993), and in particular Françoise Weil, 'La Fonction du manuscrit par rapport à l'imprimé', ibid. 17–27.

[26] Review in *Continuazione del nuovo giornale de' letterati d'Italia di Modena*, 11 (1777), 60–87.

[27] Mirri, *La lotta politica in Toscana intorno alle 'riforme annonarie'*, 28–66.

[28] Abele Morena, 'Le riforme e le dottrine economiche in Toscana', *Rassegna nazionale*, 18 (1887), 211–56, here p. 238.

summer of 1737. They had even ventilated the idea of free grain trade, at that time to no avail. Now, however, Sallustio Bandini's arguments had been put to paper, and his brother was certainly in a position to relay them to the city council. Siena requested and obtained the approval of the grand duke, and then issued an edict which was to guarantee the free exportation of grain for the next twelve years.[29]

It has been questioned whether the new legislation owed much to Bandini, mainly on the grounds that Bandini's brother left the city council in 1738, the year the new legislation was adopted, and that we have no proof of direct encounters of Bandini with the ruling class in Siena during the years 1737–8.[30] However, Pompeo Neri, one of the main defenders of the new legislation, who was also one of the most ardent disciples of Bandini, had encountered Bandini frequently both before and after the writing of the *Discorso sopra la Maremma*, of which he obtained a manuscript version. He probably even gave a version to Francis Stephen and Maria Theresa during their brief stay in Tuscany in 1739.[31] No matter what Bandini's role was in the actual shaping of legislation, it is legitimate to assume that his thought entered the circle of Tuscan administrators through this channel.

Political Economy and Government Policy: The Cases of Neri and Gianni

If Bandini very clearly belonged to the generation of jurists and administrators so characteristic of early and mid-eighteenth-century Italian states, Pompeo Neri was in many ways a mediator between generations while still retaining close ties to the juridical culture of Medici and Lorraine Tuscany. Born in 1706, he was a child when Bandini had already taken up office as a priest. When Neri was at the height of his administrative career some decades later, the young generation of Paoletti and Pelli Bencivenni in Tuscany, and Pietro Verri and Cesare Beccaria in Lombardy, were taking their first steps in the intellectual world. Neri was born in Florence, but attended school at the seminary in Siena where Sallustio Bandini exerted great influence. He went on to study at the University of Pisa, where he graduated in 1726, and subsequently became professor of public law. Several years later, in 1735, he left the academic world and entered the administration. The rest of his career was spent in administrative duties. After a stint in Lombardy, where he was responsible for the census, he moved back to Tuscany,

[29] Baker, *Bandini*, 160. [30] Ibid. 161–2.
[31] Diaz, *La Reggenza*, 81 n. 2, and Wandruszka, *Österreich und Italien*, 55.

where he was one of the main driving forces behind the law of 1767 which abolished all export restrictions for grain in Tuscany.[32]

The liberalization of the grain trade was one of Neri's great administrative successes. It certainly owed much to the reforming zeal of Peter Leopold and members of his administration. The theoretical groundwork, however, had been laid by Neri. As a tireless worker behind the scenes, he had written his *Discorso sopra la materia frumentaria*, a defence of free trade in an agricultural economy, in 1767. Tuscany, he claims, is an agrarian land, 'because it receives its main subsistence from agriculture'.[33] It is a reiteration of the point Bandini had driven home three decades earlier, when he had said of his homeland that the wealth of all its inhabitants, from artisans to merchants, depended on agriculture.[34] Bandini had sensed that the only solution to famines was free exportation. Neri, writing in a decade that had experienced devastating famines and temporary measures to liberate the grain trade, could use examples from his own experience to support Bandini's claim.[35] In fact, most of his treatise consists of variations on the theme that the liberating measures had positively affected the grain supply in Tuscany.[36] Hence, Neri's work can be seen as a late vindication and substantiation of Bandini's original thesis, and sometimes we even find direct answers to problems raised by Bandini. Bandini had noted that free trade put at a disadvantage those who had to transport their produce from afar to ports and merchant centres. His solution had been to propose tax reductions according to the distance between place of production and point of sale.[37] When Neri took up the issue, this had become superfluous because under Peter Leopold past transportation problems had been solved by an improvement of the road network in Tuscany.[38]

Neri not only shared Bandini's assessment of the nature of the Tuscan economy, he also criticized low grain prices with the very arguments

[32] Neri worked closely with Peter Leopold on other legislative projects, too. For a well-documented case, the 1773 game law, see Andrea Addobbati, 'I guastafeste: la legge toscana sul gioco del 1773', *Quaderni storici*, 32 (1997), 495–538. Overall, however, Neri remained outside the closest sphere of influence around Peter Leopold; cf. Vieri Becagli, 'Pompeo Neri e le riforme istituzionali della prima età leopoldina', in Aldo Frantoianni and Marcello Verga (eds.), *Pompeo Neri: atti del colloquio di Castelfiorentino (6–7 maggio 1988)* (Castelfiorentino, 1992), 333–76. The best account of Neri's life remains Franco Venturi, 'Pompeo Neri: nota introduttiva', in *Illuministi italiani*, i/2. 945–50.

[33] Pompeo Neri, *Discorso sopra la materia frumentaria* (1767), in *Scrittori classici*, xlix. 7–48, the quotation on p. 10.

[34] Bandini, *Discorso*, 227.

[35] On the famines in Tuscany, see Franco Venturi, 'Quattro anni di carestia in Toscana (1764–1767)', *Rivista storica italiana*, 88 (1976), 649–707.

[36] Neri, *Discorso sopra la materia frumentaria*, 21–4.

[37] Bandini, *Discorso*, 283.

[38] Neri, *Discorso sopra la materia frumentaria*, 29–30.

Bandini had used several decades earlier. Bandini had argued that low grain prices were detrimental to prosperity in Tuscany because the income of most people—landowners and peasants alike—depended on the selling of grain. That the city poor would suffer for the sake of the rural majority was a sad fact that had to be accepted. Neri shared Bandini's starting point, for high grain prices meant an increase in revenues for those with income from 'living or renewable stock', i.e. agriculture. Bandini's argument had stopped here, as he thought it sufficient to show that the majority of the population would profit from high prices. Neri, however, moved on to show that not even city-dwellers profited from low prices. According to Neri, the subsistence of the population depended on the products they sold. In the case of city-dwellers, this meant selling their labour. Now, the supply of labour was determined by its demand. Demand, in turn, depended on the ability to pay for labour. Since Neri accepted Bandini's thesis that high grain prices led to the prosperity of the majority of the population, he argued that city-dwellers would ultimately profit from high prices because their labour could actually be afforded.

Consideration for the city, and indeed industry, manufacture, and commerce, had been lacking in Bandini. Adhering to Bandini's fundamental principles, Neri managed to incorporate them into his programme for economic reform. He even went so far as to set the stage for the growing prosperity of city-dwellers through the increase in purchasing power by landowners. The more they earned, Neri asserted, the more their desire for commodities and their wish to 'satisfy fantasy' grew.[39] This effectively opened the door for a defence of luxury production by one of the most influential members of the Tuscan administrative elite. Neri, who owed so much to Bandini, in turn influenced the generation of writers that was to follow him. He had adopted his pragmatic approach to political economy and made sure that Bandini's lessons were not forgotten, but at the same time he had widened Bandini's arguments considerably. Ferdinando Paoletti, who was to draw heavily on Neri's ideas, was not the only commentator to profit from this development.

The focus on agriculture in his *Discorso sopra la materia frumentaria* should not distract from the wider scope of Neri's literary activity, however. It is not only from the *Discorso*, but from his other writings as well, that we can reconstruct his contribution to the luxury debate. It was influential because it overcame the old negative assessment of luxury that had previously dominated much of Tuscan thought. In 1748 Neri had tackled the

[39] Ibid. 33–4.

question of the role of the nobility in Tuscan society. His aim was to show historically how much the concept of nobility had become identified with the ruling classes in Europe and especially in Tuscany. He appreciated the importance of the *noblesse de robe* in running modern government, but he was well aware that this ran counter to any notion of an egalitarian society. 'In a society which is united by social contracts, there is a germ of aristocracy which contradicts any notion of the natural equality of man.'[40]

When Neri treated the issue of poverty and beggary in 1767, the year he wrote his reflections on the grain trade, he had recourse to his old concept of a society based on inequality. Inequality is now taken to mean economic inequality, rather than the social inequality Neri had outlined in his *Discorso sopra la nobiltà*. 'It is necessary that the poor live alongside the rich, for this is a natural law.' Given that poverty could not be abolished altogether, the question for Neri was how to alleviate the situation of the poor, thereby effectively restricting mendicancy in Tuscany. This had been the aim of new legislation introduced in Tuscany in 1767 to which Neri's *Memoria sulla mendicità* was a direct reply.[41] The solution to the problem of beggary, Neri argued, was not to try and ban it with new laws, but rather to increase private income. This could be achieved in two ways. One was to redistribute wealth by breaking up large patrimonies since great personal wealth meant that much money 'stagnates in the hands of the rich'. This, of course, reiterates Bandini's point that wealth depended on circulation, not on the size of the money supply. The redistribution of wealth, however, had been preached since the beginning of time, 'but it really is one of those many political dreams that cannot be put into practice'. The second method was thus much more promising. It rested on increasing, rather than splitting up, private income. His reasoning followed closely that developed in the *Discorso sopra la materia frumentaria.* Since wealth depended on agriculture, landlords had to be given the chance to increase their revenue. With growing prosperity, their consumption would increase accordingly. And since consumption was the basis of economic progress (a point made by Boisguilbert), increased consumption would help increase demand for labour. Much of the increase in revenue would flow into agriculture and commerce as investments, but it would also be used to satisfy the needs of the class of landowners. In fact, their desire for commodities and luxuries would be satisfied by city artisans. The increase in demand thus generated

[40] Pompeo Neri, *Discorso sopra lo stato antico e moderno della nobiltà di Toscana* (1748), in *Illuministi italiani*, i/2. 951–7, the quotation on p. 956; on the aim of his study, cf. Venturi, 'Pompeo Neri: nota introduttiva', 946.

[41] Pompeo Neri, *Memoria sulla mendicità* (1767), in *Illuministi italiani*, i/2. 967–78: 968.

would, in turn, draw many beggars back in to the working class because landowners would employ them directly to satisfy their luxury and their commodious living.[42]

Neri's treatment of luxury was one of the first in Tuscany that had no negative connotations. He had again adhered to the basic principles of Bandini's economic thought, but he had moved on from there. He had tried to allocate a place and a function to the luxury of the city, not as an incentive for landowners but as a means to encourage consumption. To give incentives for landowners to produce remained the task of the legislator, and the best incentive remained that proposed first by Neri's teacher Bandini—free trade. But many of Neri's arguments, I wish to argue, had been inspired not by Bandini but by Jean-François Melon.

There is strong circumstantial evidence that Neri had read Melon's *Essai politique sur le commerce*. Neri knew contemporary French literature on political economy well, as several references to French texts certify. Not only was he aware of all French laws on mendicancy from 1532 until 1764.[43] He also kept himself informed about the English and French economic situations through works translated into French.[44] And even more closely related to political economy, he asserted that Mirabeau 'had proved the necessity of free trade'.[45] Melon's text was certainly sufficiently well known in Italy for Neri to be aware of it, especially since its major arguments had been introduced into the Italian debate by Muratori. And indeed Neri's arguments bear striking similarities to those of Melon, who after all was the first to treat luxury as a purely economic, not a moral, issue—a view clearly echoed by Neri. More specifically, Melon had argued against Mandeville that the accumulation of wealth in the hands of the rich was counterproductive economically, and had urged the rich to spend their money.[46] In a similar vein Neri complained about the wealth which 'remains useless in the hands of proprietors' and which is left 'outside the account of public subsistence because the people are fed by the actual spendings' on consumption.[47] And when Melon had argued that luxury provided work for the poor, Neri had corroborated this assessment with his argument that the rich, in order to spend their surplus, will employ the poor to maintain their

[42] Ibid. 976–7. [43] Ibid. 970.

[44] By quoting, for example, John Nicholls [Plumard de Dangeul], *Remarques sur les avantages et désavantages de la France et de la Grande Bretagne par rapport au commerce* (Leiden, 1754); cf. Neri, *Memoria sulla mendicità*, 971.

[45] Neri, *Discorso sopra la materia frumentaria*, 7.

[46] Jean-François Melon, *Essai politique sur le commerce* (repr. Amsterdam, 1735), 124–7.

[47] Neri, *Memoria sulla mendicità*, 973.

luxuries and their commodious living. Finally, Melon had urged that the capital cities must sustain, rather than undermine, the countryside. Neri had followed Bandini in arguing that high grain prices were beneficial for landlords and the countryside. However, his additional argument that city-dwellers also benefited from high grain prices because their labour could actually be afforded by the landed gentry reflects Melon's conviction that it was the countryside that rendered the luxury of the city possible.[48] Once more, the key inspiration for Tuscan economic discourse proved to be France—but only in so far as it was reconcilable with Tuscany's own tradition of thought embodied by Bandini.

With the help of Melon, Neri had introduced luxury as a concept emptied of moral meaning which was instrumental in reducing unemployment. Later writers would argue that the luxury trades required skills, skills that the unemployed tended to lack. But Neri had opened a door through which he let Melon's arguments into the grand duchy while at the same time keeping up the legacy of Bandini—free trade in an agricultural economy characterized by high prices.

Another administrator who shaped economic policy in the reign of Peter Leopold was Francesco Maria Gianni.[49] Very different from Neri both in background—he had never received a proper education—and in political ideas, he nevertheless shared much of the intellectual agenda that determined the thinking of his rival Pompeo Neri. At first sight, Gianni seems unconcerned with the programme of reform and the underlying convictions of Bandini. Gianni had, for example, opposed Bandini's call for a single tax on land, which had had the support of Pompeo Neri. As one of the most important consultants to Peter Leopold, Gianni got his way, and an indirect tax on consumption was introduced.[50] Nevertheless, even Gianni owed more to Bandini and his school than he may have been prepared to acknowledge.

Gianni published nothing during his twenty-five years of service in the administration of Peter Leopold. Much of what he did publish from the end of the 1780s onwards, however, consisted of reflections on the reign of Peter Leopold, its aims and achievements, but also its shortcomings, and his own role in it. Even though his published work only appeared decades after that of Neri and other political economists, their spirit and their

[48] Melon, *Essai politique sur le commerce*, 2nd edn. (Amsterdam, 1736), ch. 22.

[49] On Gianni, see Furio Diaz, *Francesco Maria Gianni: dalla burocrazia alla politica sotto Pietro Leopoldo di Toscana* (Milan, 1966), and Eric Cochrane, *Florence in the Forgotten Centuries, 1527–1800* (Chicago, 1973).

[50] Diaz, *Gianni*, 208–25.

concerns reflect the age of reform in which Gianni had been an active member of the government. And when Gianni defended the policies he had helped to bring about, he started from assumptions that could have been copied from Bandini. 'We know', he wrote in his *Memorie e pensieri sulla ricchezza nazionale* (1791), 'that consumption determines production'. Gianni thereby placed the same emphasis on consumption that Bandini had taken up from Boisguilbert.[51] His view of taxation, furthermore, had been shaped by his acquaintance with Bandini. Gianni claimed that Bandini had caused him to think of taxes not in terms of draining resources off the population, but rather in terms of their positive effect on 'the advantages of the public'.[52] The teaching he received from Bandini had in fact become a tenet of his conception of political economy.

Neri's main achievement was to channel economic thought into the Tuscan administration. Gianni's was a retrospective and theoretical justification of government action. It remained for others to provide the wider intellectual public with economic arguments and doctrines. Reviews and annotated translations of certain foreign, and especially French, texts were important channels through which ideas were received and adapted to the intellectual debate in Tuscany; here the journals emerging in the eighteenth century were a particularly influential medium.

Translations and Reviews: The Transmission of French Ideas into the Grand Duchy

In the same year that Pompeo Neri wrote his defence of free trade, 1767, a translation of Jean Bertrand's *Essai de la législation pour encourager l'agriculture* appeared in Venice.[53] Bertrand, a Swiss priest who was a renowned agriculturalist and a prolific writer and translator—he had published a French version of Mandeville's *Fable of the Bees* in 1740—had written the *Essai* in 1765, and it earned him the prize of the economic society of Berne, of which he was secretary.[54] The Italian translation of the essay was the work of a Florentine, Giuseppe Pelli Bencivenni.[55] The interest of the work

[51] Francesco Maria Gianni, *Memorie e pensieri per formare tre ragionamenti sulla ricchezza nazionale* (1791), in *Illuministi italiani*, i/2. 994.

[52] Franco Venturi, 'Francesco Maria Gianni: nota introduttiva', in *Illuministi italiani*, i/2. 981–2.

[53] Jean Bertrand, *Essai de la législation pour encourager l'agriculture, la population, les manufactures & le commerce*, in *Mémoires et observations recuiliés par la Société œconomique de Berne* (Berne, 1765), pp. xv–139.

[54] F. A. M. Jeanneret and J. H. Bonhôte, *Biographie neuchâteloise* (Locle, 1863), i. 43–4.

[55] Jean Bertrand, *Saggio nel quale si esamina qual debba essere la legislazione per incoraggiare*

lies not so much in the content of Bertrand's treatise, but rather in the fact that its translator chose to highlight specific aspects of it and to comment critically on others. The translation, to which Pelli Bencivenni had added critical comments, is an example of the adaptation of French thinking in Tuscany, and also of the channels through which it reached the grand duchy.

Giuseppe Pelli Bencivenni was a prominent character in Florentine intellectual life in the middle of the century. Born in Florence in 1728, he had studied law at Pisa University and then made a career in the Tuscan administration. In 1760 he became a member of the commission to organize the grain supply, before moving on to become director of the art gallery in Florence. His true calling, however, was writing, and he published prolifically on various subjects ranging from art to political economy. He was also an active journalist. We shall later learn about his involvement in the running of the *Novelle letterarie* in the early 1770s. It was his interest in political economy that led him to translate Bertrand's essay on legislation in agricultural economies.[56]

The underlying conviction that had led Pelli to translate the treatise is that agriculture lies at the heart of economic progress in any country. To this assertion, which endeared Bertrand to his Tuscan readers, Pelli added the other common theme of Tuscan economic thought since Bandini: 'There is no better way to improve the human condition than freedom [of trade].'[57] Freedom, however, must not lead to licentiousness. Bertrand, the Calvinist priest, had followed the teachings of his Church and had explained that it was vital in any cultured nation to maintain moderation, frugality, and simple customs, and to ban everything that might lead to luxury. The reason why luxury must not be allowed was simple. The habits and the taste of the higher classes filter down into all layers of society. Whereas other thinkers had argued that the incentive to equal the lifestyle of the higher classes actually had a positive effect on productivity, Bertrand was careful to point out that the opposite was true. He turned the incentive argument upside down, insisting that the peasants must not be made aware of their misery through the display of luxury by the rich. Rather than employ the old argument of class distinction against luxury for the poor, Bertrand (like his compatriot Rousseau) extended his critique of a non-frugal

l'agricoltura e per favorire in rapporto a questa la popolazione, le manifatture ed il commercio, trans. and comm. Giuseppe Pelli Bencivenni (Venice, 1767).

[56] On Pelli Bencivenni, see Roberto Zapperi, 'Bencivenni Pelli, Giuseppe', in *Dizionario biografico degli italiani*, viii (Rome, 1966), 218–22.

[57] Bertrand, *Saggio*, 2–3.

lifestyle to all classes of society.[58] Pelli Bencivenni transmitted this train of thought into Tuscany, and we shall later see how it became the rival model to arguments more favourable to conspicuous consumption brought forward, for example, by Pompeo Neri. It was a poor argument intellectually, and this made it an easy target for criticism.

It is important to note at this point, however, that Pelli Bencivenni (just like Neri before him) would not have been perceived as departing significantly from the teachings of Bandini. The *Discorso sopra la Maremma* had outlined a model of economic progress based on agriculture, free export, and direct taxation. By being less outspoken about commercial activity and conspicuous consumption, it opened the way to the development of the model in two directions. The more open approach of Neri and his cautious moves in the direction of accepting luxury under specific circumstances on the one hand, and the purely agricultural model with its emphasis on frugality on the other, could both be developed under the aegis of Bandini's thought. The 'frugal' school of thought was to receive a boost by the publication of moral treatises on luxury from the clergy, which in the 1760s and 1770s either were written in Tuscany or were publicized through reviews in the widely read Tuscan journals.

The first real disagreement between Bertrand and Pelli Bencivenni arose over the question of population growth. It is significant that Pelli attempts to link population and luxury, and that this leads to an even more outspoken critique of luxury than the one attempted by Bertrand. The author and his translator and commentator agreed that population growth was vital for economic progress. This was well in line with the contemporary perception that growth was hampered by lack of labour especially in agriculture. The population issue was so important to Pelli that he deliberately distorted Bertrand's treatment of it and added paragraphs the latter had not written. Bertrand had demanded, to be sure, that any government take all possible steps to increase the population. He then outlined preconditions that had to be met in order to achieve growth. Among them he listed sound government with property guaranteed, a free society without slavery, tolerance and freedom of conscience, and privileges for the married as means to achieve this end.[59] Part of the population problem, Bertrand acknowledged, was due to an excessive number of clerics in France and especially in Italy.[60] In Pelli's translation Bertrand sounds rather different. According to the Italian version, Bertrand argued that the population had fallen for a series

[58] Ibid. 24–5, 30.

[59] Bertrand, *Essai sur l'esprit de la législation*, 75–80.

[60] Ibid. 90.

of reasons. The excessive number of clergy and their vow of celibacy were to blame in the first place. This was followed by the Church's discouragement of second and third marriages. In a plea for toleration he blamed the Church for not allowing marriages outside the rites of the dominant confession. And lastly, 'the high praise of virginity' not surprisingly led to few births.[61] Even though some of the arguments attributed to Bertrand in the translation can clearly be found in the original version, the emphasis on the shortcomings of the Church was clearly a manifestation of Pelli's creative use of the text.

Having deliberately set up a controversial issue by not doing full justice to Bertrand, Pelli could be sure that his own comments on population growth would receive their due attention. He starts apologetically and somewhat unfairly, given that he had just deliberately misrepresented Bertrand. 'He is a Protestant, so we may forgive him for what he writes.' The true reasons for a declining population, however, must be found elsewhere. Healthy population growth, he claimed, would be achieved when a pair of conditions was met. Most importantly, all land needed to be cultivated. After a mercantilist sideswipe at the import of foreign manufactured goods, Pelli moved on to blame luxury for the decline of population. When the substance of a state is sacrificed for ruinous luxury, and when marriage is discouraged through that 'ridiculous feminine ambition and the insulting pomp of the rich', that make marriages too expensive to afford for most people, then the population will never recover.[62]

The next disagreement between Bertrand and Pelli arose over the issue of sumptuary laws. Bertrand, again influenced by Calvinism, had considered them 'undoubtedly necessary'. Pelli was not so sure for the pragmatic reason that luxury could never be banned completely.[63] Instead (and taking up a theme developed by Bandini) it was better to impose heavy duties on imported goods.[64] Luxury products produced internally were to be allowed. Pelli did not offer an explanation why he supported the domestic luxury industry. His emphasis on the introduction of heavy taxes seems to suggest, however, that he saw luxury as a source of tax revenue which could, in turn, be channelled into infrastructure to improve agriculture.[65]

[61] Bertrand, *Saggio*, 38. [62] Ibid. 38–9. [63] Ibid. 48.

[64] For Bandini's emphasis on import restrictions, see Mario Mirri, 'Bandini, Sallustio', in *Dizionario biografico degli italiani*, v (Rome, 1963), 720–31. Mirri makes Bandini more of a mercantilist with protectionist tendencies than I would care to admit. Pelli favoured the import of machines to increase productivity and free up labour to be employed in agriculture; see Bertrand, *Saggio*, 74–5.

[65] Bertrand, *Saggio*, 77–8.

Luxury was not the central part of Pelli's economic programme. To some extent it remained an unwelcome source of trouble. But Pelli explicitly insisted on correcting Bertrand's all too negative assessment of luxury and drew attention to its economic benefits. His concession to allow the production of luxury goods internally indicates that the paradigm against luxury in Tuscany had indeed begun to shift. In the early part of the century thinkers like Bandini had been predominantly preoccupied with convincing the administration that Tuscany's future lay in the export of agricultural goods (and that luxury should not detract from this enterprise). Now we can detect a development towards a more positive assessment of luxury as the question arose how to provide an incentive to increase agricultural production upon which the future of Tuscany was held to depend. This subtle change of emphasis is present in Pelli's contribution, even though he did not make it quite explicit. He remained adamant in his criticism of the 'insulting pomp of the rich' and its effects on population growth. And yet the mood had changed, which indicates that Neri's consideration of luxury reflected a wider concern: he had introduced luxury as an economic concept, and Pelli accepted this lead at least in respect of internal luxury and import duties on foreign luxuries. Furthermore, it had become evident that economic thought could not afford to neglect the function of luxury. Pelli's decision to add this dimension to Bertrand's treatise (with which he substantially agreed in most other respects) bears witness to this development. Pelli was torn between the moral outrage he felt against luxury and its potential economic uses. That he ultimately refused to follow Neri uncritically only shows that the issue of the moral value of luxury was not yet settled in the grand duchy.

Despite the ambiguities in his own thought, Pelli had chosen his subject well. He had translated an author whose basic assumptions about economic growth—free export and import restrictions in an agricultural economy—were coupled with a reluctance to sacrifice morals on the altar of conspicuous consumption, which not only hindered growth but also reduced population. Bertrand thus became an important source of economic thinking in general, and the luxury debate in particular. His *Essai* was made available to Tuscan readers, but the transmission of ideas did not end with the publication of the book. Pelli, through his active participation in the running of the *Novelle letterarie*, made sure Bertrand's message was well received in Tuscany. In fact, the publication was praised in a short but encouraging review immediately after the translation had appeared.[66] But if

[66] *Novelle letterarie di Firenze*, 27 (1767), 417.

it is true that foreign, and especially French, influence played a decisive part in the development of Tuscan thought in the eighteenth century, it is equally true that the reception of foreign ideas was by no means uncritical. The filter imposed by the legacy of Bandini and his emphasis on agriculture seem to have determined the choice of what was deemed appropriate for a Tuscan audience. But even when the basic assumptions underlying a foreign text matched this requirement, reception was critical, as is shown by the two differences between Pelli and Bertrand: their treatment of sumptuary laws and their attitudes to the population debate. Differences here had been sparked off by a dispute over faith, but soon turned into something much more substantial, covering the very foundations of economic thinking. By no means outstanding intellectually, Pelli's treatment of Bertrand's *Essai* provides an illuminating insight into the transmission of ideas during the reign of Peter Leopold.

Men like Pompeo Neri and Francesco Maria Gianni had provided channels for economic thought into the administration. It was for men like Giuseppe Pelli Bencivenni to provide channels into the republic of letters, and they did this by means of their own publications, as we have seen, and by means of their journalistic activities.

By far the most important Tuscan journal in the period from the regency to the reign of Peter Leopold was the *Novelle letterarie di Firenze*. Established in 1740, the *Novelle letterarie* aimed to provide the platform for intellectual debate in Tuscany. The uncontested centre of their attention, however, was Florence, the city in which 'studies are possibly more alive than anywhere else in Italy'. This praise of Florence and its great intellectual tradition did not prevent the *Novelle letterarie* from divulging information and new literary developments from across Europe. It will, however, be helpful to keep it in mind if we want to understand the role Tuscan precedent played in the development of Tuscan thought.

The journal fashioned itself as a high-quality *Readers' Digest*, presenting extracts of books published across Europe. But the journal also prided itself on being critical, and the journal soon launched vicious attacks against the philosophy of David Hume, against Rousseau, and against the *Encyclopédie* project.[67]

Responsible for the journal's profile was Giovanni Lami, who founded

[67] Giuseppe Ricuperati, 'Giornali e società nell'Italia dell' "Ancien Regime" (1668–1789)', in Valerio Castronovo and Nicola Tranfaglia (eds.), *La stampa italiana dal '500 all'800* (Rome, 1980), 165–71, 282–97. On its readership, see Françoise and Jean-Claude Waquet, 'Presse et société: Le Public des "Novelle letterarie" de Florence (1749–1769)', *Revue française d'histoire du livre*, 22 (1979), 39–60.

the journal and ran it for nearly three decades, up to his death in 1770.[68] Lami belonged to the generation of Pompeo Neri. Born in 1697 and educated at the University of Pisa, he started his journalistic career and soon became one of the most enthusiastic followers of Ludovico Antonio Muratori in Tuscany. He devoted four reviews to *Della pubblica felicità* only months after the work came out in 1749.[69] Even after Muratori's death references to his work were frequent, especially after his biography appeared in 1756. In fact, he was to become 'the immortal Ludovico Antonio Muratori'.[70] From the late 1740s, therefore, Muratori as a writer on social, political, and economic issues received great attention in the dominant Florentine journal. It will not be surprising to find his thought taken up by political economists who struggled to find moral justifications for Bandini's economic concepts which they had learned to appreciate.

The appearance of Muratori's work on public happiness triggered a growing interest in economic writing on the part of Lami in the 1750s. An increasing number of announcements of books on agriculture, commerce, and money bear witness to this shift.[71] The *Novelle letterarie* became a forum for economic debate. In 1764, for example, a self-styled 'expert on agriculture' wrote to the *Novelle letterarie* offering his insights 'for those who care for abundant harvests'. The moral of his contribution: 'Take your hands off free trade'.[72]

The inclination towards free trade became even more pronounced in the second half of the 1770s, when the *Novelle letterarie* placed itself at the centre of the debate on behalf of physiocracy.[73] By that time, however, economic thought had ceased to be a purely economic matter. Muratori had taught his Tuscan readers that it had to be seen in the wider context of moral philosophy, and subsequent treatises on political economy should bear witness to this. It is significant that Lami, in his review of *Della pubblica felicità*, was much interested in Muratori's plans for an academy for administrative studies to educate the youth to take over government positions. Without 'having previously studied moral philosophy, that is,

68 On Lami and his intellectual formation, see Mario Rosa, 'Atteggiamenti culturali e religiosi di Giovanni Lami nelle *Novelle letterarie*', *Annali della Scuola Normale Superiore di Pisa*, 2nd ser., 25 (1956), 260–333.

69 *Novelle letterarie di Firenze*, 40, 45, 48, and 52 (1749).

70 *Novelle letterarie di Firenze*, 22 (1769), 350.

71 The growing interest seems to start with the announcement of a work by Ubaldo Montelatici, president of the Accademia dei Georgofili, on agriculture, *Ragionamento sopra i mezzi più necessari per far rifiorire l'agricoltura* (Florence, 1752): *Novelle letterarie di Firenze*, 19 (1752), 289–90.

72 *Novelle letterarie di Firenze*, 50 (1764), 790.

73 Cf. Ricuperati, 'Giornali e società', 288–9.

learned to understand man', Muratori had asserted, no one was to be admitted to the academy. A thorough knowledge of moral philosophy was a necessary precondition for being a good administrator.[74]

Moral and religious thought entered Tuscany through other channels as well. A prominent example is the Barnabite priest Sigismondo Gerdil, whose Christian works—tracts on the character of true religion and discourses on divinity—had always been praised prodigiously by Lami.[75] The reception of the Torinese writer changed drastically in tone, however, when Lami reviewed his discourse on luxury. In 1768, one year after Neri and Pelli had written on agriculture and free trade, Gerdil published his *Discours de la nature, et des effets du luxe* in Turin.

Gerdil had been born in Savoy, where he spent much of his life. He had studied theology in Bologna, and made a remarkable career in the Church which culminated in a cardinalate in 1777. His interests were wide-ranging, however, and he published extensively on philosophical and moral subjects, and against modern philosophers. His book against John Locke, for example, seems to have brought him the philosophy chair in Turin in 1749, which he held for several years before taking over the chair in moral theology.[76] He died in 1802.

Gerdil had shown a delight in attacking the philosophy of Locke, Rousseau, and Montesquieu. He showed a similar delight in repudiating Jean-François Melon's concept of luxury, which he condemned as contrary to a virtuous life. Gerdil's definition of luxury is common and straightforward. Luxury is 'an excess of delicacy and sumptuousness, be it in respect to the commodities of life, be it in respect to the rank occupied in society'.[77] It was no novelty to relate luxury to social rank, but Gerdil gave the argument special emphasis and spoke of 'the equality that luxury tends to introduce between different orders' so that all notions of social rank become blurred.[78] Morally, the problem with luxury was that it affected all layers of society, not just the wealthy few as Melon had claimed. Luxury would trickle down society and ruin the virtue of all.[79] Economically, it was negatively linked to the concepts of virtue and frugality. Against the claim that luxury was the driving force behind commerce, and the source of wealth,

[74] *Novelle letterarie di Firenze*, 45 (1749), 706–8, esp. p. 708.

[75] *Novelle letterarie di Firenze*, 22 (1769), 348–50; 33 (1769), 523; 44 (1769), 701–2.

[76] Giacinto Sigismondo Gerdil, *L'immaterialité de l'âme demontrée contre m. Locke par les même principes, par lesquels ce philosophe démontre l'existence & l'immaterialité de Dieu, avec des nouvelles preuves de l'immaterialité de Dieu, et de l'âme, tirées de l'Ecriture, des pères & de la raison* (Turin, 1747).

[77] Gerdil, *Discours de la nature, et des effets du luxe* (Turin, 1768), 8.

[78] Ibid. 11.

[79] Ibid. 77.

Gerdil asserted that states prosper through virtue and frugality. It was true that luxury brought wealth, but only to some. Those who profited from it were artisans, and their class was after all (as he knew from Montesquieu) 'the most useless class'.[80] Resources were drained off the countryside, which suffered from the prosperity of the city. Gerdil reiterated the old denunciation of the city as opposed to the virtuous countryside and towards which government attention should be directed.

Given the moralistic tone of Gerdil's work, his emphasis on agriculture as the true source of prosperity, and his belief in a state that took care of its citizens, Gerdil might have expected acclaim in Tuscany. Not so, and Lami, who was usually full of praise for Gerdil, for one criticized the *Discours* severely.

Having denied the *Discours* any originality of thought, Lami launched a fundamental critique of Gerdil's claims.[81] Luxury 'cannot but be useful for society', provided the luxury goods are not imported from abroad. The reason for this was simple. Luxury goods induced the rich to spend their 'idle money', because 'locked-up wealth is useless for the state unless it is circulated continually'. Luxury also employed the poor in 'diverse occupations'. From this starting point, which was familiar through the works of most defenders of luxury by the 1760s, Lami proceeded to treat the question of sumptuary laws. He managed to give the argument a novel and most surprising twist by turning the standard argument upside down. Most authors had hitherto either demanded sumptuary laws to keep luxury at bay, or regretted that such laws had to be abandoned because they never proved effective. Defenders of luxury had traditionally scorned sumptuary laws as a moral attempt to meddle with economic principles of spending according to desire, circulation, and consumption. Lami turned sumptuary laws into luxuries themselves. 'I know the sumptuary laws of the Romans; the sumptuary laws of many kingdoms; the sumptuary laws of the Florentines.' But the Romans, 'who plundered kingdoms and their provinces' to feed their population, 'could well afford to restrict the luxury of their citizens, because the poor did not need this support to live.' Equally the Florentines in the fourteenth and fifteenth centuries could well afford 'to issue sumptuary laws, to prescribe dress codes, limit wedding expenses', and so on, because in those times 'there was no one in the Florentine state who did not procure enough bread by his own labour'.[82] The present situation, however, was different, and luxury was needed to increase the circulation of money. People might object to this, but they would ultimately need it to survive.

[80] Ibid. 49–50 and 76.

[81] Review in *Novelle letterarie di Firenze*, 48 (1769), 762.

[82] Ibid. 763–4.

Lami almost got carried away by his enthusiasm for luxury, and went on to assert that luxury was good. It was good for a landlord to have twenty servants rather than ten, good for him to have fourteen horses rather than seven. 'I cannot see how this luxury can be detrimental to society, and contrary to the teachings of the Church, because all Christians have to direct their actions towards God, and the comfort of their neighbours (*il comodo del prossimo*).' Lami here presents us with the economic version of the Christian command to love one's neighbour as oneself. Since such behaviour is in line with Christianity, inequality can be accepted, too. Suppose a country only has 1 million *scudi* to feed its population, and that this amount is enough to feed all. 'What does it matter if one has more than the other? If those who are better off spend their money on decent luxuries, their major share passes on to those who have less, and everybody profits.' His conclusion against the old doctrine that had been repeated again by Gerdil was that the luxury he had set out to defend 'is not contrary to the Bible, and is useful for society in whatever guise it may appear'.[83]

Lami's is only a brief review of several pages. It would be inappropriate to expect a thorough treatment of luxury in all its aspects. It is nevertheless significant that he deliberately limited the scope of his review. We do not find, for instance, any direct confrontation with Gerdil's arguments. This is surprising, given that reviews in the *Novelle letterarie* usually follow the structure of the text reviewed quite closely. More often than not they are simple summaries of newly published books, occasionally preceded by a positive or disapproving comment. After introducing Gerdil's book, and after some preliminary remarks on its author, Lami launches immediately into a treatment of luxury, without sparing much thought for the work he had set out to review. The point against sumptuary laws, which Lami makes so forcefully, for example, cannot have been directed against Gerdil, because the latter had criticized them as well.[84] Neither do we find any reference to Gerdil's sources, which is all the more surprising if we bear in mind that Gerdil had composed his *Discours* as a direct answer to, and a refutation of, Melon, who, in turn, had stood at the centre of Muratori's treatment of luxury. All this increases the suspicion that Gerdil's tract on luxury was not really the target of Lami's wrath. It rather provided the occasion for a contribution by Lami to the luxury debate that had been gaining momentum in Tuscany. And the most appropriate forum for such a contribution proved to be the review section of his widely read journal.

[83] Review in *Novelle letterarie di Firenze*, 48 (1769), 765–6.

[84] Gerdil, *Discours*, 87.

What explains Lami's sudden abandonment of Gerdil, whom he had previously praised so prodigiously? Gerdil had criticized a text that was only just coming to be accepted in Tuscany. After Muratori's introduction, Neri's endorsement, and even Pelli's reluctant concessions to some of its arguments, Melon's *Essai politique* was on its way to becoming assimilated into the thought of the Tuscan elite because it provided answers how to improve Tuscany's troubled economy. But the violence with which the otherwise quite mild-mannered Lami attacked Gerdil indicates that the acceptance of Melon's doctrines in the grand duchy was not unanimous, and that the attack was not only directed against Gerdil (after all, his book did not receive much detailed attention in the review) but also served to convince the sceptics at home. The battle was not yet over.

Lami's review had several consequences. First, and despite its neglect of most of the book's subject matter, it made Gerdil's treatise known in Tuscany because it provided full bibliographical details of the book, and gave an outline of its argument. Secondly, it heated up the debate about luxury with a positive assessment that had not hitherto been heard in Tuscany in such force. The assertive tone of Lami's contribution decisively moved luxury towards the centre of economic debate. But (and here we come back to the deliberate limitation of the review), Lami presented the luxury issue as a purely economic one. It is true that he acknowledged that people might find luxury morally objectionable. But these concerns are brushed aside with a view to finding a solution to the economic problem of starvation and unemployment. What Lami's review did, then, was to increase the interest in the luxury issue without providing a full answer to the problems it raised. His economic reasoning stopped half-way, which is perhaps understandable given the brevity of his contribution. The moral side of the issue is barely touched upon. But whatever the shortcomings of Lami's review, the field was now open for debate in Tuscany. It may not be exaggerated to claim that Lami's review had as similarly disturbing yet unsatisfactory an effect as Mandeville's treatment several decades earlier. After all, the two had both claimed that moral considerations had to be put aside when the solving of economic problems became more pressing.

6

The Tuscan Luxury Debate between Morals and Economics

> We . . . are indebted to the profound observations and the useful research of Sig. Quesnai.
>
> (Ferdinando Paoletti, *Dei veri mezzi*, 1772)

Ferdinando Paoletti was one of the authors who intervened several times in the Tuscan luxury debate. His contributions cemented a trend that had been started by Pelli and Lami. After the closed ministerial culture of the first half of the century, the debate became increasingly public. It was carried out in widely read journals (as in the case of the *Novelle letterarie*) or in published treatises on political economy (as in the case of Paoletti). Characterized by more open public discussion, this is the age of the Tuscan Enlightenment. Peter Leopold had just moved to Florence as the new grand duke. An era of reform was clearly in the offing, and people from outside the administration or the Florentine ruling classes began to intervene in the great debates of the time. It is in Paoletti's thought, I shall argue, that the threads outlined so far—the influence of Sallustio Bandini and Ludovico Muratori, the constant indecision about how to insert luxury into the picture of an agricultural economy based on free export, the shaky balance between economic reasoning and moral arguments, Lami's provocative contribution—are joined together for the first and last time in eighteenth-century Tuscany.[1]

Ferdinando Paoletti: Economic Progress as Christian Duty

Ferdinando Paoletti was born near Florence in 1717. After having studied in Florence, he was appointed priest in Villamagna, a little village near Florence, when he was around 30 years old. It was here, in the heartland of

[1] Paoletti has long been unduly neglected. The only work on him is Mario Mirri, *Ferdinando Paoletti: agronomo, 'georgofilo', riformatore nella Toscana del Settecento* (Florence, 1967). See also Till Wahnbaeck, 'Ferdinando Paoletti georgofilo e il dibattito sul lusso nel Settecento', *I Georgofili: atti della Accademia dei Georgofili*, 45 (1998), 367–89, which the following account supplements.

the Chianti region, that Paoletti developed an interest in agriculture because his parish responsibilities included the supervision of a small farm of three families.[2] He had some notable successes as a farmer, and managed to double the yield of his lands within a few years.[3] In fact, it was because of his practical work on his model farm that he was elected a member of the Accademia dei Georgofili in 1770.[4] His fame soon spread abroad, and he was visited by the English agriculturalist Arthur Young during his travels in Italy.[5]

But his most lasting achievement was in the field of agricultural and economic treatises such as the *Pensieri sopra l'agricoltura*, begun in 1768 and published the following year in Florence. With the *Pensieri*, Paoletti aimed to establish the appropriate moral and economic climate to foster the growth of Tuscany's agricultural economy and to improve the situation of its population.[6]

Paoletti found his teacher in Ludovico Muratori, whom he discovered while he was being trained at S. Miniato. For Paoletti, as for Muratori before him, economic growth and morally sound behaviour were closely linked.[7] It was this link that led Paoletti to the heart of the issue of economic stagnation and peasant misery. The causes of all economic problems were (he argued against the defenders of conspicuous consumption in Tuscany) luxury, fashion, and absenteeism.[8]

In placing his emphasis solely on peasant misery and the improvement of the countryside, he followed the route of economic thinking which Bandini had outlined several decades earlier. More pressingly, he took issue with treatments of the luxury question that appeared in the 1760s. The first to address the issue in a treatise of its own in Florence was Bindo Peruzzi. In 1767, shortly before Paoletti set to work on his *Pensieri*, Peruzzi addressed

2 For details on his farm, see Arthur Young, *Travels during the Years 1787, 1788, and 1789; Undertaken More Particularly with a View of Ascertaining the Cultivation, Wealth, Resources, and National Prosperity of the Kingdom of France*, 2 vols., 2nd edn. (London, 1794), i. 253.

3 Giuseppe Sarchiani, 'Elogio del Pievano Ferdinando Paoletti, letto nell'Adunanza del dì 28. Febbrajo 1803', *Atti della Reale ed Imperiale Accademia Economico-Agraria dei Georgofili di Firenze*, 5 (1804), 47.

4 Marco Tabarrini, *Degli studi e delle vicende della Reale Accademia dei Georgofili nel primo secolo della sua esistenza* (Florence, 1856), 68.

5 Young, *Travels*, 253.

6 Ferdinando Paoletti, *Pensieri sopra l'agricoltura* (Florence, 1769). A first review is in *Novelle letterarie*, 1 (1770), 179–80.

7 'That man is happy, who does not lack the necessaries to survive and live commodiously (*viver comodamente*), as long as he is capable of limiting the excess of his desires' (Paoletti, *Pensieri*, p. iv).

8 Ibid. 3–8. On the defence of luxury, see e.g. Giovanni Lami, who claimed that luxury 'cannot but be useful for society', in *Novelle letterarie di Firenze*, 48 (1769), 762–6.

the Accademia dei Georgofili in Florence and gave a lecture about the right use of luxury relating to agriculture and commerce. The title of the lecture alone must have been disagreeable enough for Paoletti, who, as a member of the academy with a keen interest in its proceedings, can be expected to have attended on the occasion. Peruzzi's is a shallow treatment of luxury, and he did not venture to defend or criticize luxury in any convincing manner. What he did do, however, was establish 'luxury' as the principal link between the city and the countryside, through which the two could and must benefit from each other.[9] We do not learn how this link was to operate precisely, but it is important that Peruzzi acknowledged the importance of the city for improvement in the countryside, and that he presented arguments in favour of luxury production for export purposes, and reiterated the point that the consumption of luxury goods might increase the circulation of money.[10] By way of conclusion, Peruzzi presented luxury as potentially beneficial for economic development, but effeminizing in its moral aspects and leading to ruin if not regulated wisely.

Peruzzi's lecture was not outspoken enough to lend itself to a direct confutation. It did, however, increase awareness among the Tuscan agricultural elite as represented in the Accademia dei Georgofili of the importance of luxury in economic matters. And even though Peruzzi had not taken a clear position in favour of luxury, at least he had hinted at its potentially positive function in society. Neri's efforts at re-evaluation were slowly beginning to bear fruit.

Whether or not Paoletti actually attended the lecture, it is clearly against the likes of Peruzzi that Paoletti directed his arguments in his *Pensieri*, which he began only shortly after Peruzzi had given his lecture. Luxury was not a topic he could choose to ignore. Indeed, he would have none of Peruzzi's weighing up of the advantages or disadvantages of luxury. Instead, he chose luxury as his main target with which to explain both moral decadence and economic decay. Contrary to Peruzzi, he also chose to focus solely on the countryside. That this focus was predetermined by the great tradition of Tuscan economic thought has already been mentioned. In fact, it was a focus that few Tuscan thinkers abandoned in the second half of the eighteenth century, and almost all shared Paoletti's scepticism towards the role of commerce and manufacture in Tuscany, where the climate was favourable and agricultural products were sought after abroad.[11]

[9] Bindo di Bindi Simone Peruzzi, *Dissertazione accademica letta nell'Accademia de' Georgofili il dì 2. Settembre 1767 sopra l'uso giusto del lusso relativamente all'agricoltura, arti e commercio* (Florence, 1768), 9–10. [10] Ibid. 16–17.

[11] See e.g. Giuseppe Sarchiani, *Regolamento sul commercio, arti e manifatture della Toscana*

The main thrust of Paoletti's argument against luxury is that it detracts from efforts to make agriculture profitable. Once agriculture is singled out as the way to economic growth, and as long as agriculture does not yet yield the profits that are necessary to develop it over time, all efforts have to be directed at improving the situation. The main problem with luxury is that it keeps landowners away from their land and insensitive to the need for improvement. Far from constituting a link between the city and the countryside, as Peruzzi had claimed, luxury is exclusively associated with the 'the pleasures of the city'. And landlords, who are needed most to ensure the prosperity of agriculture, are most prone to succumb to these pleasures and leave their farms. In other words, luxury does not constitute a danger per se, but as a cause for absenteeism. This might be tolerated under more favourable economic circumstances. In its present state, however, the Tuscan economy simply could not afford it.[12] But Paoletti's argument does not end here. So far it had been one of mere pragmatism in the face of economic problems. But using Peruzzi's image that luxury led landowners to forget both their duties as agriculturalists and their civic duties, Paoletti went one step further and equated the two. The civic, and indeed moral, duties of the landlord consist precisely in increasing the revenue of his land. 'Pomp and gorgeous display do not make up the good citizen.' He has to be useful to his *patria* (a concept of usefulness that had been coined by Muratori), and that is best achieved by providing food to satisfy the needs of the population.[13]

Once this frame of reference had been established, Paoletti could make a case for the study of agriculture by landlords residing on their lands that would ultimately lead to prosperity. The chief modern text that Paoletti recommended for study was Bertrand's *Essai de la législation pour encourager l'agriculture*, which had appeared in translation the year before he wrote his *Pensieri*. In fact, Bertrand offered most of what Paoletti considered necessary for the education of the landlord.[14] What is more, Bertrand had the right approach to political economy. 'Modern politicians only speak of commerce and money.' Instead, you need to consider custom and virtue, and Bertrand got it right when he praised frugality and sought to banish everything that could lead to luxury.[15]

There was thus a need for Pelli's translation of Bertrand's *Essai* because it offered a moral account of economic activity with an emphasis on virtue

(Florence, 1781), 107; cf. also the review in *Giornale dei letterati di Pisa*, 42 (1781), 130–5; Saverio Manetti, 'Lezione accademica', *Magazzino toscano*, 1 (1770), 15; Giovanni Battista Landeschi, *Saggi di agricoltura* (Florence, 1775); review in *Giornale dei letterati di Pisa*, 19 (1775), 100–37.

[12] Paoletti, *Pensieri*, 5–8. [13] Ibid. 10. [14] Ibid. 18–20. [15] Ibid. 46–7.

rather than wealth. This seemed all the more necessary as some influential thinkers were increasingly inclined to accept luxury as a guarantor of prosperity regardless of specific circumstances. In fact, Paoletti had argued against what seemed set to become a new hegemony, and his treatment met with strong resistance. His contemporaries criticized him for offering an all too simplistic account of the economic problems faced by Tuscany. It seemed to his critics that 'he did not sufficiently explain the reasons for Tuscany's agricultural decline by concentrating solely on luxury, fashion, and absenteeism, without even suspecting that trade restrictions for agricultural produce might have played a role'.[16] The criticism seems somewhat unjust. It is true that Paoletti had not considered trade regulations to be of paramount importance for his argument. But he had deliberately set out to make a moral case for economic development, linking the virtuous life and civic duties with agricultural work. In this framework, there was little room for free trade and export activities. This is not to say, however, that these considerations could not have been accommodated in Paoletti's thought. In fact, when he did so in his following work, he had little need substantially to alter his previous assumptions.[17]

Paoletti developed his theory in two stages. At first, in the *Pensieri*, he was concerned with the mindset conducive to production and economic progress. First of all, this entailed drawing attention to the landlords' civic duties, which were to be fulfilled through the provision of agricultural produce. The moral assumptions underlying this demand correspond with Muratori's insistence that it was man's duty to help one another (and, on a utilitarian level, entice help from others in return), to contribute one's share to public happiness. And once the moral groundwork had been laid, it was vital to discover what stood at the centre of the economic process that guaranteed the landlords' fulfilment of their deeds. This led Paoletti to urge landowners to abandon luxury and concentrate on practical measures to improve agriculture. The second stage was based on different assumptions altogether. Here the central concern was how to keep up the momentum, what to do once the internal situation was improved, and how to provide an incentive to assure *continued* development. If the aim of Paoletti's first book,

[16] U. de' Nobili, 'Elogio del sacerdote Ferdinando Paoletti, pievano di S. Donnino in Villamagna', *Nuovo giornale dei letterati di Pisa*, 5 (1803), 13.

[17] I take issue here with Mirri's contention that a big change took place in Paoletti's economic thought around 1770. I would argue rather for a change in emphasis within an essentially unchanged moral and economic framework. Mirri, *Paoletti*, 4–6. The homogeneous nature of Paoletti's thought has been observed, albeit from a different perspective, by Eric Cochrane, *Tradition and Enlightenment in the Tuscan Academies, 1690–1800* (Chicago, 1961), 236.

namely to outline the first stage, could be achieved with the help of Muratori's insertion of economic activity into enlightened Catholicism and with the help of manuals such as Bertrand's *Essai*, the second stage necessitated a different approach and a new book. He did not change his mind from one work to the next, but he did draw on different authors to achieve his new aim.

Political Economy and Physiocracy

Paoletti's next intervention in the field of political economy (which incidentally brought Bandini back into the frame) was not only the necessary continuation of his project. It was also caused by a variety of specific developments in Tuscany. First of all, the publication of Paoletti's treatise had received only modest attention in learned circles. The *Novelle letterarie* in Florence printed a short notice; the *Nuovo Giornale de' letterati* in Pisa ignored the work; the *Giornale d'Italia* spoke of a satisfactory attempt of an author who was well versed in the details of agriculture and the principles of politics.[18] Apart from this, nothing. To make matters worse, Lami launched his defence of luxury only months after the *Pensieri* came out. That at least part of the dissatisfaction with Paoletti's work (of which his biographers give notice) was caused by his treatment of the question of luxury is suggested by two facts.[19] First, Paoletti addressed the critique of his views in *I veri mezzi di render felici le società*, an apologetic appendix to the *Pensieri*, published independently in 1772.[20] Secondly, Paoletti returned to the question of luxury when he added a new chapter on luxury in the second edition of his *Pensieri* published in 1789.

It is in this local context that we have to place Paoletti's subsequent treatments of political economy in general, and luxury in particular. His answers, however, owe much to outside influences. For his new book, Paoletti found the most fruitful inspiration in France, and he became the mouthpiece of physiocracy in Tuscany.

When the *Veri mezzi* came out in 1772, 'the beautiful work' was immediately hailed as a major contribution to the doctrine of economic freedom in Tuscany.[21] The agricultural focus remained the same as in his previous

[18] *Novelle letterarie di Firenze*, 1 (1770), 179–80; *Giornale d'Italia*, 50 (1770), 393–4.

[19] On the animosities caused by his controversial views, see Sarchiani, 'Elogio', 43–4.

[20] Ferdinando Paoletti, *I veri mezzi di render felici le società: appendice apologetica al libro 'De' pensieri sopra l'agricoltura'* (Florence, 1772), 2–4.

[21] Reviews in *Giornale d'Italia*, 46 (1772), 362–4, and *Novelle letterarie di Firenze*, 3 (1772), 225–9, and 6 (1772), 271–5.

work, but rather than considering the necessary preconditions for economic development, he moved on to outline the conditions for a continuous success of his model.

Once the basic conditions were met—landowners with a keen interest in agriculture residing on their lands, and an industrious, well-fed, and educated peasantry—Paoletti could move on to explain how development could be sustained. Sustained growth depended on investment. This required money, which was best acquired through export. Once money started coming in through export, owners could spend more, and ultimately cultivate more. Through the 'profusion' of money, the population would grow, and with it consumption. This, in turn, would lead to the progress of agriculture.[22] Commercial activity did not feature prominently in this account, and indeed Tuscany was again described as an 'agricultural land'. Paoletti had calculated, he claimed, that commerce did not play a significant role in the Tuscan economy. His example is the correctly observed decline in the silk industry. The memory of Florence's glorious past, where the wool trade alone would bring millions into the city, should not distract its inhabitants from facing reality in the eighteenth century.[23] Those old manufactures were gone, and even if they still existed, competition from across Europe would be too strong for them to strive. Hence, the arts alone were incapable of feeding the population. The competitive advantage that Tuscany now enjoyed lay in its territory. The extent of the land, the quality and diversity of its produce, the industriousness of its inhabitants, and a supply outstripping internal demand all led to the conviction that the Tuscan economy had to be based on agriculture.[24]

This line of thought, which was predominantly inspired by Paoletti's own observations as a farmer, was given a theoretical foundation by his recourse to physiocratic doctrine. Tuscany was fortunate in having such a prospering agriculture because the arts were ultimately 'sterile and infertile'. It might well be true that the products of the arts sold at higher prices than agricultural produce, but the higher margin was eaten up by the labour employed in the process of production. In fact, the products of the arts are not even products, but 'only form, only modification' of prime materials.

[22] Paoletti, *I veri mezzi*, 29 and 34–5.

[23] On Florence's privileged position during the Renaissance, see Richard A. Goldthwaite, *Wealth and the Demand for Art in Italy, 1300–1600*, pbk. edn. (Baltimore, 1995), 13–67.

[24] Paoletti, *I veri mezzi*, 55–61. On the fate of the silk industry, see Paolo Malanima, *La decadenza di un'economia cittadina: l'industria a Firenze nei secoli XVI–XVIII* (Bologna, 1982), 305–21. On the growing competitiveness of agriculture especially in northern Italy, see Domenico Sella, *Crisis and Continuity: The Economy of Spanish Lombardy in the Seventeenth Century* (Cambridge, Mass., 1979).

The only genuine production and reproduction is to be found in agriculture, and since political economy is interested in physical production, it is only agriculture that does the trick.[25] Furthermore, agriculture enjoys the additional benefit of turning the 'gifts of nature' such as sun, soil, and rain into profit. Manufacture, by contrast, gets nothing for free, and any gain in this field can only ever be a restitution of expenses incurred and a recompense for labour and risk.[26] Even the high prices commanded by fashion goods are mere chimeras. Taking up a line of argument developed by Muratori, he argues that the 'price of opinion' contains hidden costs that were all too often neglected. High prices are paid for singular goods of rare craftsmanship and fashion. The year-long efforts that lead to excellence are costly and need to be offset against the ultimate selling price. In the case of fashion, prices are short-lived because so is fashion, and imitators are quick to move into the market.[27]

The inspiration Paoletti drew from physiocratic writings is visible enough. He himself acknowledged that 'we are indebted to the profound observations and the useful research of Sig. Quesnai'.[28] Contrary to what Paoletti makes us believe in the introduction to his work, however, his real debt lies elsewhere, namely in the works of Mirabeau, and more precisely in his *Ami des hommes*, published in 1756 but only distributed a year later in France. Paoletti had acquired a familiarity with physiocratic doctrines by having the Tuscan agent in Paris, Niccoli, send him packs with the sect's latest publications.[29] Paoletti himself corresponded with Mirabeau, which probably enhanced his understanding of the central issues of contemporary French debate.[30] But why did he choose Mirabeau as his correspondent and not Quesnay? The answer is that Mirabeau's premisses and his outlook on the economy were much more congenial to the Tuscan situation, to its intellectual tradition, and thus ultimately to Paoletti than those of the founder of the school.

Mirabeau's influence on the formulation of physiocratic doctrine was certainly greater than has long been thought. Nevertheless, there are

[25] Paoletti, *I veri mezzi*, 65–6. [26] Ibid. 43–4.

[27] Ibid. 71–80. On Muratori's concept of the *prezzo d'opinione*, see Ludovico Antonio Muratori, *Della pubblica felicità oggetto de' buoni principi*, ed. Cesare Mozzarelli (Rome, 1996), 171–2.

[28] Paoletti, *I veri mezzi*, p. lxi.

[29] Mario Mirri, 'Per una ricerca dei rapporti fra "economisti" e riformatori toscani: l'abate Niccoli a Parigi', *Annali dell'Istituto Giangiacomo Feltrinelli*, 2 (1959), 55–120.

[30] The correspondence is mentioned by his biographer. The contact between the two was established by a Tuscan monk in Paris, Niccoli; cf. de' Nobili, 'Elogio del sacerdote Ferdinando Paoletti', 27–8. Most of the correspondence is lost. See, however, one letter to Paoletti by Mirabeau printed in Mirri, *Paoletti*, 101–11.

striking differences between Quesnay, the founder, and Mirabeau, the not-so-willing convert.[31] As one of his admirers put it, Mirabeau had a literary or historical rather than an analytic mind; his was a work of social rather than political economy. Unlike Quesnay, who was obsessed with the generation of a net product, Mirabeau never lost sight of the broader picture. For him, the social system mattered as much as the economy, and religion constituted an indispensable element of an ordered society. In fact, in the words of Fox-Genovese, 'Mirabeau probably . . . did not favor economic growth' and had no interest in price mechanisms. He even saw monetary circulation more in moral than in economic terms.[32] Furthermore, Mirabeau did not share Quesnay's view of agriculture as a source of capital accumulation. Rather, he preferred to see it simply as a source of revenue. Finally, Mirabeau was an outspoken critic of Cantillon, who had conceived of proprietors as luxury consumers whose spending stimulated the economy. Mirabeau, by contrast, saw proprietors as guarantors of social hierarchy.

It is easy to see how these ideas appealed to Paoletti. The principal assumptions such as the focus on agriculture and free trade and the notion of the sterility of the arts he shared with the whole physiocratic school, but Mirabeau's insertion of economic activity into a larger frame of an ordered society governed by religious principles blended well with Paoletti's previous attempts in the *Pensieri* to apply economic principles to the Muratorian quest for public happiness. Mirabeau's view of agriculture as a source of revenue, and his scepticism towards unrestricted economic growth (as opposed to a development of a nation's capacities), were much closer to Paoletti than Quesnay's approach.

There is also another reason for the attractiveness of Mirabeau to Paoletti, and this takes us back to the role of Bandini in the development of Tuscan thought. Bandini exerted a strong influence on Paoletti, and this further enhanced the appeal of physiocracy because Mirabeau and Bandini's economic thought can be traced back to the same source, to Boisguilbert. The thought of the two need not necessarily be similar in all details (Bandini accorded far greater importance to money than Mirabeau, for example), but a common heritage served to bridge the differences.

The influence of Boisguilbert on Bandini has already been discussed. But Boisguilbert's role for the development of physiocratic thinking, and

[31] The following account is based on Elizabeth Fox-Genovese, *The Origins of Physiocracy: Economic Revolution and Social Order in Eighteenth-Century France* (Ithaca, NY, 1976), 146–65.

[32] Ibid. 162.

that of Mirabeau in particular, was equally pronounced. As Mirabeau wrote to the Milanese law professor and one-time priest Alfonso Longo in 1775, 'Boisguilbert is the true and only precursor of the *économistes*.'[33] And Forbonnais, in turn, asserted that Mirabeau had found in Boisguilbert's *Détail de la France* 'his guide and his perpetual model, even though he never cites it'.[34]

If Boisguilbert was a precursor of both Mirabeau and Bandini, and if Paoletti adopted Mirabeau's teachings, then we should look for a connection between Paoletti's thought and that of Bandini as well. And it is indeed striking how similar the *Veri mezzi* is to the *Discorso sopra la Maremma*. The chain reaction leading to economic prosperity is a case in point. Bandini had argued that money stood at the centre of economic development. The money supply had to be increased through free export and high prices, and the increase would lead to an increase in consumption. The boost in demand would, in turn, push up production and ultimately guarantee growth. Paoletti had followed a similar path. Development required money, which could only be achieved through free export. The availability of money, in turn, spurred consumption and ultimately production—a reiteration of Bandini's argument. But the influence of Bandini on Paoletti reaches even further, although the reception was not always uncritical.

Bandini's argument for high prices had been suspiciously missing from Paoletti's account. For the former, high prices were necessary to provide an incentive for landowners and peasants alike. Their purchasing power was assumed to be proportional to the price of grain because their income almost exclusively depended on selling grain. Acutely aware of the economic reality and the strains high prices placed on the peasant population, Paoletti had already taken issue with the underlying assumption in his *Pensieri*. High prices, he had argued, were not beneficial for the population at large, and not even for the peasantry, because the peasants had to keep the overwhelming part of their produce for their own subsistence anyway.[35] In the *Veri mezzi* Paoletti refined, and somewhat changed, his argument in response to a pamphleteer who had effectively repeated Bandini's arguments for high grain prices. Paoletti at first asserted again that the flaw of the argument was that peasants had little if any surplus to sell.[36] But a case for

[33] Letter, 5 Sept. 1775, quoted in Henri Ripert, *Le Marquis de Mirabeau: Ses théories politiques et économiques* (Paris, 1901), 64. According to Mirabeau's judgement, Quesnay completely took over Boisguilbert's teachings and only added his concept of net product to the edifice.

[34] Quoted in Louis Salleron, 'Boisguilbert précurseur des physiocrates', in *Pierre de Boisguilbert, ou, La Naissance de l'économie politique*, 2 vols. (Paris, 1966), i. 44.

[35] Paoletti, *Pensieri*, 60.

[36] Paoletti, *I veri mezzi*, 7–11.

high prices could indeed be made. His argument was based on the assumption that peasants receive a salary from their landlords, and that this salary is proportional to the grain price. Low prices reduce the need for labour, and consequently cause a decline in pay and lucrative jobs. It was, therefore, not humanitarian considerations about an increase in *peasant* revenue which should lead to the defence of high prices (because the peasant still had little surplus grain to sell), but rather the effect on employment through an increase in *proprietor* revenue. Under circumstances where landlords pay their peasants a salary proportional to the grain price, high prices will translate into high salaries. When grain is dear, in other words, the peasant will benefit from an increase in disposable income since he will only spend a portion of his higher salary on high-priced bread.[37]

The issue of high prices had first been brought up by Bandini. It continued to be discussed well into the 1770s, and Paoletti's contribution to the debate can be viewed in this context. The line of argument that artificially low grain prices had to be avoided had shifted considerably over the decades, but Bandini's original claim still held true when Paoletti wrote his *Veri mezzi*. On a wider scale, it is useful to note that Paoletti's intervention in the grain price debate cannot be explained by his recent reading of Mirabeau, who was largely uninterested in price mechanisms. When he did mention prices, he usually complained that they were too high.[38] The price debate is yet another example of a clearly Tuscan frame of reference in which Tuscan authors operated, a frame that had been shaped by Sallustio Bandini. The debate need not always have been inspired by a direct confrontation with Bandini's work. It is significant, however, how many issues first raised by him continued to shape the contours of debate well into the second half of the eighteenth century.

The link that has figured so prominently in the account so far was explicitly acknowledged in 1775, when Ferdinando Paoletti reviewed Bandini's *Discorso sopra la Maremma*, which had finally appeared in print that year.[39] In one of his very few reviews Paoletti praises the work that had shaped so much of Tuscan thought while still circulating in manuscript form. The review itself is of little interest intellectually because it is too positive and affirmative for any serious analysis of contrasting views. It is, however, a reminder that Paoletti felt the connection with, and his indebtedness to, Bandini as clearly as many a Tuscan writer. The dual influence of pre-physiocratic thinking on Bandini, and of Bandini on Paoletti and

[37] Paoletti, *I veri mezzi*, 45–8.
[38] Fox-Genovese, *The Origins of Physiocracy*, 163.
[39] *Giornale de' letterati di Pisa*, 19 (1775), 138–78.

Tuscan thought in general, facilitated the ease with which Tuscans looked to France for advice in economic matters.

Few economic doctrines could be found in Europe at the time that could have appeared more congenial, more genuinely 'Tuscan', than physiocracy in Mirabeau's vein. The Tuscan tendency to pick up only those aspects of foreign thought to which they could relate, which has been convincingly shown by Eric Cochrane in the case of botany, archaeology, and medicine, can also be observed in the field of economic thought. But here it was not the experience of famines that made Tuscans look to physiocracy for help as Cochrane has argued and as Lucio Villari has repeated. Both give the misleading impression that Tuscany's own intellectual tradition played a negligible role in the assimilation of physiocratic thought.[40] It is true that the famines of the 1760s increased the urgency with which physiocratic ideas were received in Tuscany. But the channel through which economic thought was to pass in the course of the century had been dug decades earlier by Bandini's assimilation of Boisguilbert, and it was only through this groundbreaking work that physiocratic ideas could be received a generation later.

THE ECONOMIC LANGUAGE OF THE CATHOLIC ENLIGHTENMENT

Paoletti's earlier treatment of luxury in the *Pensieri* was predominantly inspired by Italian sources—Neri and Peruzzi's uncritical interventions locally, and Muratori and enlightened Catholicism more generally.[41] In the *Veri mezzi* he had looked further afield to France, and this focus can be discerned not only in his general frame of reference but in his treatment of luxury as well. It is not certain whether Paoletti knew of the *Encyclopédie* article on luxury. Several copies of it were available in Florence, however, and given that Paoletti kept up a lively correspondence with Mirabeau in addition to receiving information about the latest developments in French provided by Niccoli, it is legitimate to assume that he was aware of Saint-Lambert's article.[42] After all, the group of the *encyclopédistes* was still very

[40] Eric Cochrane, 'French Literature and the Italian Tradition in Eighteenth-Century Tuscany', *Journal of the History of Ideas*, 23 (1962), 61–76, esp. pp. 69–70, and Lucio Villari, 'Teoria economica e rapporti sociali', in *Immagini del Settecento in Italia* (Bari, 1980), 54–61, esp. p. 57.

[41] For a discussion of the similarities between Paoletti and Antonio Genovesi's stance towards sumptuary laws and luxury as related to social status, see Wahnbaeck, 'Ferdinando Paoletti', 384–7.

[42] More than 100 copies of the *Encyclopédie* were available on the peninsula; see Daniela Parisi Aquaviva, *Il pensiero economico classico in Italia (1750–1860)* (Milan, 1984), 119.

close to that of the *économistes* at this time, as even Ferdinando Galiani, a follower of the first and outspoken critic of the second, acknowledged.[43] The similarities between the *Encyclopédie* and Paoletti's physiocratic treatment indeed confirm such an assumption and serve as further circumstantial evidence. One of the lessons to be learned from the *Encyclopédie* article had been that the language used to discuss luxury was too ambiguous to allow for generalizations, and Saint-Lambert had heeded his own observation by considering luxury in relation to specific situations and economic systems. Paoletti followed this lead. In his contribution we find none of Peruzzi's uncritical and ultimately unhelpful generalizations. Nor is Paoletti prepared to judge Tuscan luxury without constant reference to specific situations. Indeed, what could be detrimental in one stage of economic development (the '*Pensieri* stage') may well be unavoidable in another (the '*Veri mezzi* stage'). And just as Saint-Lambert had done, Paoletti argued the case for a vigorous government paying due attention to agriculture. He too presented the countryside as the starting point for the desirable taming of luxury's excesses and their transformation into public benefits.

The second probable strand of French influence comes from the physiocrats, of whose writings Paoletti was well aware. Quesnay's attack of the 'luxury of decoration' draining money away from the countryside is of course reflected in Paoletti's own agricultural focus. And Mirabeau's concern about luxury's detrimental effect on the social order can similarly be found in Paoletti's writings.[44] As a member of the Accademia dei Georgofili, he was indeed (at least in some respects) a 'mouthpiece of the landowners'.[45] On a more theoretical level Paoletti's considerations of the effects of luxury implicitly accept Baudeau's neutral definition of the term. To be sure, luxury was still criticized on moral grounds. But he endorsed Baudeau's assertion that everything was luxury 'which increases the amount of non-productive expenditure at the expense of that expenditure which serves towards production, and, at the same time, at the expense of

[43] The close connection between the two groups until the end of the 1760s is analysed by Jean A. Perkins, 'The Physiocrats and the Encyclopedists', *Studies in Eighteenth Century Culture*, 8 (1979), 323–36. Denis Diderot similarly acknowledged his debts to the physiocrats in a letter to Grimm in November 1769; Diderot, *Correspondance*, ed. Georges Roth (Paris, 1955–70), ix. 210–12. See in a similar vein Marco Minerbi, 'Diderot, Galiani e la polemica sulla fisiocrazia', *Studi storici*, 14 (1973), 147–84, which (albeit ultimately concerned with Galiani and Diderot's critique of physiocracy) stresses Diderot's 'profound intellectual sympathy for the physiocrats' up until 1770 (p. 149).

[44] Most explicitly in the additional chapter on luxury in the second edition of the *Pensieri*; cf. Ferdinando Paoletti, *Opere agrarie*, 2 vols. (Florence, 1789), i. 116–24.

[45] Stuart Woolf, *A History of Italy 1700–1860: The Social Constraints of Political Change*, new edn. (London, 1991), 107.

production itself'.[46] Like Baudeau, Paoletti separated the notion of luxury from specific objects of conspicuous consumption. He did not go as far as to strip it of its moral connotation—the Muratorian influence remained too strong for such a move—but with Baudeau he justified conspicuous consumption under special circumstances and provided it was kept within limits that did not threaten agricultural development.

Paoletti's interventions mark the culmination of the Tuscan luxury debate. Like no one else he epitomizes the development and the various inspirations of Tuscan economic thought. He was influenced by Bandini, and adhered to his model of a free-trading agricultural economy. At the same time he became the mouthpiece of physiocracy in Tuscany, and not only because the sect's doctrine seemed tailored to the specific situation of the grand duchy. Perhaps more importantly, many of the physiocratic teachings seemed genuinely Tuscan because of the influence Boisguilbert had exerted on Bandini, who 'Tuscanized' the precursor of the French physiocrats. In the realm of luxury, however, there was more room for development because Bandini had remained vague in his treatment. Paoletti used this freedom and drew on French precedent just as Pompeo Neri had drawn on different French authors before him. Again he took up physiocratic positions. But he had also learned about the ambiguities of luxury, and this helped him avoid facile generalizations. While adhering to the moral reservations against luxury as expressed by Catholicism, he could develop a model in which there was a stage where luxury could be needed and employed beneficially to safeguard agricultural growth.

Is Eric Cochrane's judgement justified that 'the Tuscans were mercantilists, liberalists, free-traders, and protectionists all rolled into one—to which perhaps the term "eclectics" can be applied, but to whom no coherent "system" can be attributed'?[47] Is there no discernible common thread? If we take Bandini's legacy seriously and accept the close relationship between Boisguilbert and Bandini on the one hand, and Boisguilbert and Mirabeau on the other, then it becomes apparent that the Tuscans had a clear understanding of what was important and what ideas should be taken up and developed. It was determined by the school of economic thought in which they had grown up. But this legacy left considerable freedom, as the developments of Bandini's price theory to accommodate luxury, and the arguments over luxury itself, have demonstrated. Tuscan intellectuals used this freedom within well-defined limits, but they used it nevertheless.

[46] Nicolas Baudeau, *Principes de la science morale et politique sur le luxe et les lois somptuaires* (1767), ed. A. Dubois (Paris, 1912), 14. See above, Ch. 2.

[47] Cochrane, *Tradition and Enlightenment*, 233.

Cochrane's charge of a somewhat random eclecticism overlooks the complex influences and traditions that determined the development of Tuscan economic thought.

In one respect, moreover, the development of Tuscan thought left tradition behind. If Bandini and Neri had still operated in the rather closed world of ministerial memorandums, the discussion became increasingly open and public in the second half of the century. Paoletti is just one of the many who now made their voices heard in public, yet he is again representative of a new trend. Hitherto, the most promising way to exert influence had been to become an administrator and to gain access to the centre of power. Now, influencing opinion appeared to be an equally effective way to achieve this end. People like Paoletti, whose job as a parish priest prevented him from becoming an administrator, increasingly turned to this new option and disseminated their views in treatises, pamphlets, and journals.[48] Their opinion was all the more valuable because the growing importance of the countryside made first-hand advice especially necessary. It seemed a promising strategy since the person one ultimately wanted to influence was Peter Leopold, who had already proven that he was prepared to translate enlightened ideas into practice.[49]

If the new mode of discussion allowed new groups to influence discussion, this explains the renewed shift of emphasis in economic discussion towards moral concerns. The parish priests had different objectives from the administrators: their concern for the moral life stands against Bandini, Neri, and Gianni's analysis of money and taxation. But the moral critique of luxury was no longer voiced in moral language, and this explains why Paoletti's thought developed to the '*Veri mezzi* stage'. He conceded that the 'pragmatic school' had set the terms for the debate; it had laid out the terrain on which discussion took place. In order to defend the moral stance of the Catholic Enlightenment, Paoletti employed the tools and the language of the members of the 'pragmatic school'. Their language as well as their central concern, prosperity, had monopolized discussion.

[48] See in a very similar vein Giuseppe Ippoliti, *Lettera parenetica, morale, economica di un Parroco della Val di Chiana a tutti i possidenti o comodi, o ricchi scritta nell'anno* MDCCLXXII *concernente i doveri loro rispetto ai contadini* (Florence, 1774), and Landeschi, *Saggi di Agricoltura*.

[49] The reform of Tuscan institutions, for example, seems to have been based on the 'Politics' article in the *Encyclopédie*; cf. Furio Diaz, '"La philosophie" e il riformismo leopoldino', in Diaz, *Per un storia illuministica* (Naples, 1973), 280–3.

EPILOGUE

It was only in the next century that Tuscans became engaged in the quarrel about luxury again. Like a flash in the pan, emotions were to be swept up at the Accademia dei Georgofili in 1819. By then, however, the focus of the debate had shifted and 'luxury' had ceased to be an economic concept. What was at issue was 'peasant luxury', and this was understood as a symbol for the more comfortable living of the poor in the countryside. The debate thus concentrated on the moral effects of a comfortable life. Lapo Ricci, who started the debate, judged that the dire straits of the peasantry were a thing of the past and that they should be allowed to indulge in the fruits of their labour, which were the outcome of Tuscany's fortunate economic situation. In Ricci's contribution there is no feeling of unease any more about luxury, no quarrel over its meaning. The whole debate simply becomes a question of logic: when freedom reigns and enriches proprietors, it is only natural that the peasant population will also benefit and raise their living standards accordingly.[50] The rebuke came promptly, and within months Aldobrando Paolini, another member of the academy, reasserted the moral approach to luxury and upheld the old notion that it was not the spending as such, but the moral duties of the spenders, that needed to be focused on. Economic arguments had lost their force for Paolini: 'As both private and public ethics condemn luxury, the issue merits the same ruling from the court of political economy.' And furthermore, 'Who sleeps in a bed of roses will not work in the field of thorns'.[51]

The debate of 1819 was polemical at best, and it was short-lived. It generated two more contributions within the Accademia dei Georgofili, both of them compromising in tone and arguing for moderation and decency for peasants and proprietors alike. But the flame of the previous century had gone out, and the controversy finally died a silent death with a shallow call for caution not to employ peasants for any work other than agriculture.[52] The most heated phase of the Tuscan luxury debate, which had profited so much from the transmission of French ideas and the new mode of discussion, had taken place in the age of Neri, Gianni, and Paoletti.

[50] Lapo Ricci, 'Del lusso delle vesti dei contadini', *Atti della Reale ed Imperiale Accademia Economico-Agraria dei Georgofili*, C.2 (1819), 332–9.

[51] Aldobrando Paolini, 'Discorso sul lusso dei contadini nei suoi rapporti con i costumi, e con la pubblica economia d'un popolo agrario', *Atti della Reale ed Imperiale Accademia Economico-Agraria dei Georgofili*, C.2 (1819), 452–90, the quotations on pp. 471 and 465.

[52] Michelangelo Buonarroti, 'Sul lusso dei contadini: memoria letta il dì 7 gennaio 1821', *Atti della Reale ed Imperiale Accademia Economico-Agraria dei Georgofili*, C.4 (1825), 220–32, and Filippo Gallizioli, 'Sul servizio personale dei contadini. Memoria . . . letta nell'adunanza de' 2 maggio 1830', *Atti*, C.8 (1830), 109–18.

III

The Development of a New Language of Political Economy

7

Lombardy: Enlightenment from Above and from Within

Lombardy as a Habsburg Land

Like Tuscany, Lombardy was ruled by Austria for most of the eighteenth century. The Habsburgs obtained the state first in 1707, but continual wars threatened Austrian hegemony until the 1740s.[1] Unlike the grand duchy, which enjoyed considerable freedom of action after the ascent of Peter Leopold, Lombardy was much more closely linked to the core lands, and Maria Theresa and Joseph II had it governed through plenipotentiaries who received their orders from Vienna.[2] Nevertheless, the state of Milan was not strongly integrated into the territories of the Habsburg monarchy. Conquered only recently, it retained pronounced political autonomies, even though the guidelines for political reform were formulated in Vienna. When a reform movement took shape in Lombardy between 1742 and 1771, the initial impulse—in Vienna as well as in Milan—came from the precarious financial situation.[3] Especially at the beginning of the century the Austrian finances offered 'the spectacle of a state tottering in truly suicidal fashion on the brink of a precipice'.[4] It was in the field of taxation that

[1] A helpful starting point for the political and social history of Austrian Lombardy is Domenico Sella and Carlo Capra, *Il Ducato di Milano dal 1535 al 1796* (Turin, 1984), 153–663 (Carlo Capra, 'Il Settecento') with an extensive bibliography. See also Franco Venturi, *Settecento riformatore*, i (Turin, 1998), 645–747 (ch. 9: 'La Milano del Caffè'), and v/1 (Turin, 1989), 425–824 ('Gli uomini delle riforme: la Lombardia'). For a concise orientation in English, see Dino Carpanetto and Giuseppe Ricuperati, *Italy in the Age of Reason, 1685–1789* (London, 1987), chs. 11 and 15.

[2] Influence was not only exerted in one direction, however. For the influence of Italians and Italian thought in Vienna, see Elisabeth Garms-Cornides, 'Zwischen Giannone, Muratori und Metastasio. Die Italiener im geistigen Leben Wiens', in Friedrich Engel-Janosi, Grete Klingenstein, and Heinrich Lutz (eds.), *Formen der europäischen Aufklärung. Untersuchungen zur Situation von Christentum, Bildung und Wissenschaft im 18. Jahrhundert* (Vienna, 1976), 224–50.

[3] Adam Wandruszka, *Österreich und Italien im 18. Jahrhundert* (Munich, 1963), 47–58, esp. p. 51.

[4] B. Holl, 'Hofkammerpräsident Gundaker Thomas Graf Stakenberg und die österreichische Finanzpolitik der Barockzeit, 1703–1715', *Archiv für österreichische Geschichte*, 132 (1976), 437.

reforms first took root. In order to achieve a state-controlled, rational, efficient, and broadly based tax revenue, the tax farm was unified and a new fiscal law was introduced in 1760 which was based on official assessment of the land rather than personal declaration. In 1765 the reform of customs duties initiated the development towards free trade. On the whole, however, economic policies were still generally influenced by mercantilism, while the role of the state in running the economy became more evident.

Most of the reforms were decided upon in Vienna or by the imperial officers in Milan. The initial phase of Theresian reforms such as the restructuring of the administration in the name of lean management, for example, is linked with the powerful count Gian Luca Pallavicini, who became plenipotentiary in 1745 after having been in charge of the military economy. Under his governorship between 1750 and 1753 the first attempts were made to solve the financial crisis.[5] Attempts at administrative unification were continued under his successor, until Count Carlo di Firmian took up office in 1759.[6] It is with him in particular that the decisive shift in policy towards enlightened principles which occurred in the 1760s is associated. Recent scholarship suggests, however, that it was not so much Firmian and Kaunitz, his superior in Vienna, or indeed the Milanese intellectuals, who were primarily responsible for reform. As Pietro Verri wrote to his brother in 1771, the real centre of influence was the Dipartimento d'Italia in Vienna.[7] It was there, he claimed, that the reports on Lombardy were drafted. State Chancellor Kaunitz (who, according to the famous, if exaggerated, anecdote, governed Lombardy in the morning while putting on his stockings) merely signed them, and Maria Theresa, who had little interest in Lombard affairs, merely followed Kaunitz's advice.[8]

[5] Mario Romani, 'Gian Luca Pallavicini e le riforme economiche nello Stato di Milano', in Romani, *Aspetti e problemi di storia lombarda nei secoli XVIII e XIX* (Milan, 1977), 355–91.

[6] On Firmian, see Elisabeth Garms-Cornides, 'La destinazione del conte Firmian a Milano: analisi di una scelta', in *Economia, istituzioni, cultura*, ii. 1015–29, and her 'Un trentino tra Impero, antichi stati italiani e Gran Bretagna: l'anglomano Carlo Firmian', in Cesare Mozzarelli and Giuseppe Olmi (eds.), *Il Trentino nel Settecento fra Sacro Romano Impero e antichi stati italiani* (Bologna, 1985), 467–93.

[7] Pietro and Alessandro Verri, *Carteggio*, ed. Emanuele Greppi, Alessandro Giulini, *et al.*, 12 vols. (Milan, 1923–42), iv. 322–3. In fact, Verri lobbied successfully to get a trusted friend into an important position at the department; cf. Carlo Capra, 'Un intermediario tra Vienna e Milano: Luigi Lambertenghi e il suo carteggio con Pietro Verri', *Römische historische Mitteilungen*, 31 (1989), 359–76.

[8] On the importance of the department and its head, Luigi Giusti (1709–66), see Carlo Capra, 'Luigi Giusti e il Dipartimento d'Italia a Vienna (1757–1766), in *Economia, istituzioni, cultura*, iii. 365–90. The standard account on Kaunitz is Grete Klingenstein, *Der Aufstieg des Hauses Kaunitz* (Göttingen, 1975); see also Franz A. J. Szabo, *Kaunitz and Enlightened Absolutism 1753–1780* (Cambridge, 1994).

Compared with Tuscany, then, the local elite played a much less important role in the formulation of policy, and this lay behind the growing discontent of Lombard intellectuals with the enlightened absolutism embodied mainly by Joseph II. In fact, the lack of local participation and thus support is one of the reasons why Josephism in Lombardy did not have long-lasting cultural or social results. The amount of passive resistance became apparent when, after the death of Joseph II in 1790, all the forces that he had repressed regained authority. A telltale example of the absence of Lombard involvement in important ventures is the Supreme Council of the Economy, which was installed in 1765 in order to manage all economic and financial affairs of the state of Milan. Even though Pietro Verri became a member from its inception, the council was dominated by non-Milanese in an attempt, it has been suggested, to reduce the influence of the Milanese ruling class.[9] Equally, when the University of Pavia was to be restructured and locals volunteered to propose reform, Maria Theresa entrusted the project to her own men, and the restructuring was eventually carried out by Kaunitz and Firmian.[10]

Jurisprudence and the Lombard Ruling Classes

To be sure, the Lombard elite held important positions in the state of Milan from which influence could be exerted. Franco Arese has provided us with lists of all major office-holders in Lombardy in the eighteenth century, and it emerges from his research that more than half of all senators and *questori* in the first half of the century belonged to the Milanese patriciate.[11] Pietro Verri explained the unfortunate situation which many foreign officials found themselves in.

> Unable to speak the language, unacquainted with customs and the system; at the head of a government which was an intricate labyrinth in which even the nationals were often adrift . . . up against the powerful body of the senates and the *noblesse de robe* . . . [and] up against the no less powerful body of the nobility . . .—a governor in such a system often returned [home] as ignorant as he had been when he arrived.[12]

The Milanese ruling classes occupied an intricate position after the Habsburgs had assumed power. Dependent on orders and favour from Vienna

[9] Carpanetto and Ricuperati, *Italy in the Age of Reason*, 167. [10] Ibid. 230.

[11] Franco Arese, 'Le supreme cariche del Ducato di Milano e della Lombardia austriaca, 1707–1796', *Archivio storico lombardo*, 105–6 (1979–80), 535–98.

[12] Pietro Verri, *Pensieri sullo stato politico del Milanese nel 1790*, in Pietro Verri, *Scritti vari*, ed. Giulio Carcano (Florence, 1854), vol. ii, app., pp. 3–4.

on the one hand, acutely aware of their power and influence as knowledgeable magistrates on the other, they strove to make the best of their situation. Traditionally, this was to be achieved within the 'noble' professions, namely law and medicine, which were supervised by the colleges of noble jurists and noble medical doctors. So close was this connection that it was precisely the college of Milanese jurists that was primarily responsible for formulating rules of admission to the patriciate.[13] If it was difficult to bypass the jurists on the way to advancement in society, they were an equally limiting factor in the development of intellectual life in the first half of the century. Private academies and learned circles were dominated by nobles and clergymen, which made it difficult for new philosophical currents to take root. Remote from public life and often hostile to developments in the universities, the academies did not foster enthusiasm for reform.[14] As Carlo Capra has recently argued, the 'cultural hegemony of the Milanese patriciate, which was reflected in a socio-economic hegemony with few parallels in Italy at the time, depended on their practical and ideological knowledge of jurisprudence on the one hand . . . and on the exclusion of the lower classes from the circulation of ideas' and the deliberate rejection of enlightened ideas from elsewhere across Europe on the other.[15]

It was this culture, with its reliance on jurisprudence and privilege to safeguard class interests, that a new movement struggled to overcome after the 1750s. When political and economic reform had started a decade earlier with the first efforts of Pallavicini, cultural change had not followed suit immediately. But now, at the beginning of the 1760s, a new generation of intellectuals emerged that was to shape the remaining years of the reign of Maria Theresa and that of her son and successor, Joseph. Pietro Verri and Cesare Beccaria were the major protagonists of the new era, and it was in the Verri household that the new group gathered and plans for reform were hatched.[16] One of the prime goals of the new group was the substitution of legal thought by political economy. Again it was Pietro Verri who lent his voice to the new approach when he lamented in 1760 that in Milan 'all is in

[13] Cf. Sella and Capra, *Ducato di Milano*, 195. On noble professions, see most recently Elena Brambilla, 'Il "sistema letterario" di Milano: professioni nobili e professioni borghesi dall'età spagnola alle riforme teresiane', in *Economia, istituzioni, cultura*, iii. 79–160.

[14] Cf. Ugo Baldini, 'L'attività scientifica nelle accademie lombarde del Settecento', in *Economia, istituzioni, cultura*, ii. 503–32.

[15] Sella and Capra, *Ducato di Milano*, 195–8.

[16] Franco Venturi has made the emergence of the Milanese Enlightenment, the *école de Milan*, one of his major research interests; see *Settecento riformatore*, i. 645–747, and v/1. 425–575. His contention that the years between 1765 and 1771 are to be seen as the 'turning point' in Lombard history (v/1. 474–80) is now universally accepted; see e.g. Sella and Capra, *Ducato di Milano*, ch. 3, pp. 329–431, entitled 'La svolta degli anni sessanta'.

the hands of the doctors, who—infatuated with the ideas of the times of Bartolo—either have no idea about political economy, or they have ideas it would be better not to have'. And retrospectively, in a late account of his career, he outlined the dominant culture in Milan at the time when he set about to change it: 'A bit of Latin, a dreamy theology, pedantic and trivial jurisprudence: these are the only studies that were being praised; the rest was the object of hatred or ridicule.'[17]

The Break with Tradition and the Enlightened Decades: The 1760s and 1770s

In Tuscany we could observe the continuous evolution of local intellectual participation in government activity, where the education provided by universities such as Pisa was put into practice in the administration. In Lombardy the situation was different. The new rulers first drew upon the old patriciate with their traditional training in jurisprudence. Against this class the newcomers had to fight in order to establish themselves, and the struggle was as much a discontinuity in government participation as a break between generations. Nowhere does this become clearer than in the case of Pietro Verri and his father, Gabriele.[18]

Pietro Verri was born in 1728 into a family well respected in Lombardy without, however, belonging to the highest level of the ruling class. That the Verri name had become one of the best known by the time of Pietro's first steps into public life was the merit of his father. The conservative jurist, interested in history and shaped by the Roman law tradition—about which he once remarked that it was similar to the laws governing Lombardy—was appointed senator in 1749. The appointment marked his ascent into the highest sphere of influence within Habsburg Lombardy, and the father wanted his son to follow in his footsteps. A legal career seemed certain, and might even have brought a senatorial seat to Pietro. Because the son resented all that his 'vain, insecure, untrustworthy' father represented, however, and because he already sensed that the economic and social problems of his time could not be solved with Roman law alone, he opposed his father's plans. Breaking with his family, he spent his youth with literary

[17] Pietro Verri, letter from Vienna, 20 Dec. 1760, and the manuscript Memoria del conte Pietro Verri in cui si espongono i motivi per i quali venne impiegato e poi dopo vent'anni congedato, both quoted in Sella and Capra, *Ducato di Milano*, 351.

[18] The account of this conflict of generations was first given by Franco Venturi, *Settecento riformatore*, i. 648–64, and has been repeated many times since.

studies in Parma, Rome, and Milan. When the Seven Years' War broke out in 1757, the young Verri joined the Austrian army—'the bad treatment at home made me become a soldier', as he was to say later.[19] The time in the army shaped Pietro Verri more than anything previously, and in this respect he owed more to his family, which had pushed him into the army, than he may have been aware of. In long conversations with friends he became increasingly interested in political economy, and when he left his regiment and returned to Milan in 1760, he began to read Hume, Melon, Forbonnais, and Montesquieu.[20]

Back in Milan it was difficult not to miss a forum for intellectual debate in which the new ideas could be discussed and developed. From the winter of 1761–2 onwards a group of friends drawn mostly from the aristocratic class in Lombardy began to gather in the Verri home to start an academy for this purpose.[21]

The Accademia dei Pugni, whose name, 'Academy of Fists', was said to derive from their often heated debates, had no statute and no official programme and was meant to provide an opportunity for the friends to exchange ideas, and discuss books and manuscripts by any member of the group: not a society established with a fixed and determined aim, as Cesare Beccaria explained, but a coterie.[22] The membership of the academy comprised the intellectually most active thinkers, and some of the more successful future administrators and university teachers, in Lombardy. Pietro Verri (1728–97) was the uncontested head, organizer, and *spiritus rector* of the group; Cesare Beccaria (1738–94) the best-known thinker in enlightened Europe. The two were joined by Pietro's brother Alessandro (1741–1816), who made his name as a historian; Giuseppe Visconti (1731–1803) and Giambattista Biffi (1736–1807) from Cremona; and later Alfonso Longo (1738–1804), who was to become successful as a professor of public law and political economy. It was here that most of the economic treatises of the members of the group first saw the light and it was here that Cesare Beccaria wrote his major work, *Dei delitti e delle pene*, which he read out to Pietro Verri in the evenings to invite his criticism.

It is indicative of the role of the Church in intellectual debate that no Catholic academy managed to establish itself as an antidote to the circle

[19] Quoted by Venturi, *Settecento riformatore*, i. 664.

[20] The role of his British friend and comrade in arms Henry Lloyd was decisive in his conversion; cf. Franco Venturi, *Le vite incrociate di Henry Lloyd e Pietro Verri* (Turin, 1977).

[21] On the academy, see Nino Valeri, *Pietro Verri*, 2nd edn. (Florence, 1969), ch. VIII: 'L'Accademia dei Pugni'.

[22] Quoted by Venturi, *Settecento riformatore*, i. 683: 'Nous ne formons pas une société établie sur un plan fixe et déterminé, mais une coterie.'

around Pietro Verri and that none of the members of the Accademia dei Pugni belonged to the clergy. The only exception is Alfonso Longo, but he was a disillusioned priest who was later in his life to launch ferocious attacks on his former colleagues. In fact, the Church had been losing its voice in the realm of imperial politics ever since the Habsburgs had decided to subdue Roman influence in imperial affairs. This began with the taxation of the clergy and the need for imperial approval of clerical appointments in 1762, and led to the transfer of the right of censorship from the Church to the imperial Deputazione per gli Studi. This did not guarantee the liberty of the press any better than before (in fact, Pietro Verri remarked that 'the press is under greater pressure now than it was under the Inquisition'), but it marked the victory of *Staatskatholizismus* in Lombardy.[23] In 1769 Firmian could sigh: 'the tedious affair is over'.[24] If Tuscany was characterized by a vivid participation of parish priests in an increasingly public debate, and if Neapolitan thinkers understood political economy as a Christian enterprise well into the second half of the century, in Lombardy religious concerns were all but absent in the circles of the Milanese Enlightenment. No doubt, this was partly driven by the fact that the clergy had more pressing things to do than engage in debate about luxury and political economy (regain their sources of income, for example, after Church property had been literally confiscated in 1767). But it also meant that they left the field of debate to those thinkers who were as distant as one could imagine from Muratori's quest for public happiness embedded in Catholic thought.

The Mouthpiece of the Enlightenment: The *Caffè* Journal

One single journal stands out in Lombardy in the second half of the century, *Il Caffè*, which appeared every ten days from 1764 to 1766.[25] Pietro Verri was the driving force behind the project, and he recruited most members of the Accademia dei Pugni as contributors to the journal. *Il Caffè*, then, was the work of a group of young intellectuals who prepared themselves to take up responsible positions in the political and economic realm in their country. Almost all were from aristocratic backgrounds, but many

[23] Verri and Verri, *Carteggio*, iii. 172. [24] Capra, *Il Ducato di Milano*, 382–96: 394.

[25] For a useful introduction into history, background, and content of *Il Caffè*, see Sergio Romagnoli, '"Il Caffè" tra Milano e l'Europa', in *Il Caffè, 1764–1766*, ed. Gianni Franconi and Sergio Romagnoli, 2nd edn. (Turin, 1998), vol. i, pp. xiii–lxxix. The editorial history of the journal is treated by Gianni Francioni, 'Storia editoriale del "Caffè"', ibid. pp. lxxxi–cxlv.

were in conflict with their families and their conservatism. They saw the new journal as a means to voice new ideas which hardly found their way into other papers. The Milanese journalistic scene was dire around the middle of the century. Some learned journals existed, it is true, but mostly they were concerned with local affairs and archaeology, the diffusion of language, magic, and the origins of idolatry. The *Raccolta milanese* (1756–7) is a case in point. Erudite research into the medieval and Renaissance past prevailed; long articles described the lives of poets and artists of fifteenth-century Lombardy. Antonio Genovesi's economic ideas were ignored, and Franco Venturi has counted only one reference to the *Encyclopédie*, and none to publications from across the Alps.[26] It was in this context that *Il Caffè* was established as the mouthpiece of enlightened ideas in Lombardy. Modelled on the English *Spectator*, it treated questions of law, economics, agriculture, medicine, and natural sciences, as well as literature, morals, and the arts, until it ceased publication in 1766.[27]

The *Caffè* journal was a forum for debate, and in this sense the title—'The Coffee House'—was programmatic because it was the place for conversation par excellence. It was also decidedly cosmopolitan in its approach. A clear indication of this attitude was the choice of the Greek owner of the coffee house, Demetrio, as the character around whose table the contributors united and conversed. It was also made explicit by Pietro Verri's criticism of Gianrinaldo Carli's article 'Della patria degli Italiani', which he nevertheless published in his journal. As he told his younger brother Alessandro, he did not like the article. To Carli, he complained that—apart from the fact that it carried the risk of being understood as a call for sedition from foreign rule—'the love of the fatherland prejudices [the] impartiality of a good cosmopolitan'.[28] The cosmopolitan approach was to serve a very concrete purpose, however, namely the improvement of the cultural and economic situation of the state of Milan. As early as 1760 Pietro Verri had explained to his brother that he wanted to occupy himself 'seriously with the local condition of my country, with domestic issues relating to . . . commerce, the mint, etc.'.[29] In his journal Verri consequently devoted his attention to political economy. The principal articles on the subject, such as the 'Elementi di commercio' and the 'Considerazioni sul lusso', were written by him, and he in particular introduced the themes of

[26] Venturi, *Settecento riformatore*, i. 645–7. [27] Ibid. 735.

[28] Verri, letter to Carli, 17 Apr. 1765, quoted in Romagnoli, '"Il Caffè" tra Milano e l'Europa', p. lxv.

[29] Verri, letter from Vienna, 2 Sept. 1760, in Pietro and Alessandro Verri, *Lettere e scritti inediti di Pietro e di Alessandro Verri*, ed. Carlo Cassati, 4 vols. (Milan, 1879–81), i. 146.

politics and reform and used the new forum as a 'fighting instrument' for his 'battle for innovation', as Giuseppe Ricuperati has observed.[30] Cesare Beccaria and Alessandro Verri were in charge of the literature and culture section of the journal.

The content of the journal reflects the intention of the editors to publish 'various things . . . all directed towards public utility'.[31] In the first year twenty articles were concerned with political economy and science, and ten in the second year; twenty-nine and then nineteen on literature; fourteen and then twelve on moral issues. Even though political economy still received less than half the space allotted to literary subjects, the change in emphasis compared to other Italian journals of the time cannot be overlooked. The *Frusta letteraria di Aristarco Scannabue*, for example, published by Giuseppe Baretti in Venice and Ancona between 1763 and 1765 and one of the main adversaries of *Il Caffè*, contained twenty-eight articles on literary subjects, five on morality and religion, four on history and philology, ten on medicine, and only three on law and economic subjects.[32]

Il Caffè was an immediate success. Reprints appeared almost simultaneously with the original edition, and the first partial translations into French were published in 1766 in the *Gazette littéraire de l'Europe*.[33] Nevertheless, the journal ceased publication after only two years. Partly it fell victim to its own success, or rather to the success of its contributors. They had made a name for themselves and went their own ways. Cesare Beccaria had become a famous man and travelled to Paris together with Alessandro Verri; Gianrinaldo Carli was appointed president of the Supreme Council of the Economy in the State of Milan; Alfonso Longo would soon become a professor in Milan; Giambattista Biffi returned to his native Cremona. Moreover, Pietro Verri sought the opportunity to turn his ideas into practice. In 1765 he had been asked to compile the trade balance for Lombardy, and he was appointed to the council headed by his collaborator Carli. A laconic preface to the second year of *Il Caffè* announced the end of the enterprise. 'The small society of friends that has written these pages has been dissolved; some have undertaken travels, others are taken by business; necessity dictates that a work has to be finished that, according to the wishes of its

[30] Giuseppe Ricuperati, 'Giornali e società nell'Italia dell' "Ancien Regime" (1668–1789)', in Valerio Castronovo and Nicola Tranfaglia (eds.), *La stampa italiana dal '500 all'800* (Rome, 1980), 211.

[31] 'Introduzione', in *Il Caffè*, i. 11.

[32] On the clashes between the two journals, see Francioni, 'Storia editoriale', pp. xcv–cix. The analysis of the *Frusta letteraria* is by Ricuperati, 'Giornali e società', 211–12 and, more generally, pp. 202–8.

[33] On subsequent editions, cf. Francioni, 'Storia editoriale', pp. cxxiii–cxxiv.

authors, should not have ended so soon.'[34] Verri in particular bemoaned the fate of his journal. Ten years later he was complaining that he had not been able to keep *Il Caffè* alive. But he was also confident that *Il Caffè* had been a success. 'I think', he told his brother, 'that if there was a way to improve the new generation, then it was that of *Il Caffè*.'[35] Decades later he remembered the times of *Il Caffè* as the happiest of his life.[36]

Despite their frustration about the premature death of the project, the group around Pietro Verri had managed to initiate discussion on a broad range of subjects, from language to the proper role of the nobility and from moral philosophy to the value of rural life. But political economy was the area Pietro Verri and some of his most ardent collaborators remained most interested in.[37] If the aim of the group was to solve Lombardy's most pressing problems, this should be done through economic improvement. Thus, political economy claimed a prominent place in many debates, because the economy was an area in which reform was both needed and likely to occur. Indeed, the state of the economy in the eighteenth century promised no bright future for Lombardy unless measures were taken to reinvigorate it and provide a framework for economic growth.

The Economic Reality: Towards an Agricultural Economy

If the Tuscan economy had been severely affected by the economic decline of the previous century, the outlook in Lombardy was little more positive.[38] The seventeenth century had brought about a de-industrialization of the economy from which the duchy had not recovered in the eighteenth century.[39] The trend towards a predominantly agricultural economy was not reversed until the nineteenth century and in fact continued even after the

[34] 'Al lettore', in *Il Caffè*, ii. 407.

[35] Pietro Verri, letter, 14 Aug. 1776, in *Carteggio*, x. 171.

[36] Cf. Venturi, *Settecento riformatore*, i. 738–40.

[37] For Verri's ability to impose his agenda on other members of the academy, see Christof Dipper, *Politischer Reformismus und begrifflicher Wandel. Eine Untersuchung des historisch-politischen Wortschatzes der Mailänder Aufklärung (1764–1796)* (Tübingen, 1976), 58–9.

[38] Asciano Caracciolo, 'La storia economica', in *Storia d'Italia*, iii (Turin, 1973), 533–54.

[39] Angelo Moioli, 'La deindustrializzazione della Lombardia nel secolo XVII', *Archivio storico lombardo*, ser. 11, 3 (1986), 176–85. The deindustrialization argument partly contradicts Domenico Sella's claim of a *shift* of industrial production to the Lombard countryside in the 17th century; cf. Domenico Sella, *Crisis and Continuity: The Economy of Spanish Lombardy in the Seventeenth Century* (Cambridge, Mass., 1979).

Italian unification.[40] Efforts were made, it is true, to revive industrial production in the state of Milan in the first half of the eighteenth century, but mostly to little avail. In the case of silk production, for example, import prohibitions were renewed in the years 1713 to 1720 in order to stimulate home production. Owing to the hostility of the merchants and the inability of the public authorities to enforce the laws, however, the new provisions were rarely adhered to, and in 1724 the government responded with a change of direction from prohibition to the tacit acceptance of imports. Customs duties were raised as a consequence.[41] Even though some specialized industries resisted the transition, most were unable to cope with the shift of commercial routes away from the Mediterranean to northern Europe. English, French, and Dutch competition proved disastrous for Lombardy. In addition to this, the Milanese merchants failed to adapt to the new nature of commerce which implied selling goods cheaply and reducing costs. In this setting, Milan ceased to be a centre of production and finance and became a centre of consumption.[42]

On the whole, and given the futility of reviving Lombard industry in the face of growing European competition, Lombardy responded to the economic challenges of the eighteenth century by re-enforcing the primacy of agriculture and improving it in several respects. The return to the land was fuelled by widespread distrust in the financial system. 'The little confidence', wrote Pietro Verri in a letter to his brother in 1775, 'that people have in the Monte Camerale has pushed the wealthy to invest in the improvement of the land.'[43] But specific government measures further accelerated the flow of money into the countryside. When a new financial policy was introduced which reduced the rate of repayment on state bonds, capital moved to private enterprise. Part of the savings thus released went into productive investments, and part went into the consumption of luxury goods, thus affirming Milan's function as a centre of consumption. It was this dual process—the freeing up of funds and the low returns on industrial investments—that offered new opportunities to Lombard agriculture.

The new census was perhaps primarily responsible for the lavish flow of money into the countryside. It was perhaps the most successful project of Lombard economic policy in the middle of the century. Planned and

[40] Mario Romani, *L'agricoltura in Lombardia dal periodo delle riforme al 1859: struttura, organizzazione sociale e tecnica* (Milan, 1957), 11.

[41] Mario Romani, 'L'economia milanese nel Settecento', in Romani, *Aspetti e problemi*, 145–9.

[42] Massimo Amato, 'Il decentramento dell'economia mediterranea: il caso di Milano fra crisi e riconversione (secoli XVI e XVII)', *Rivista storica italiana*, 106 (1994), 622–50.

[43] Verri and Verri, *Carteggio*, vii. 230.

attempted for a long time, the census only translated into new legislation in 1760. Against strong resistance, Pompeo Neri (who had been in charge of the project since 1749) pushed through the proposal that land was now to be assessed by officials rather than by personal declaration. Since fiscal reform was linked with administrative reform, communal affairs were to be run by elected administrators regardless of birth or social condition. The effects of the new provisions were twofold. On the one hand, they made ownership secure and fixed a tax on it. On the other hand—since the capital value of each property was defined as the value of its produce at the time of the survey—every subsequent increase in productivity was virtually tax-free. Linking the tax to land and not to income provided a productivity stimulus that can hardly be overestimated.[44] Cesare Beccaria's observation of the effects of the new census on one particular aspect of agriculture, namely that 'the fixed assessment of the land [has] encouraged the cultivation of mulberry trees', applies to the development of agriculture at large.[45] So successful was the Milanese model that it exerted influence even abroad, as François Veron de Forbonnais used the census to argue for similar measures in France.[46]

It has long been thought that this development caused a proper agrarian revolution. But whereas it is beyond doubt that the reforms from 1760 onwards gave a boost to agriculture in late eighteenth-century Lombardy, recent research indicates that the rural sector was characterized by substantial stability of land-ownership and contractual relationships.[47] The system succeeded simply in adapting to the increase in foreign and domestic demand for some goods. This adaptation took place with only minor changes to the system. The average peasant remained very poor indeed, and from mid-century the misery of the rural population became commonplace among reformist writers.[48]

It is true that agricultural production improved. Of all the Italian states, Lombardy was probably the one where agriculture made most headway

[44] Carlo Capra, 'The Eighteenth Century, I: The Finances of the Austrian Monarchy and the Italian States', in Richard Bonney (ed.), *Economic Systems and State Finance* (Oxford, 1995), 303–4. See also Daniel Klang, *Tax Reform in Eighteenth-Century Lombardy* (New York, 1977).

[45] Cesare Beccaria, *Opere*, ed. Sergio Romagnoli (Florence, 1958), ii. 396.

[46] Mainly that taxation of land should be based on fixed sums and that profits of land improvement should go to the proprietor. Forbonnais did, however, modify Neri's census model in that he argued for an assessment of the land by village communities or individuals. Cf. Antonella Alimento, 'Véron de Forbonnais tra Spagna, Francia e Lombardia', *Annali della Fondazione Luigi Einaudi*, 19 (1985), 171–94.

[47] Romani, 'L'economia milanese', esp. p. 180.

[48] Francesco Carpani, *Bilancio dello Stato col quale a priori si fa la dimostrazione del suo attivo commercio*, in *Economisti minori*, 137.

and proved most adaptable to the new conditions.[49] A number of landlords supported innovations such as new forms of land tenure. Whereas the sharecropping system continued to stifle progress in most of central Italy, Lombardy contained an increasing number of tenant farmers and peasant proprietors who employed wage-earners dispossessed by the agrarian depression of the previous century. They also employed capitalist measures of land management, and invested in irrigation, new tools, and the elimination of fallow. In some of the more fertile areas of Lombardy, such measures could result in wheat yields as high as anywhere in Europe. Visitors from abroad were impressed by the level of wealth and culture that was rendered possible by an agricultural economy. When Arthur Young visited Milan and saw La Scala, he remarked that it was 'quite astonishing for a city located in the interior, and which has neither commerce nor manufacture. The ploughshare alone makes such luxury possible.'[50] On the whole, however, adequately capitalized modern farms remained the exception in Lombardy, and the average yield of wheat was probably no higher in the eighteenth century than it had been in the sixteenth. As one historian put it, 'Capitalism had yet to triumph throughout the northern Italian countryside.'[51]

The enthusiastic observations made by Arthur Young should not be overvalued. In any event, such luxury was restricted to comparatively few people: less than 2,000 families out of 30,000 in Milan divided over half of the net product among themselves in 1770. Half to two-thirds of working class families lived at or below subsistence level.[52] According to Mario Romani's estimate, in the eighteenth century about 85 per cent of the population of the state of Milan lived in the countryside, i.e. dwellings and small cities with less than 10,000 inhabitants.[53] Most of these were peasants who were dependent upon their landlords.

The countryside was also the main source of state income. In 1740, 74 per cent of the state income was derived from land and house taxes, 24 per cent from taxes paid by country-dwellers (or their landlords), and only 2 per cent from manufacturing and commercial activity.[54] Even though these figures changed during the course of the century, they provide an accurate insight into the relative importance of the cities and of the countryside. The

[49] For a recent attempt to put Lombard agriculture into a European perspective, see Robert S. Duplessis, *Transitions to Capitalism in Early Modern Europe* (Cambridge, 1997), 153–4.

[50] Arthur Young, *Voyage en Italie pendant l'année 1789* (Paris, 1796), 62.

[51] Duplessis, *Transitions to Capitalism*, 154.

[52] For these estimates, see Sella and Capra, *Ducato di Milano*, 581–2.

[53] Romani, *L'agricoltura*, 13.

[54] Ibid. 14.

ruralization of economic power, visible in Lombardy but existent in other parts of Italy as well, was certainly one of the big problems facing reformers.

Lombardy in the eighteenth century was too small to establish a sufficient internal market and it was highly dependent on foreign raw materials. This dependence was exacerbated by the economy's failure to produce goods which had a strong exchange value.[55] On the whole, an improvement of the agrarian system was of vital importance to the Lombard economy.

In the case of Tuscany we have seen that the sharecropping system caused peasants to concentrate cultivation on what they needed for their subsistence. A similar shift towards interculture can be observed in Lombardy, albeit out of more competitive reasoning. The decline in grain consumption and consequently falling prices had led farmers to branch out into new areas. Some moved into dairying; and the fame of Parma's cheeses dates from those times. Others planted rice and maize in addition to traditional wheat. Rice soon accounted for a large part of northern Italian agricultural production, and the high yield and low price of maize helped it become a staple of the northern diet; both the traditional *polenta* and the *risotto alla milanese* still bear witness to this development. The growing importance of rice to feed the population at home also had a positive economic side-effect for large farmers who continued to grow wheat. Not only could famines be largely avoided, but it was now possible to produce more wheat for export. With the prices of the main cereals going up by 50 per cent in Milan between the middle and the end of the century, it was clear that profits were again to be made from the land.[56] Finally, the planting of vines and other crop-bearing trees in grain fields further increased both range and quantity of agricultural production. It was precisely this development that Beccaria had hinted at in his remark about the effects of the Theresian census.

The Fate of Industry and Manufacture

By the second half of the eighteenth century, manufacture and commerce had lost the privileged position they had enjoyed during the Renaissance period. Internal demand was stable but limited, and the remaining foreign

[55] Bruno Caizzi, *Industria, commercio e banca in Lombardia nel XVIII secolo* (Milan, 1968), 134–5.

[56] Aldo de Maddalena, *Prezzi e mercedi a Milano dal 1701 al 1806* (Milan, 1974), 427. In Mantua prices went up 40 per cent over the same period; cf. C. Vivanti, 'I prezzi di alcuni prodotti agricoli a Mantova nella seconda metà del XVIII secolo', in Ruggero Romano (ed.), *I prezzi in Europa dal XVIII secolo a oggi* (Turin, 1972), 419–36.

demand for primary goods sparked off more production and higher export rates, which in turn led to higher imports. It is true that the manufacturing sector to an extent benefited from this development, even though its dependence on the 'agricultural–commercial equilibrium' became ever more apparent.[57] At the same time, however, the coalition between producers and merchants hampered industrial growth. Foreign demand increasingly concentrated on primary goods, and this led to a comfortable alliance between big landowners, who produced those goods, and the merchants specializing in imports, who would exchange primary for foreign goods.[58] In addition to foreign competition, the limited internal market, and the scarcity of qualified workforce, this meant that the manufacturing sector remained depressed.

Some sectors did show resilience and even experienced reasonable development. Even though silk-spinning declined rapidly at the beginning of the eighteenth century, silk-weaving reversed the previous decline to gain strength from 1715 onwards. Despite a marked downturn in the 1730s, when Lombard industry reached the lowest point of the century, the silk industry enjoyed a reasonable development in the course of the century. Cotton was the only other industry that had developed significantly by the end of the century, even though the growth rates of the cotton industry were much smaller compared to the development of silk.[59] The other traditional Lombard industries, such as mining and metallurgy, merely survived.

One general trend can be observed in the development of industry and manufacture. As in Tuscany, the ruralization of the economy shifted economic power increasingly to the countryside. The decline of silk-spinning, for example, affected mainly the big towns. Mills were increasingly set up in the hinterland, and often closer to borders so that their produce could be more easily exported to the major textile-producing areas in France, Switzerland, and Genoa.[60] Villages and small towns also took over much of the production of other more refined goods. Lombard peasants, for example, took to producing felt hats—the equivalent to Tuscany's export hit, straw hats—as the craft disappeared from Milan. As manufacture became dominated by rural enterprises producing cheaper items from raw

[57] Angelo Moioli, 'L'economia lombarda verso la maturità dell'equilibrio agricolo–commerciale durante l'età delle riforme', in Sergio Romagnoli and Gian Domenico Pisapia (eds.), *Cesare Beccaria tra Milano e l'Europa* (Rome, 1990), 330–1.

[58] Caizzi, *Industria, commercio e banca*, 137.

[59] Cf. Sella and Capra, *Ducato di Milano*, 573–7, on the silk industry, and pp. 577–8, on cotton.

[60] Cf. Carpanetto and Ricuperati, *Italy in the Age of Reason*, 37.

materials and often relying on peasants and their families as workforce, it became increasingly difficult to compete in the export market for fully processed goods. Consequently, industry was thrust back on the home market, with its need for cheap goods for mass consumption. In fact, the mass market was the only one that seemed to promise growth.[61] What had made some sense in the seventeenth century—keeping high-quality standards for a high-price foreign market—now had to be questioned. Equally, stagnating purchasing power, a result of falling salaries and rising prices for staple food, now seemed an impediment to development and became a problem that had to be dealt with if growth through mass consumption was to be attained.

Most aspects of economic life in eighteenth-century Lombardy can be viewed in the light of the city–countryside dichotomy. Originally, this dichotomy had denoted the relationship between industry and agriculture. The ruralization of eighteenth-century society and the shift of industry to the countryside added new dimensions to this. Population growth in Lombardy in the second half of the century was mainly due to an increase in rural areas; the relative importance of the cities declined.[62] The urbanization of the countryside was partly propelled by the growing role of manufacture and industry outside the cities, but mainly by the growing importance and profitability of agriculture.

If economic growth was to be achieved, then, it was beyond doubt that the revival had to begin in the countryside. It was equally clear that any programme for reform had to take the agricultural nature of the Lombard economy as its starting point.

[61] Moioli, 'L'economia', 339.

[62] Mario Romani, 'Il movimento demografico in Lombardia dal 1750 al 1850', in Romani, *Aspetti e problemi*, 3–47.

8

Pietro Verri, Cesare Beccaria, and the Beginning of the Debate

Our aim is . . . to give an exact account of how luxury is to be understood as an economic phenomenon.

(Cesare Beccaria, *Elementi di pubblica economia*, 1769)

In an atmosphere increasingly open to local expertise to solve the region's pressing problems, the precarious state of the Lombard economy generated a large amount of treatises and contributions to a wide range of subjects by the educated classes in Milan.

Pietro Verri is the central figure in the intellectual debates that occupied the members of the Milanese Enlightenment—or, to be more precise, the group of mostly aristocratic thinkers that formed the Accademia dei Pugni in the 1760s. While Tuscany had witnessed a shift from a ministerial to an increasingly public culture around the middle of the century, the Accademia dei Pugni acted as the single mouthpiece of the Enlightenment in Lombardy. Its members met regularly and published widely, but their frame of reference was never as dominated by local intellectual conflicts and inspirations as those of their colleagues further south. In fact, the Accademia dei Pugni was very much a self-sufficient organ that drew inspiration from the European republic of letters. The academy's journal, *Il Caffè*, had a wide target group. It was complemented by more targeted publications written expressly for the rulers (Pietro Verri gave a copy of his textbook on political economy to Joseph II) or for future administrators (Cesare Beccaria developed his political economy in his lectures as professor at the Palatine Schools). Discussion within the Accademia dei Pugni developed among its own members, and the detachment from wider spheres of public life could hardly have been more pronounced. It is for this reason that the shaping of political economy in Lombardy can be examined by a predominant focus on the Accademia dei Pugni. If economic thinking in Tuscany and Naples alike could be traced back to precedents from the first decades of the century, Lombard intellectuals drew a line around 1760, left tradition behind, and started anew.

This radical new beginning was made possible by Pietro Verri. Not only did he formulate the basic tenets of economic thinking in Lombardy (as well as set the precedent of treating luxury predominantly as an economic phenomenon). He was also, I wish to argue, the first to overcome the luxury debate a decade later at the beginning of the 1770s. In a ground-breaking attempt at systemization of economic phenomena, Verri offered an alternative solution to the stalemate between economic praise and moral condemnation that had come to characterize the European luxury debate.

Pietro Verri's Early Economic Thought: The Economic Foundation of Luxury

Pietro Verri wrote his first economic tract in 1760. The 'Elementi del commercio', a short dissertation about the nature of commerce, was subsequently published in the third issue of *Il Caffè* in 1764. In the 'Elementi', Verri defined commerce as 'an exchange of one good with another one', which was driven by the interplay of needs and abundance. It was 'active commerce' (and consequently a positive balance of trade), Verri argued, which accounted for the wealth of nations, and the desire for gain provided the incentive to engage in it.[1] Commercial society was thus a product of man's inclination to better his position. The role of government was to facilitate this natural inclination by providing economic freedom, guaranteeing private property, and fostering competition.

The 'Elementi di commercio' was a short and unsystematic treatise, but it outlined three basic elements of Pietro Verri's early economic thought. The first was his mercantilist belief in wealth generation through the export of manufactured goods while limiting both the export of prime materials and the import of manufactured goods. The second, his early adherence to state intervention, which was required to channel man's selfishness into a direction conducive to national wealth. This entailed the rule of law to set the parameters for economic activity. In fact, 'freedom has to stem from the law, not from licence'. But it also entailed the abolition of privilege, which was 'perfectly opposed to the spirit of commerce'.[2] Verri himself was later to remark in a letter to his brother that he had perhaps believed too strongly

[1] Pietro Verri, 'Elementi del commercio' (1760), in *Il Caffè, 1764–1766*, ed. Gianni Francioni and Sergio Romagnoli, 2nd edn. (Turin, 1998), i. 30–1.

[2] Ibid. 35–6. For Verri's view of economic freedom not as *laissez-faire* but as liberty guided by the law and by state intervention, see Christof Dipper, *Politischer Reformismus und begrifflicher Wandel. Eine Untersuchung des historisch-politischen Wortschatzes der Mailänder Aufklärung (1764–1796)* (Tübingen, 1976), 65–6.

in the need for state intervention at the time when he wrote the 'Elementi'. 'I believed too much in science. I was like a German doctor who wants to treat everything with medicine.' Moderate guidance of human inclinations was better, he now realized, than 'pulling man in this or pushing him in that direction'.[3] The third element was his view of luxury, which was the central category of Verri's early economic thought. In fact, 'without luxury, there can be no industry'. Luxury was so important because 'the majority of artisans live from' it. Not only did luxury increase the circulation of money, it also provided an incentive for the poor to work harder. Verri further recognized luxury's positive effect on population growth.[4]

Most of these arguments are taken directly from Jean-François Melon's *Essai politique sur le commerce*, a treatise he knew, as direct citations elsewhere in *Il Caffè* testify.[5] Melon's defence of the economic role of luxury at the expense of moral considerations as well as his argument that luxury was necessary in a modern state because it provided work find their direct reflection in Verri's first economic writings. Melon had argued that, once agriculture, defence, and industry were catered for, 'it is useful that the surplus workforce is being employed in the luxury trades, because what is left is either this, or idleness'.[6] He had then presented the circulation and incentive arguments, which Verri took up in his 'Elementi'. But whereas Melon had claimed that luxury stimulated manufactures, Verri underlined its positive effects on agriculture. Only conspicuous consumption, Verri argued, would provide strong enough an incentive for rich landowners to make agriculture more profitable and sustain it in the long run. And while the peasants themselves were excluded from conspicuous consumption, they would nevertheless profit from it because it guaranteed both their jobs and their income.

In his first writings on the functioning of commerce, Verri thus accorded a pivotal role to luxury. Not only did it guarantee the employment of much of the urban population and facilitate the circulation of money. Luxury also served as the principal engine of commerce and thus of economic development and national wealth. Only through the incentive provided by the availability of luxury goods could landowners be motivated to cultivate their land and to export excess produce. The economic function of

[3] Pietro Verri, letter, 24 Nov. 1770, in Pietro and Alessandro Verri, *Carteggio*, ed. Emanuele Greppi, Alessandro Giulini, *et al.*, 12 vols. (Milan, 1923–42), iv. 71.

[4] Verri, 'Elementi del commercio',. 36–8.

[5] Pietro Verri, 'Considerazioni sul lusso', in *Il Caffè*, i. 162.

[6] Jean-François Melon, *Essai politique sur le commerce* (Amsterdam, 1735; first edn. Bordeaux, 1734), 124. See above, Ch. 2.

consumption itself was of limited importance in Verri's economic model. What was important about luxury was not that it stimulated internal demand, but rather that it fostered supply for potential export. The fact that luxury was important only as a means to an end—an incentive to produce and export—and not as a factor of economic development in its own right points to a potential fault line in Verri's economic model. A decade later, as we shall see, it was to lead Verri into abandoning luxury as the built-in engine of economic development. But the 1760s marked the early phase of his economic thinking, in which luxury still occupied centre-stage. Consequently, he devoted another article in *Il Caffè* exclusively to the praise of luxury.

In his 'Considerazioni sul lusso' of 1764 Verri repeated the economic benefits of luxury, but he accompanied his arguments with an assessment of the moral status of luxury, which he had excluded in his earlier treatment. The *Considerazioni sul lusso* is both an engagement with Mandeville's *Fable of the Bees* and an attempt to incorporate the concept of luxury into the tenets of his utilitarian philosophy as developed in his philosophical works on the nature of happiness and pleasure.[7]

Just as Mandeville had not justified luxury morally, Verri argued that luxury remained a vice.[8] In fact, to indulge in luxury 'is a vice against which Christian orators have rightly preached'. Verri did not deny that luxury had brought down families and that its effects on individuals could be devastating. But, and here he endorsed the same Epicurean and Augustinian assumptions as Mandeville, these very vices were needed for society to run and to prosper economically. Having asserted the moral grounds upon which luxury was to be judged, Verri could afford a quasi-mechanical treatment of its effects, repeating the arguments for a chain reaction in the direction of prosperity which he had outlined in his 'Elementi del commercio'.[9]

But the 'Considerazioni sul lusso' is not only an engagement with Mandeville. Verri also linked the concept of luxury to the principles of his utilitarian philosophy, which he was to develop more fully in his philosophical work *Discorsi sull'indole del piacere*.[10] His definition of public happiness—

[7] Although Verri never cited Mandeville explicitly, his indebtedness becomes clear in almost literal translations of some of Mandeville's arguments. See e.g. Verri, 'Considerazioni sul lusso', 155: 'a private vice is not necessarily a political vice'.

[8] Bernard Mandeville, *The Fable of the Bees, or, Private Vices, Public Benefits*, ed. F. B. Kaye, 2 vols. (Indianapolis, 1988), preface, p. 10. See above, Ch. 2.

[9] Verri, 'Considerazioni sul lusso', 155–6.

[10] Pietro Verri, *Discorsi sull'indole del piacere e del dolore*, in *Discorsi del conte Pietro Verri dell'Istituto delle Scienze di Bologna . . . Riveduti ed accresciuti dall'autore* (Milan, 1781), esp. pp. 1–24.

the true object of political economy—was the 'maximum happiness shared by the largest number of citizens'.[11] Public happiness as defined in utilitarian terms necessitated a more equal distribution of wealth, but conspicuous consumption was only rendered possible by its unequal distribution. Paradoxically, luxury spending of the rich reduced inequality because it reduced their patrimony, circulated their money, and thus spread wealth among a larger group of the population. Thus, the beneficial but paradoxical effect of luxury was that it acted as 'the remedy for the evil that had caused it in the first place'.[12]

With Verri's two interventions in 1764, the terms for the luxury debate in Lombardy were set. First of all, Verri had presented the luxury issue as a predominantly economic phenomenon. Just like Muratori's summary of Melon a decade earlier, Verri's treatment established Mandeville and Melon as the main inspirations in the Lombard luxury debate. Verri's two articles in *Il Caffè* set the parameters for discussion for almost a decade until Verri himself overcame them with a new model of economic development in his *Meditazioni sulla economia politica* of 1771.

That Verri's interest in luxury was predominantly economic needs explanation. It could have been expected that Verri would consider luxury politically. After all, Montesquieu had written an extremely influential political account of luxury that considered luxury in relation to various forms of government, and Verri had read the *Esprit des lois* various times while he was in Vienna in 1760.[13] In fact, he even repeated Montesquieu's arguments that republics were built on equality and thus had no place for luxury and that the reward system in monarchies was built on inequality that made luxury characteristic of the government of one.[14] And yet, Verri merely summed up Montesquieu's definition without further development and moved on to concentrate fully on the economic nature of luxury. He never took up the connection between luxury and political systems again.

[11] On precursors of this line of thought (e.g. Helvétius's 'l'interêt public, c'est à dire celui du plus grand nombre') and their influence on the Milanese Enlightenment, cf. Gianni Francioni, 'Beccaria filosofo utilitarista', in Sergio Romagnoli and Gian Domenico Pisapia (eds.), *Cesare Beccaria tra Milano e l'Europa* (Rome, 1990), 69–87, esp. pp. 73–4.

[12] Verri, 'Considerazioni sul lusso', 157–8. The same argument had been advanced by Helvétius, whom Verri had read; Claude-Adrien Helvétius, *De l'Homme, de ses facultés intellectuelles et de son éducation* (London, 1772), ch. 13; see above, Ch. 2, 'Physiocracy and its Critics'.

[13] Peter Groenewegen, 'Pietro Verri's Mature Political Economy of the *Meditazioni*: A Case Study in the Highly Developed International Transmission Mechanism of Ideas in Pre-Revolutionary Europe', in Manuela Albertone and Alberto Masoero (eds.), *Political Economy and National Realities* (Turin, 1994), 107–25.

[14] Verri, 'Considerazioni sul lusso', 161–2. On Montesquieu, see above, Ch. 2.

The exclusive focus on the economy can be explained by a variety of factors: by Verri's conviction that Lombardy's most pressing problem was the economy (in fact, he remarked that what interested him most was 'the local condition of my country . . . domestic issues relating to . . . commerce, the mint, etc.'[15]); furthermore, by the acknowledgement that the economy was the only field in which the Lombard patriciate could hope to yield influence in Vienna in the face of censorship and the monopolization of political initiatives in Vienna; and finally by his belief that political economy was an area in which he could best distance himself from the generation of his father with its focus on jurisprudence.

The focus on the economy which we can detect not only in his treatment of luxury but also in the majority of his other writings is complemented by extreme caution in the realm of political judgement. We know that Pietro Verri censored the contributions to *Il Caffè* and made sure that too direct and explicit critical references to the Habsburg monarchy were cut out.[16] Even though recent research has stressed Pietro Verri's republican inclinations after the French revolution, Verri clearly believed that absolutist rule promised the necessary strength to carry out reform in the 1760s and 1770s.[17] If changes were to occur under the reform-minded government of Maria Theresa, it was best not to question the political authority of this government. As one Lombard thinker explained: 'Without doubt the worthiest occupation of a citizen who loves the government with all his heart is the study of economic affairs.'[18] And Gianrinaldo Carli, president of the Supreme Council of the Economy in the state of Milan, exclaimed that 'the remedy' against corruption as the inevitable consequence of property and contractual freedom 'is the sovereign'.[19] It may be exaggerated to claim, as has been done, that the Lombards were simply not interested in 'the nature of the political problem'.[20] It is clear, nevertheless, that the Lombards were champions of political economy. The new science that spread across

[15] Verri, letter from Vienna, 2 Sept. 1760, in Pietro and Alessendro Verri, *Lettere e scritti inediti di Pietro e di Alessandro Verri*, ed. Carlo Cassati, 4 vols. (Milan, 1879–81), i. 146.

[16] Francioni, 'Storia editoriale', in *Il Caffè*, vol. i, pp. cxxxix–cxlvi.

[17] On Verri's republicanism, cf. Carlo Capra, '"La mia anima è sempre stata repubblicana": Pietro Verri da patrizio a cittadino', *Pietro Verri e il suo tempo: quaderni di Acme*, 35 (1999), 519–40. On his endorsement of absolutism to initiate reform, see Pietro Verri, *Meditazioni sulla economia politica*, 6th edn. (Livorno, 1772), ch. 38.

[18] Luigi Lambertenghi, *Su' mendici e sugli oziosi* (1763), quoted in Dipper, *Politischer Reformismus*, 59.

[19] Gianrinaldo Carli, *Dell'uomo libero*, quoted in Franco Venturi, *Settecento riformatore*, v/1 (Turin, 1989), 797.

[20] Giuseppe Zarone, *Etica e politica nell'utilitarismo di Cesare Beccaria* (Naples, 1971), 153.

Europe not only promised to solve the region's most pressing problems. It also served as a means to assert their claim to power against the generation of their fathers, who were trained in, and dominated, not the field of economics but that of jurisprudence and politics.

But the development of political economy in Lombardy cannot be explained by lack of alternatives or in terms of strategies of social advancement alone. In fact, this was the one area in which the Milanese could make a difference because agriculture and economic policy were an area of devolved government, whereas all attempts at administrative reform had been monopolized by Vienna.[21] Pietro Verri and most members of the Accademia dei Pugni realized this and sought to influence the political leaders in this area. Such an endeavour seemed to have good auspices. In Milan the plenipotentiary Firmian was particularly receptive to new developments in political economy. His large library (he possessed over 3,000 works in English alone) contained many books on economic subjects. He seems to have been interested in political economy especially at the time when Verri and Beccaria wrote their economic treatises because most editions of the economic titles in Firmian's library date from the 1760s.[22]

Firmian's influence was limited, however. As a plenipotentiary he was increasingly powerless.[23] Aware of this development, Pietro Verri directed his efforts at Vienna. He went to considerable lengths to place his friend Luigi Lambertenghi at the Dipartimento d'Italia, the centre of policy formulation in Vienna (even though his efforts did not in the end pay off for Verri because Lambertenghi only cautiously, if at all, intervened in favour of his former benefactor).[24] But even in the highest spheres of government the Milanese political economists met with a keen interest in their work. The state chancellor, Kaunitz, was particularly open to new ideas in the field of political economy. He was familiar with the works of the members of the Accademia dei Pugni, and let himself be influenced by their thought. It was due to his initiative, in fact, that many of the academy's members

[21] At least from 1765 onwards Vienna left the Lombard administration considerable freedom in matters of economic policy; see Franco Valsecchi, 'Le riforme teresiane in Lombardia', in *Economia, istituzioni, cultura*, i. 37–8.

[22] Elisabeth Garms-Cornides, 'Un trentino tra Impero, antichi stati italiani e Gran Bretagna: l'anglomano Carlo Firmian', in Cesare Mozzarelli and Giuseppe Olmi (eds.), *Il Trentino nel Settecento fra Sacro Romano Impero e antichi stati italiani* (Bologna, 1985), 467–93.

[23] Elisabeth Garms-Cornides, 'La destinazione del conte Firmian a Milano: analisi di una scelta', in *Economia, istituzioni, cultura*, ii. 1015–29.

[24] Carlo Capra, 'Un intermediario tra Vienna e Milano: Luigi Lambertenghi e il suo carteggio con Pietro Verri', *Römische historische Mitteilungen*, 31 (1989), 359–76.

obtained high positions in government and (in the case of Pietro Verri and Cesare Beccaria) membership of the Supreme Council of the Economy.[25]

The Milanese political economists wanted to make themselves heard in Vienna. This does not explain the specific proposals they put forward. But it does help to explain why they should have opted for an area which was perhaps the only one where they could hope to be heard: political economy.

Cesare Beccaria: The Role of Consumption in an Agricultural Economy

Cesare Beccaria accepted the economic frame of reference which Pietro Verri had chosen in his treatment of luxury, but the language he used and the conclusions he drew were different. The two had a difficult relationship. Beccaria, undoubtedly the most famous of the Milanese group, was widely admired across Europe. His *Dei delitti e delle pene* was an extremely influential work on penal reform. Published in July 1764, the book was an immediate success with new editions both legitimate and pirated appearing within the year; by 1767 the work had been translated into both French and English.[26] This single work planted Milan on the map of the European Enlightenment, and Verri had inspired his protégé to write it. It seems that he never got over Beccaria's success, which, he felt, was really due him. The friendship between the two never recovered, and when Beccaria established himself as a political economist in 1769–70, Verri again could not accept the success of his former friend. He wrote his own treatise on political economy and he confided his motives to his brother: 'The revenge I am taking will put the professor of political economy in his place.'[27]

Beccaria was appointed to the chair of political economy at the Palatine Schools in Milan in 1769. For three years, from 1768 (when Beccaria charted the outline of his lectures in the expectation of the Milanese chair) to 1771 (when he left academia in order to take up administrative duties),

[25] Franz A. J. Szabo, *Kaunitz and Enlightened Absolutism 1753–1780* (Cambridge, 1994), 33–5.

[26] On the publishing history, see the introduction to Cesare Beccaria, *Dei delitti e delle pene. Con una raccolta di lettere e documenti relativi alla nascita dell 'opera e alla sua fortuna nell'Europa del Settecento*, ed. Franco Venturi, 2nd edn. (Turin, 1994), as well as the letters relating to the conception of the work; ibid. 113–26.

[27] Letter to Alessandro Verri, in Verri and Verri, *Carteggio*, iv. 17. On the *Meditazioni sulla economia politica* and their genesis out of competition with Beccaria, cf. Franco Venturi, 'Le *Meditazioni sulla economia politica* di Pietro Verri: edizioni, echi e discussioni', *Rivista storica italiana*, 90 (1978), 530–94.

Beccaria devoted his energies to the development of his economic thought. The first outline, the *Piano d'istruzioni per la cattedra di scienze camerali o sia di economia civile*, was written at short notice in 1768 after Kaunitz and Firmian had decided to appoint him to the newly endowed chair. The *Piano d'istruzioni* draws heavily on Cantillon, whose *Essai sur la nature du commerce en général* (1755) had come out in an Italian translation in 1767.[28] It was based on Beccaria's understanding of political economy as legislation aimed at increasing public wealth. In fact, 'cameral science is that part of the legislation . . . which increases the opulence of the state and its subjects, and which teaches the most just and useful administration of . . . the revenue'. This was a practical, not an abstract, endeavour, because Beccaria's students were to be trained as future administrators who needed 'to be shown the concrete application of abstract theory'.[29] Consequently, Beccaria planned to teach the general principles of political economy (starting from the concept of value and the importance of population growth for economic development). These were to be followed by practical lectures on agriculture (where he would argue in favour of free grain trade), commerce (where he underlined the importance of the circulation of money for economic development), manufacture (where he would argue against prohibitive laws which would lead to monopolies), and finance (where he championed simple and universal taxation).[30]

While not yet fully developed, the central assumptions of Beccaria's economic thought are already clear in the outline of his proposed lectures: the importance of agriculture and of economic freedom, the central role of consumption for economic development via the role of the circulation of money, and the belief in limited but clear state intervention in the field of finance. The central role of luxury in his economic edifice can likewise already be observed. In fact, his analysis of the general principles of political economy ultimately 'leads to an . . . answer to the question if luxury is of use in a nation'.[31] Beccaria did not yet give an answer to the question in his outline. But, as promised, he made luxury a central element of his lectures over the coming two years.

Beccaria's inaugural lecture, held in January 1769 and soon published across Europe, positioned political economy against jurisprudence.[32] It is

[28] Cesare Beccaria, *Piano d'istruzioni per la cattedra di scienze camerali o sia di economia civile* (1768), in Beccaria, *Opere*, ed. Sergio Romagnoli (Florence, 1958), 337–47. On the influence of Cantillon, see Augero Mauri, 'La cattedra di Cesare Beccaria', *Archivio storico italiano*, 41 (1933), 237.

[29] Beccaria, *Piano d'istruzioni*, 341–2. [30] Ibid. 343–7. [31] Ibid. 344.

[32] Cesare Beccaria, *Prolusione letta il giorno 9 Gennaio 1769 nell'apertura della nuova cattedra di scienze camerali nelle scuole palatine di Milano*, in Beccaria, *Opere*, 361–77. On the early

indicative of the same urge to leave the jurisdictional tradition of the generation of their fathers behind that had inspired Pietro Verri in his economic treatment of luxury. Against the bureaucratization of commerce and the rule of privilege over economic freedom, Beccaria argued for an economic science based on quantitative methods and deduction as a means to unite private utility with public interest.[33] In the lectures themselves he was to combine a mathematical approach to the science of economics with the moral impetus of bettering the condition of the population at large.

Beccaria gave his lectures over the course of three years, from 1769 to 1771. Meant as university lectures, he never gave them to the press, and it was only in 1804 that Pietro Custodi published the lectures as *Elementi di pubblica economia* in his multi-volume edition of Lombard economic texts.[34] As he had already announced in the *Piano d'istruzione*, the *Elementi* have an eminently practical thrust. Conceived as a teaching course for future administrators, they link general principles of the economy with concrete examples drawn from the Lombard economy and demographic information as well as concrete policy proposals. The art Beccaria had set out to train his students in was 'to conserve and grow the riches of a state, and to make the best use of it'.[35] His economic thought was based on the assumption that it was consumption (or demand, in today's terminology) rather than manufacture and industry (or supply) which was the prime engine of economic development. For Lombardy, his preferred model of economic development was what would later be called 'capitalist agriculture': an economic model based on primary goods, produced at cheap cost achieved via productivity increases which were made possible by the division of labour. Incidentally, it was precisely the need to employ the excess labour freed up in this process that lay at the centre of Beccaria's economic treatment of luxury. It was in the luxury trades that 'unproductive labour' should be employed and contribute to economic development in its own right.

Beccaria argued the case for the primacy of home consumption over the foreign market. The reasons for this choice were economic and followed from his axiom that the economy could only thrive if profits were 'restored'

diffusion of the inaugural lecture, see Pier Luigi Porta, 'Le lezioni economiche di Cesare Beccaria', in Sergio Romagnoli and Gian Domenico Pisapia (eds.), *Cesare Beccaria tra Milano e l'Europa* (Rome, 1990), 356.

[33] Beccaria, *Prolusione*, 368–9.

[34] I quote from Beccaria, *Elementi di pubblica economia*, in Beccaria, *Opere*, 379–649, which is more reliable than Custodi's first edition.

[35] Beccaria, *Elementi di pubblica economia*, 383.

to the economy by way of consumption. Though of little value individually, the accumulated effect of home consumption would by far outweigh the seemingly bigger benefits derived from foreign trade. Suppose, Beccaria argued, we have an economy with many refined products—the sort of products designed for the foreign market—and with little simple manufacture. Now one manufacturer of refined goods (whose value is equivalent to more foodstuff compared to that of simple products) earns as much as many manufacturers of simple products would. The single manufacturer will restore some of this value to the economy through consumption, and he will spend more than less well-off manufacturers individually. But taken together, their spending will exceed that of the few manufacturers of refined goods. All this led Beccaria to champion those industries that 'are closest to representing foodstuffs' and essential goods. The economy had first to provide proper clothing and other affordable goods for the common man before moving on to more refined products. To concentrate exclusively on refined goods would be 'ruinous'.[36]

Beccaria had initially been sceptical about an agricultural path towards economic development in Lombardy. In the first outline of his lectures he had drawn heavily on Cantillon, with whom he shared the belief that agriculture alone would not be enough to feed the people. It was true, Beccaria conceded, that the size of a population was always proportional to 'the means of subsistence that the land supplies' and that the population would fall when the land was not cultivated. But equally important, he added, was the help of industry, without which the population could not be kept up either.[37] Perhaps it was this initial scepticism that led Franco Venturi to stress Beccaria's lack of enthusiasm for agriculture.[38] But by the time he gave his lectures in 1769, he had changed his mind. Now agriculture enjoyed the right of first place, and economic reform had to start here. In fact, he urged countries with fertile lands to devote themselves to its cultivation. The 'artisan and industrial economy' had to come second to this.[39] Rather than accusing Beccaria of lack of enthusiasm for agriculture, we should appreciate his *Elementi* as a strong case for the agricultural development of Lombardy.

[36] Ibid. 538–40.

[37] Beccaria, *Piano d'istruzioni*, 343.

[38] Venturi, *Settecento riformatore*, v/1. 469.

[39] Beccaria, *Elementi di pubblica economia*, 383 and 390. He even became a member of the Tuscan Accademia dei Fisiocritici in Siena; cf. Renato Pasta, 'Istituzionalizzazione della scienza e controllo del sapere: il contributo di Pompeo Neri alla rinascita dei Fisiocritici', in Aldo Frantoianni and Marcello Verga (eds.), *Pompeo Neri: atti del colloquio di Castelfiorentino (6–7 maggio 1988)* (Castelfiorentino, 1992), 217–38, esp. p. 231.

Contrary to Italy on the whole (where agricultural themes were prominent because Italian society was to a large extent based on agriculture and it was here that thinkers could best prove their reforming spirit),[40] the widespread belief in eighteenth-century Lombardy was that there was not enough money to be made with agriculture and that industry had therefore to be preferred. Some, it is true, argued for the primacy of agriculture. Paolo Simonini, a self-professed follower of Beccaria, for example, considered agriculture the sole creator of wealth. He propagated an agricultural model of small holdings operating in complete freedom, and for an encouragement of the 'arts close to the prime materials'.[41] Other authors echoed his concerns. It was agriculture, one of them argued, that made a life of luxury and pleasure possible, that increased the circulation of money, and thus filled the public purse with income from taxes and duties. 'If a well-conceived financial policy helps agriculture by facilitating internal circulation, consumption and export, then agriculture in turn will allow the citizens . . . to enjoy goods of luxury and pleasure.'[42]

But occasional praise of Lombardy's agricultural economy notwithstanding, the preference for industry, manufacture, and commerce over agriculture was much more typical of the Lombard approach to political economy.[43] As early as 1760 the Lombard thinker Muttoni had assessed the economic power of the state of Milan and had reached the conclusion that 'agriculture comes second to commerce'.[44] A similar confidence in industry was echoed more than a decade later by another political economist, Giuseppe Biumi, when he remarked that 'agriculture alone cannot bring perfect happiness to a state'.[45]

In order to rebut such concerns, Beccaria argued that sufficient profits from agriculture could indeed be made if the cost of agricultural labour could be reduced. This was to be achieved by the division of labour because

[40] Enzo Piscitelli, 'Il pensiero degli economisti italiani del '700 sull'agricoltura, la proprietà terriera e la condizione dei contadini', *Clio*, 15 (1979), 245–92, esp. pp. 247–53.

[41] Paolo Simonini, *Sulla ricchezza in pubblica economia* (1773), in *Economisti minori*, 422–4.

[42] Anon., *Sopra lo studio dell'agricoltura con un saggio sull'agricoltura logigiana*, in *Economisti minori*, 196. Neither place nor year of publication are known. However, reference to Maria Theresa suggests that it was written in Lombardy before 1780, probably in the early 1770s; cf. ibid. 212.

[43] In fact, most works on agricultural themes published in Lombardy during the reign of Maria Theresa were translations of foreign publications; cf. Rosalba Canetta, 'Gli studi agronomici in Lombardia durante l'età teresiana', in *Economia, istituzioni, cultura*, i. 59–75, esp. p. 65.

[44] Filippo Muttoni, *Dissertazioni intorno alle rendite dello Stato di Milano* (1760), in *Economisti minori*, 24–72: 31.

[45] Giuseppe Biumi, *Piano di scienza politico economica* (1773), in *Economisti minori*, 371.

'everybody knows from their own experience that when he does one specialized and particular thing all the time' rather than a whole range of tasks, 'his work becomes faster and better'. Unlike Adam Smith, who was to introduce the concept of the division of labour in the context of industry and manufacture, Beccaria explicitly chose examples from the realm of agriculture: 'whereas some pasture the sheep, others shear the wool, and others again weave; some grow the grain, and others bake the bread'.[46] The potential drawback of this model (which Beccaria would later address by arguing the case for luxury) was that it led to underemployment. Free trade, Beccaria argued, increased the need to be competitive in a market free of privileges. In such an environment the main obstacle to success was the high cost of labour driven by the high cost of foodstuffs.[47] Productivity increases could solve this disadvantage by reducing manufacturing time, but this would ultimately lead to a reduction in the need for manpower, in other words unemployment.[48] 'With less working time *and* less people we can do a larger number of jobs.'[49]

The concept of productivity increases brought about by the division of labour allowed Beccaria to embark on a route of economic progress that would later be called 'capitalist agriculture'. And indeed Beccaria argued against a subsistence economy of small farms because if the land is divided among too many people this 'prevents those grand expenditures which alone make agriculture grow'. It was large-scale agriculture that provided an incentive for the rich to invest and thus 'bring fresh capital to the land'.[50]

If the encouragement of agriculture (together with a growing industry in the countryside) was the way forward for the Lombard economy; if, furthermore, the development of agriculture depended on productivity increases made possible by the division of labour; and finally, if this led to a reduction in demand for manpower and potential underemployment, what then was to be done with the labour freed up in this process? At this point, Beccaria's model of economic development merges with his treatment of luxury, where he combined philosophical and economic reasoning. In the *Elementi* Beccaria based his discussion of luxury on the Epicurean pleasure–pain principle he had outlined in *Dei delitti e delle pene*.[51] According

[46] Beccaria, *Elementi di pubblica economia*, 387–8. [47] Ibid. 522.

[48] Ibid. 561. [49] Ibid. 390 (my emphasis). [50] Ibid. 442–3.

[51] A further link between the two works, namely the relationship between economic activity and punishment, is explored by Gian Paolo Massetto, 'Economia e pena nell'opera del Beccaria', in Romagnoli and Pisapia (eds.), *Beccaria tra Milano e l'Europa*, 279–328, esp. pp. 285–95. On Beccaria's transformation from a jurist into a political economist, see Daniel M. Klang, 'Cesare Beccaria and the Clash between Jurisprudence and Political Economy in

to Beccaria, 'pleasure and pain are the motive forces of all sentient beings'. This meant that 'the proximate and efficient cause of actions is the flight from pain, their final cause is the love of pleasure'.[52] The search for pleasure was a never-ending process for two reasons. First, the duration of pleasure can never be taken for granted and man is thus driven by constant fear of loss to accumulate pleasures. Secondly, any pleasure will soon cease to satisfy because there are always greater pleasures to be attained. The resulting feeling of dissatisfaction is 'a pain like any other'.[53] In his lectures on political economy Beccaria linked these axioms to conspicuous consumption as an equally never-ending and expanding process. Defining luxury as 'every expense incurred to rid us of the pains that are privations of pleasures', conspicuous consumption becomes an innate part of man's natural quest for pleasure. Since any pleasure will loose its appeal (turn into pain, in Beccaria's words) in the sight of even greater pleasures to be attained, there is no limit to man's urge to indulge in luxuries.[54] Whereas Mandeville and Melon had pointed to the fact that indulgence in luxury was an inextricable component of any well-governed *society*, Beccaria went one step further and placed luxury at the heart of the nature of the individual.[55] To 'try to root out luxury would be tantamount to trying to destroy one of man's innate faculties'.[56]

Having established the ineradicable inclination of man towards luxury, Beccaria then showed the economic consequences of such behaviour. First (and here Beccaria repeated the standard arguments of the European luxury debate), luxury acted as an incentive to produce, and conspicuous consumption increased the circulation of money. Secondly (and here Beccaria advanced a new argument which tied his theory of productivity increases to the economic need for luxury), it was in the luxury trades that excess labour could be employed.[57] It is within the context of potential underemployment generated by the division of labour and the reduction of manpower in a

Eighteenth-Century Lombardy', *Canadian Journal of History / Annales canadiennes d'histoire*, 23 (1988), 305–36.

[52] Cesare Beccaria, *On Crimes and Punishments and Other Writings*, ed. Richard Bellamy (Cambridge, 1995), 21 and 157. On the Epicurean origin of the principle, see Michael Erler, 'Epikur', in Hellmuth Flashar (ed.), *Die Philosophie der Antike*, iv/1: *Die hellenistische Philosophie* (Basel, 1994), 29–202, esp. pp. 153–70, 190–4.

[53] The pleasure–pain principle became a common theme in Beccaria's writings. See e.g. his *Ricerche attorno alla nature dello stile*, in Beccaria, *Opere*, 297–8.

[54] Beccaria, 'On Luxury', in Beccaria, *On Crimes and Punishments*, 161–9, esp. p. 163. See also Richard Bellamy, 'Introduction', ibid., pp. xv–xvi.

[55] Mandeville, *Fable of the Bees*, 27–37; Melon, *Essai politique*, 122.

[56] Beccaria, 'On Luxury', 165.

[57] Beccaria, *Elementi di pubblica economia*, pt. iv, ch. 33, pp. 617–18.

large-scale agriculture that we can understand Beccaria's remark that luxury was beneficial in a free economy because it was needed to employ the excess labour made available through productivity increases.

Not only had Beccaria incorporated his treatment of luxury into the utilitarian philosophical model employed in the development of both his legal and his economic thought. He had also shifted luxury to the centre of the discussion about the role of consumption in economic development, about modes of production, and about the employment of labour. It was on this ground that Lombard political economists responded.

The Lombard Debate about Luxury and Consumption

One of the most accomplished contributions to the debate that Pietro Verri and Cesare Beccaria had sparked off came from Alfonso Longo, who succeeded Beccaria as professor of political economy in Milan in 1773. Born in the same year as his predecessor, he had been a member of the Accademia dei Pugni from the very beginning. A priest, he had published in *Il Caffè* before embarking on a career in ecclesiastical law in Milan, where he used his chair to launch biting attacks against the Church, before he turned his attention towards political economy. A follower of physiocracy, he was in correspondence with Mirabeau in France, whose book *Les Devoirs* he helped publish in Milan in 1780.[58]

In his lectures on political economy, published posthumously as *Istituzioni economico politiche*, Longo postulated that consumption was the engine of economic development. The 'insatiable nature of man' constantly requires more goods to consume, which in turn leads to an increase in production, sparking off yet new desires and new needs. The virtuous cycle of economic growth is being set in motion, and it leads in turn to the refinement of the arts. Indeed those arts develop that 'serve to satisfy the exquisite senses and the pleasures of the imagination' and their 'needs will give birth to elegance, symmetry and perfection'.[59] Longo further underlined the importance of domestic consumption with historical arguments, citing a common theme in the European luxury debate, Asia's past greatness, which was due to commerce and luxury. But Longo linked this to domestic

[58] Franco Venturi, 'Alfonso Longo: nota introduttiva', in *Illuministi italiani*, i/1. 215–22. Some of Mirabeau's letters to Longo are reproduced in the *Mémoires biographiques, littéraires et politiques de Mirabeau: écrits par lui-même, par son père, son oncle et son fils adoptif*, iii (Paris, 1834), 134–7 and 443–79.

[59] Alfonso Longo, *Istituzioni economico politiche* (1773), in *Illuministi italiani*, i/1. 272–5.

consumption by insisting that 'their commerce was probably only internal'. Not only did luxury thus contribute to the greatness of the Asian empires. What is more, their very prosperity was generated by home demand.[60]

Shortly after Beccaria had lectured on political economy, Giuseppe Biumi supported Beccaria's argument about the importance of consumption. 'Everything in the economic system begins and ends with spending,' and 'the consumption of products . . . restores to the productive class the means of production'.[61] Another Lombard political economist, Giuseppe Gorani, argued against this position. A self-professed follower of Beccaria, 'who had the courtesy to read my notes', Gorani nevertheless did not share his teacher's belief in the role of consumption as the engine of economic development.[62] Gorani believed that the competitive edge of the Lombard economy lay in the export of its high-quality agricultural produce and in less refined manufactured goods. Home consumption, in other words, was detrimental to economic development because it harmed potential export. Incidentally, his emphasis on agriculture and low-quality manufacture led him to consider the practical consequences of the growth of the luxury trades on the structure of the labour market. Tempted by the prospect of big profits, 'the smith, the carpenter, the bricklayer and similar rustic professions' would abandon their trade or encourage their children to become goldsmiths and jewellers. It was precisely the desire to emulate, in other words, that would drain off resources from necessary production to the luxury sector. The downturn of agriculture and commerce would be accelerated because of the lack of labour for the production of necessities.[63]

Different though all these attempts were in the thrust of their arguments, they have one thing in common. All contributors to the luxury debate in Lombard shared the conviction that luxury was predominantly an economic phenomenon. They may have differed over the role of domestic consumption and export in economic development, and over the primacy of agriculture or manufacture. But they all agreed that it was impossible to talk about economic development without talking about luxury.

[60] Longo, *Istituzioni economico politiche*, in *Economisti minori*, 332–3.

[61] Biumi, *Piano di scienza politico economica*, esp. p. 373.

[62] Quoted by Franco Venturi, 'Guiseppe Gorani: nota introduttiva', in *Illuministi italiani*, i/1. 484. See also his memoirs: Guiseppe Gorani, *Dal dispotismo illuminato alla rivoluzione (1767–1791)*, ed. Alessandro Casati (Milan, 1942).

[63] Guiseppe Gorani, *Saggio sulla pubblica educazione*, in *Illuministi italiani*, i/1. 526–7.

The Moral Value of Luxury

Such a focus on the economy raises the question whether the Milanese economists paid any attention to the moral dimension of luxury. The widening range of meaning to encompass moral–religious and economic connotations clearly made luxury a potential conceptual link between the moral and the economic realm. It is one of the outcomes of the eighteenth-century luxury debate, however, that the two worlds increasingly grew apart. Luxury as a morally reproachable concept continued to prosper. But it was confined to the institution that had most audibly railed against its corrupting effects: the Church.

Despite preoccupation with economic problems, the Milanese political economists were nevertheless concerned with the wider issues of refinement, self-improvement, and moral status raised by the issue of political economy, and most notably luxury. It was Pietro Verri who first spoke of luxury in the context of refinement. In 1763 he remarked that 'luxury and the love of pleasure have contributed to refine men, and to stabilize fraternity and good faith'.[64] Even before Antonio Genovesi took up Hume's views on refinement in his *Lezioni di commercio*, thus, Verri endorsed the arguments of the Scottish philosopher and presented refinement as beneficial to the social fabric.[65] Alfonso Longo saw a similar connection. For him, the advantage of the city was that enviable 'refinement of the senses'. But refinement was not only a feature of urban life. Refinement brought about by the consumption of luxury goods became the guarantor of sociability and the *doux commerce* Montesquieu had called for. As Longo explained, 'the delicacy of living and luxury sweeten the mind and render man sociable'.[66]

Unflinching defences of refinement had met with fierce resistance elsewhere in Europe. Jean-Jacques Rousseau, for his part, was surprised at Hume's endorsement of luxury and inequality. How could this not, he wondered, be regarded as the source of moral and political decline?[67] In Italy, Rousseau may have been scorned, but many Italian authors at least

[64] Pietro Verri, *Considerazioni sul commercio dello Stato di Milano* (1763), ed. C. A. Vianello (Milan, 1939), quoted in Dipper, *Politischer Reformismus*, 186.

[65] On Genovesi's use of Hume, see Till Wahnbaeck, 'Ferdinando Paoletti georgofilo e il dibattito sul lusso nel Settecento', in *I Georgofili: atti della Accademia dei Georgofili*, 45 (1998), 373–5.

[66] Longo, *Istituzioni economico politiche*, in *Illuministi italiani*, i/1. 274, and in *Economisti minori*, 351.

[67] On Rousseau's reaction to Hume, see Donald Winch, *Riches and Poverty: An Intellectual History of Political Economy in Britain* (Cambridge, 1996), 52–6.

tried to follow him in combining ancient and modern political philosophy, that is, morals and virtue with commerce and money.[68] Antonio de Giuliani was one of his followers and endorsed his dream to go back 'to that initial happiness, those times in which, with fewer needs, men were richer and more happy'.[69] And Giambattista Biffi even went so far as to hail Rousseau as 'my father, my escort, my master, my idol'.[70] Consequently, there were attempts in Lombardy to assess the moral nature of luxury spending, albeit seldom as critical in tone and negative in judgement as the ones brought forward by Rousseau himself. Paolo Simonini, for example, did attempt to provide a moral justification of the accumulation of wealth. What he ended up with, however, was a curious explanation of the circulation of money by which 'the rich man in his noble spirits makes others share his wealth', as if he bought goods out of a humanitarian interest. The less wealthy will then try to emulate the rich and at the same time teach the latter about 'the justice of spending'. Even though his reasoning remains somewhat cryptic, we can at least sense a preoccupation with a moral assessment of the nature of spending and the virtues of inequality.[71]

More often than not, however, the Lombard political economists accepted inequality and the indulgence in luxury it gave rise to. Again, Alfonso Longo is a case in point. He had endorsed the equation between luxury and refinement wholeheartedly, and it is not surprising that he found inequality quite natural, too. His entire philosophical edifice is based on inequality. Having asserted a natural imbalance of power in the family because men have 'both more mental and more physical power' than women, he observed 'an even greater one in the state of war which comes very close to the origin of the civil state'.[72] Now, it is the very inequality—natural and inescapable—that leads to luxury, and luxury in turn helps ease some of the evil effects of inequality. If, Longo argued, inequality meant that society was divided into rich and poor, it also meant that some of the poor could

[68] On Rousseau's fate in Italy, see Luigi Firpo, *Rousseau in Italia* (Turin, 1963), esp. pp. 19–31. The most outspoken critic of Rousseau was Gianrinaldo Carli, *Della disugualianza fisica morale civile fra gli uomini ossia ragionammento sopra l'opera di Rousseau 'Discours sur l'origine & les fondamens de l'inégalité parmi les hommes'*, in Carli, *Opere*, 19 vols. (Milan, 1784), xix. 97–238. On his particularly ardent attack, see Antonio Trampus, 'L'illuminismo e la "nuova politica" nel tardo settecento italiano: l'uomo libero di Gianrinaldo Carli', *Rivista storica italiana*, 106 (1994), 42–114.

[69] De Giuliani, *Saggio politico sopra le vicissitudini inevitabili delle società civili*, in *Illuminista italiani*, i/2. 690–1.

[70] Giambattista Biffi, *Cose notabili accadute in Cremona dal 1° Ottobre 1777 al 24 Ottobre 1781*, in *Illuministi italiani*, i/1. 412.

[71] Simonini, *Sulla ricchezza*, 424–5.

[72] Longo, *Istituzioni economico politiche*, in *Economisti minori*, 292–4.

only survive by providing services and goods for the rich. Since the rich have no need for further necessities, new products have to be invented to make life easier, 'and thus came about the commerce in commodities and finally that of luxury goods'. Given that 'commodities and luxury are continuous occasions for both spending and earning', luxury helps bridge the financial gap that had caused it in the first place.[73] It is this type of reasoning that underlies Beccaria's swift phrase that 'the rich man's opulent and haughty liberality differs from a genuinely compassionate and discriminating charity only in its motives'.[74]

There was one field, however, where luxury was always morally reproachable, and this was the luxury of the Church. Recent scholarship has paid specific attention to the deteriorating relationship between the state and the Church, much of which can be attributed to the state's growing desire to assert authority that had previously been exerted by the Church. Book censorship is a case in point. Some measures, like the expropriation of Church property, have also to be seen in the light of economic advantages for the state.[75] But the revolt against Rome had moral undertones as well, and it is in this respect that luxury was used to condemn the decadence of the Church. Alfonso Longo (who had been so understanding of inequality and indulgence in luxury goods as long as they served to further public happiness through economic mechanisms) launched a ferocious attack on the luxury of the Church in his inaugural lecture as professor of ecclesiastical law. A disillusioned priest himself, he spared his former colleagues no criticism. The Church had been degenerating for centuries, ever since it had abandoned the care of the poor and begun to amass ecclesiastical goods. It was clear for Longo that 'opulence gives birth to weariness of prayer and piety' and that 'ambition enters the human mind and everybody aims to outdo the others, praising no longer virtue but luxury'. Longo had had no problems with such a chain of events in civil society. But the Church, he maintained, had to be judged on different grounds because 'it was not founded by human consensus with the aim to further public happiness in this world'. It 'is not based on force, power or wealth' but rather on the word of Christ and his example. What was laudable in civil society (where vices had to be accepted and be put to good use) became a target of attack in the clergy.[76]

[73] Ibid. 333.

[74] Beccaria, 'On Luxury', 161.

[75] A good bibliography of the vast literature on Church–state relations and ecclesiastical reform in the age of Maria Theresa can be found in Sella and Capra, *Ducato di Milano*, 651–3.

[76] Alfonso Longo, *Prolusione tenuta l'anno MDCCLXIX dal marchese Alfonso Longo, canonico teologo della Basilica di Santo Stefano, regio professore di diritto pubblico ecclesiastico presso le Scuole Palatine Milanesi*, in *Illuministi italiani*, i/1, esp. pp. 247–9.

Similar views were endorsed by other Lombard thinkers. Carlantonio Pilati, for example, joined Longo in an attack on the clergy. He too admonished the lavish luxury of the Church, and blamed missionaries for introducing luxury into native societies and subsequently profiting from its devastating effect on the populations.[77] But on the whole, moral concerns were of secondary importance to the Lombard political economists. They endorsed Hume's equation of luxury and refinement, and at times even attempted a moral critique of luxury. Following the path outlined by Melon and Muratori, who had chosen to exclude a moral justification of commercial society in their treatments of luxury, they—unlike their Tuscan counterparts—decided to concentrate their efforts on its economic effects. Luxury may have been a vice, but it was necessary for the well-functioning of society. Its moral status was only discussed in the case of the clergy because the Church was founded on different grounds from the ones that had allowed Mandeville to formulate his paradox.

Outside the realm of the Church, all Milanese political economists agreed with Pietro Verri's initial claim that luxury was to be understood as the cornerstone of economic development. All, that is, except for Pietro Verri himself, who removed this very cornerstone from the new economic edifice he erected at the beginning of the 1770s.

[77] Carlantonio Pilati, *Riflessioni di un italiano sopra la chiesa in generale, sopra il clero sì regolare che secolare, sopra i vescovi ed i pontefici romani, e sopra i diritti ecclesiastici de' principi*, in *Illuministi italiani*, i/2. 601–12.

9

The Shaping of Political Economy in the Milanese Enlightenment

From the interest rate, one can calculate the happiness of a nation.
(Pietro Verri, *Meditazioni sulla economia politica*, 1771)

The Luxury Debate Overcome: Pietro Verri's Principles of Political Economy

Pietro Verri had sparked off the economic debate in Lombardy. He had made political economy the field in which the thinkers of the Milanese Enlightenment predominantly engaged. He had set the terms for the luxury debate in Lombardy, a lead that was followed by the members of the Accademia dei Pugni. Pietro Verri, however, was also the thinker who abandoned the focus on luxury at the beginning of the 1770s in his account of the principles of economic development. His systematic treatment of political economy replaced luxury as the cornerstone of growth with the concept of productive investment driven by low interest rates.

The *Meditazioni sulla economia* was written in less than a month in October 1770, and published half a year later.[1] It constituted, Verri was convinced, the culmination of his thought, destined, he hoped, to secure him 'a European name, and it seems to me that this is not a vain hope'.[2] It was a vain hope. Even though Verri sent dozens of copies of the work to his colleagues in the republic of letters and even though the work was swiftly reviewed in the main Italian journals, his influence on the development of economic thought remained limited.[3] Only in the case of Say, and perhaps the English political economist McCulloch, has *direct* influence been

[1] Franco Venturi, 'Le *Meditazioni sulla economia politica* di Pietro Verri: edizioni, echi e discussioni', *Rivista storica italiana*, 90 (1978), 530–94.

[2] Pietro Verri, letter to Alessandro, 17 Oct. 1770, in Pietro and Alessandro Verri, *Carteggio*, ed. Emanuele Greppi, Alessandro Giulini, *et al.*, 12 vols. (Milan, 1923–42), iv. 25.

[3] Reviews in *Novelle letterarie*, 21 (1771), 326, and *Giornale de' letterati di Pisa*, 4 (1771), 81–109.

established.[4] The one Milanese author with 'a European name' continued to be Cesare Beccaria. But despite the limited success of the *Meditazioni*, the work was an outstanding piece of economic writing, and it prepared the grounds for the development of economics as a systematic science. It is tempting to think that Adam Smith, who owned a copy of the work, found more inspiration in it than has previously been acknowledged.[5] At any rate, the systematic nature of the work, which deduced economic rules from only a handful of principles, marked an advance from previous economic writings not only on the Italian peninsula, but in Europe at large.

The guiding question of the *Meditazioni* is how to foster economic development, which Verri defined as an excess of production over consumption. The limited context he had in mind was the Lombardy of the eighteenth century (which he knew from years of administrative service), but the wider context was modern commercial society, characterized by growing needs and international trade, which was carried out with money as 'the universal good'. The two elements of his answer are the idea of an economic equilibrium and the central role of money in the birth of commercial society.

The idea of equilibrium Verri had taken directly from Newtonian science. In a letter to his brother he explained that he 'considered the elements of national prosperity in the same way as we consider the laws of motion'.[6] The equilibrium principle affected all areas of economic activity, if at times only by a slow process. Most importantly, national production and consumption were linked and naturally strove to reach equilibrium. A decrease in production would ultimately lead to diminishing consumption. In a society where many members lived at subsistence level such as in Lombardy, this signified depopulation in the long run.[7] The secret to economic growth lay in the slow process of adaptation of internal demand to supply. As long as supply was higher than demand, the nation could export and invest the profit productively in order to further increase supply. A virtuous cycle was thus set in motion, which guaranteed equilibrium at ever rising levels of prosperity. The secret to this success lay in an economic model based on the

[4] Peter Groenewegen, 'The Significance of Verri's *Meditazioni* in the History of Economic Thought', in *Pietro Verri e il suo tempo: quaderni di Acme*, 35 (1999), 693–708. On Say's use of Verri's concept of value, see André Tiran, 'Pietro Verri: Aux origines de la théorie de la valeur et de la loi des débouches de Jean-Baptiste Say', *Revue d'economie politique*, 103 (1993), 445–71.

[5] James Bonar, *A Catalogue of the Library of Adam Smith* (London, 1932), 190.

[6] Letter, 17 Oct. 1770, in Verri, *Carteggio*, iv. 25.

[7] Pietro Verri, *Meditazioni sulla economia politica*, ed. Renzo De Felice (Milan, 1998; reproduction of the 2nd edn. Naples, 1771), 25.

primacy of the supply side. In fact, one of the general principles of the economy was to 'increase as much as possible the number of vendors', in other words to boost supply.[8]

A similar equilibrium mechanism was at work in the determination of prices. The equilibrium price, the *prezzo commune*, was defined as the price of a commodity which allowed for an exchange of goods in which neither buyer nor seller would be worse off after the transaction. Importantly, this applied only to commodities and staple goods. Rare products had no equilibrium, but variable prices, because both demand and supply were restricted and depended upon variable factors such as fashion.[9]

The idea of equilibrium both in the interplay between supply and demand and in the nature of prices led Verri to argue in favour of economic freedom. In the economy at large, freedom meant the absence of privilege, corporations, and sumptuary laws. Privilege and corporations hindered economic development because they hampered competition and reduced the number of potential vendors, and hence supply.[10] Sumptuary laws had the dual effect of restricting both demand and supply. While the former was not necessarily bad (after all, national wealth was defined as the balance between supply and demand, and low demand was thus conducive to national wealth), the combination of low demand and supply would deprive the population of all incentives to increase production.[11] In sharp contrast with his early economic writings, Verri thus abandoned his old arguments in favour of state intervention. If he now saw room for intervention at all, it consisted in tearing down prohibitions and safeguarding freedom. The principal duty of government in economic matters was 'above all else to be active in destroying' privilege and trade restrictions as well as all obstacles that caused friction to the interplay of economic forces in their natural tendency towards equilibrium.[12]

That the mechanical law of economic equilibrium could lead to long-term prosperity was guaranteed by the introduction of money, which Verri regarded as instrumental in the birth of commercial society. Exchange of goods had always taken place, but in a non-monetary society it had been hampered by the absence of an objective measure of value (because human needs differed and so did the value perception they accorded to any

[8] Ibid. 33.

[9] Ibid. 27–8.

[10] Ibid. 37–8 and 46–7. On the critical reception of Verri's stance against government intervention (which was considered as not wide-ranging enough) in 19th-century Italian economic thought, see Giuseppe Bognetti, 'La teoria della finanza pubblica: il pensiero politico di Pietro Verri', in Alberto Quadrio Curzio (ed.), *Alle origini del pensiero economico in Italia*, ii: *Economia e istituzioni: il paradigma lombardo tra i secoli* XVIII *e* XIX (Bologna, 1996), 68–71.

[11] Verri, *Meditazioni sulla economia politica*, 48.

[12] Ibid. 118.

particular good that was offered for exchange) and by the fact that future desires could not be satisfied with the exchange of goods (because the goods received in return were often perishable).[13] The introduction of money overcame both obstacles. On the one hand, money as the universal measure helped to make the concept of value more objective because everybody used the same measure. On the other, commercial transactions no longer depended on the immediate desires of both parties because money could be stored to satisfy future desires. Following Hume's arguments for commercial society as civilized society, Verri argued that the introduction of money resulted in increased trade between nations and, as a direct consequence, the process of civilization.[14]

From Luxury and Consumption to Investment and Low Interest Rates

If economic freedom led to ever-rising levels of prosperity and equilibrium between demand and supply; if national wealth was determined by an increase in supply which could be used for export; and finally, if money played the central role of facilitating commerce, the question remained how exactly economic development was to be achieved. What was the key engine to drive economic development, and how could it be fuelled? The luxury debate had introduced the luxury trades and conspicuous consumption as engine and fuel. Verri himself had endorsed this view in the early 1760s when he argued in favour of an economy driven by consumption, propagated the incentive function of luxury goods, and presented luxury as the cornerstone of his economic model. In the *Meditazioni*, however, he overcame the focus on luxury. While he endorsed the beneficial economic effects of luxury that had been rehearsed for three decades in the European luxury debate, these were no longer the drivers of economic development. The new engine was money and the desire for profit; its fuel, low interest rates which led to productive investment.

One historian of economic thought has claimed that 'the thinkers of the Enlightenment' perceived consumption to lie at the heart of economic progress via the idea of productive consumption. According to this line of argument, the Enlightenment was the only moment in the history of economic thought when the idea of development was based on increased consumption of the productive class.[15] At first sight, contemporary accounts

[13] Verri, *Meditazioni sulla economia politica*, 19–20. [14] Ibid. 22.

[15] Cosimo Perrotta, 'Le teorie del consumo prima di Smith: dalla polemica sul lusso all'idea

seem to confirm such a contention. 'We all know', wrote Francesco Carpani in his treatise on the value of the Milanese lands, 'that the great wealth of a state . . . depends on the consumption of goods.' Carpani related this to the growth of the luxury market, 'which boosts the circulation of money more and more every day' and hence provided the money needed for consumption.[16] Giuseppe Biumi launched an even more outspoken defence of consumption in his brief *Piano di scienza politico economica*. 'Everything in the economic system begins and ends with spending', and 'the consumption of products . . . restores to the productive class the means of production'.[17]

Pietro Verri's *Meditazioni* challenged those standard accounts of the role of consumption in direct response to Cesare Beccaria's lectures on political economy. In the 'Considerazioni sul lusso', Verri had still been strongly in favour of consumption, which he perceived as increasing the market for luxury goods. His newly developed model called into question Beccaria's view on, as well as his own previous adherence to, consumption as the primary engine of economic development.

A change of tone can already be detected in Verri's assertion that 'at first sight, the consumers seem to be a useless burden for the state' because without them all produce could be exported. Even though consumption played a role as an incentive for landowners, a growing market was not created by the mass demand of consumers. Rather, *producers* (that is, landlords and manufacturers) received an incentive to increase productivity through their own quest for luxury goods. The increased supply would then generate consumer demand, rather than vice versa. Desires produced new needs, which provided a boost to manufacture, and incidentally caused growing consumption.[18] But internal consumption, it is important to note, was a *result* of profits from the export economy, not a spur to industry in its own right. Dismissing widespread consumption as a means to achieve economic growth, Verri thus adhered to a concept of luxury that had not been alien to mercantilist writers in the seventeenth century. The arguments in favour of luxury that he had expressed in *Il Caffè*, and which had been inspired by contemporary British and French thinking, had been relegated to second place at the expense of the model of an export-based economy in which luxury could play an economic role as an incentive only for a very restricted

di capitale umano', *Quaderni di storia dell'economia politica*, 6/3 (1988), 35–6. See also G. Beccattini, 'La posizione del consumo nel pensiero degli economisti classici', in *Scienza economica e trasformazioni sociali* (Florence, 1979), 143.

[16] Francesco Carpani, *Bilancio dello Stato col quale a priori si fa la dimostrazione del suo attivo commercio*, in *Economisti minori*, 115.

[17] Giuseppe Biumi, *Piano di scienza politico economica* (1773), in *Economisti minori*, 373.

[18] Verri, *Meditazioni sulla economia politica*, 79.

group of producer–consumers, the landowning class and manufacturers. What they needed were domestically produced luxuries (ideally also designed for export) rather than foreign luxury in order to keep the money supply in the country.

Verri supported his argument with the theoretical consideration that the aim of political economy was to increase the number of vendors or to decrease the number of consumers. What he meant was that the aim of political economy was to encourage foreign commerce, which could best be achieved through low prices. Low prices were guaranteed by competition on the supply side, and this implied either increasing the number of vendors or decreasing the number of consumers. Influenced by the debate about depopulation, Verri did not argue the case for a decrease in the number of consumers, but he did want to keep consumption constant in order to export excess products.[19] And the emphasis on the supply side is also the reason why Verri condemned sumptuary laws: not because they prevented the incentive mechanism to take root or because they had proved ineffective, as the standard arguments had it, but mainly because they restricted the supply side and effectively reduced the number of vendors.[20]

Verri thus attacked the conventional wisdom in favour of consumption from two sides, from a mercantilist stance in favour of foreign export and from an analysis of price mechanisms in the face of growing consumption. Both arguments still accepted the positive role of luxury as an incentive to production, but they no longer constituted the centrepiece of his model. The first step in the transition from the economic model based on luxury and consumption to his new concept of a supply-driven economy dependent on productive investment had thus been taken. The next step was the introduction of low interest rates as the key driver of investment.

The introduction of money had intensified commerce and facilitated an objective measure of value. At the same time, it had become the universal measure of prosperity and a store of potential wealth for future consumption for individuals and nations alike. The three means of employment of money were immediate spending for consumption, accumulation with the expectation of interest generation, and finally investment.

Consumption was necessary, as we have seen, but conceptually it did not contribute to the growth of 'annual reproduction', or rather public wealth.[21] The other two means were more promising, and Verri tied them into a general model of the drivers of savings and investment. Verri divided

[19] Verri, *Meditazioni sulla economia politica*, 40 and 76. On the population debate in Italy, see Gabriella Gioli (ed.), *Le teorie della popolazione prima di Malthus* (Milan, 1987).

[20] Verri, *Meditazioni sulla economia politica*, 72–3.

[21] Ibid. 23.

the subjects of his analysis into the group of those who already had money to deploy and those who sought money for investment. Starting from the theoretical premiss that active commerce would lead to a rising money supply, Verri postulated that it was part of human nature to employ one's money 'because to keep it in custody is a burden that only a few are prepared to carry for fear of losing it'. Savings were an option, but only so long as the high interest rates promised a sufficient return. However, the higher the money supply due to active commerce, the lower the interest rate because interest was defined as the price of money. In other words, just as a rising supply of any good at constant demand tended to reduce prices, so did interest rates go down with an increasing money supply. The practical consequence of low interest rates was that savings no longer guaranteed as high a return as other forms of employment, which Verri divided into agricultural and industrial investment.[22] Industrial investment was promising. In explicit rebuttal of physiocratic arguments that manufacture was sterile, Verri held that manufacture was prone to generate high returns because it created value above the combined cost of raw materials and the work employed. 'The artisan . . . is not only reimbursed for his consumption, but he obtains an additional portion, and that portion is new value created in the field of annual production.'[23] The employment of money in manufacture thus had a dually beneficial effect. On the one hand, it provided a higher return for an individual than savings in the context of a high money supply and low interest rates. On the other, the nation at large benefited from an increase in annual production and thus public wealth. Agricultural investment was equally beneficial. Low interest rates led to an increasing demand of land for agricultural production. New land would be made arable, produce would be increased, and both the individual landowner and the nation would benefit from increased annual production.[24]

If low interest rates proved an incentive to transfer savings into productive investment, they were equally beneficial for investors who sought money. In fact, low interest rates facilitated 'bigger enterprises both in commerce and in agriculture because the landowner and the manufacturer alike can borrow money more easily for bolder actions' and pay the interest from the return of their investment.[25] This is the origin of the capitalist notion of investment.

[22] Ibid. 56–7.

[23] Ibid. 23–4. *Pace* Franco Venturi's claim that Pietro Verri was deeply influenced by the ideas of physiocracy; cf. Venturi, *Italy and the Enlightenment: Studies in a Cosmopolitan Century*, ed. Stuart Woolf (London, 1972), 290.

[24] Verri, *Meditazioni sulla economia politica*, 56–7.

[25] Ibid. 57.

The attractiveness of investment as an alternative to savings only worked as long as interest rates were low. In commercial society with its rising money supply, this was normally the case (if government intervention did not distort the picture). But if interest rates were not low, this was the one area where state intervention was necessary through reducing the interest rate of the national bank, or rather 'the banks from which those who lend to the state receive their interest'. Additionally, political stability and the protection and enforcement of contracts reduced the risk of losing one's money. This, in turn, helped reduce interest rates, which was always a dual compensation for both the forfeit of returns from productive investment and the risk of the loss of savings through instability.[26]

In the *Meditazioni sulla economia politica* Verri had constructed an economic model that left his earlier economic writings behind. It was a model that deduced economic rules from a limited set of principles. And contrary to current claims, Verri no longer considered political economy as an exercise in moral and social science.[27] Inspired though his thought was by the moral impetus to better the situation of his compatriots in Lombardy, he deliberately distanced himself from previous accounts of political economy, which linked considerations of human nature, social status, moral needs, and political circumstance with economic principles. These still play into his treatise, but only as his motivation for the development of principles. 'Cold reason has convinced me', Verri wrote, 'to further the well-being of mankind not with the language of sentiment, but with a tranquil analysis of things, [which] shows the identity of common interest' with private interest.[28] Verri's economic treatise paved the way for a separation of moral and economic science, a separation that was to gain wide acceptance only in the nineteenth century.

This parting of ways also helps to explain why Verri abandoned the concept of luxury as the cornerstone of economic development, and why a chapter on luxury is missing in Verri's entire work—contrary to most other treatises on political economy of the time. The economic benefits of luxury (that it provided an incentive to produce, that it employed excess labour, and that it facilitated the circulation of money) were well accepted by the time Verri wrote the *Meditazioni*. The moral arguments were less easily digestible, especially after the moral debate had been rekindled by Rousseau.

[26] Verri, *Meditazioni sulla economia politica*, 58–61.

[27] Bognetti, 'La teoria della finanza pubblica', 87–8; Pier Luigi Porta and Roberto Scazzieri, 'Il contributo di Pietro Verri alla teoria economica', in *Pietro Verri e il suo tempo: quaderni di Acme*, 35 (1999), 813–52.

[28] Verri, *Meditazioni sulla economia politica*, 81.

But Verri no longer had a need to engage in the debate. He accepted luxury (in fact, the desire to indulge in luxury was 'natural') and rescued its public benefits (by acknowledging the incentive function for landed gentry to intensify agriculture), but he subordinated it to what made wealth grow: the accumulation of money and its productive investment driven by low interest rates.[29]

Within the wider context of the republic of letters Verri had found a way out of a luxury debate that looked increasingly as if it had reached an impasse. In France, Saint-Lambert had written his essay on luxury for the *Encyclopédie* after Verri's first economic writings had appeared in print, and a few years before Verri developed his new economic model in the *Meditazioni sulla economia politica.* Verri took seriously Saint-Lambert's position that the recent discussion about luxury had been misplaced because the moral language of needs and necessities was too ambiguous to allow for a clear-cut answer about the value of luxury. Saint-Lambert's solution had been to focus on the *political* preconditions for economic development rather than on luxury as the guarantor of wealth. Verri's approach was different. He accepted Saint-Lambert's warning and refused to engage in a moral evaluation of luxury. At the same time he followed the physiocratic lead of considering luxury in purely *economic* terms, not least because of the Milanese context of enlightened absolutism in which he wrote. But whereas the physiocrats had struggled to make economic sense of luxury and combine it with the notion of investment, Verri eventually got rid of luxury as the engine of economic development altogether. He had realized that the debate had run out of steam, and had determined to leave it behind.

A New Language of Political Economy

Both Pietro Verri and Cesare Beccaria introduced new theories of economic development into the Italian discussion—the concept of savings, productive investment, and the pivotal role of the cost of money for Verri; 'capitalist agriculture' and the division of labour in a demand-driven economy for Beccaria. But they not only furthered the understanding of the mechanisms underlying economic development. They also helped develop a language in which these mechanisms were to be expressed, a language which Cesare Beccaria called the 'new language of economic reason'.[30]

[29] Ibid. 112 and 79.

[30] Cesare Beccaria, *Prolusione letta il giorno 9 Gennaio 1769 nell'apertura della nuova cattedra di scienze camerali nelle scuole palatine di Milano*, in Beccaria, *Opere*, 376.

Pietro Verri's attempts at systematization, the postulation of principles of political economy, and the deductive method in extracting economic rules from general principles are one strand of this new approach. The other strand was provided by Cesare Beccaria's mathematical approach to political economy, which allowed him to show 'how the science of economics can be considered analytically'.[31]

In 1764 Beccaria had developed a language of mathematics which he later applied to his economic writings. In an article in *Il Caffè* he calculated the probability of winning a popular game of chance, Il Faraone, a simple card game where players put money on specific card values similar to today's roulette. The bank then draws two cards at a time, one bank card (*carte de face*) and one for the players (*carte anglaise*). If the player had put money on the *carte de face*, he loses. If on the *carte anglaise*, he wins. The bank's advantage comes from two special cases, a 'pair', or *doppio* (where both cards drawn have the same value and the bank wins half the players' bet), and the last card drawn, or *nulla* (where the players cannot win). Now, Beccaria calculated the probability of the occurrence of those two special cases because they determine the bank's long-term advantage, which he quantified at about 5 per cent. While interest in probability theory was widespread in the Enlightenment, and while Beccaria drew on French precedent for his analysis, his approach claimed novelty.[32] His aim was to translate the algebraic treatment of probabilities into 'common language... so that any man of common sense can understand it'.[33] The concern to make the language of mathematics intelligible and thus applicable more widely was to guide Beccaria's approach to mathematics in all his later writings. He did so first by establishing the general mathematical rules in a limited case (four cards in the case of Il Faraone, two merchants in his later account of the development of prices in a free market), and then by applying those basic rules to a more complex environment. This method of beginning analysis with a limited number of factors or players is the foundation of undergraduate teaching in economics to this day.

From probability theory and card games it was but a short step to mathematics and the economy. In fact, in a new article of the same year Beccaria introduced differential calculus for an analysis of import taxes.

[31] Beccaria, 'Tentativo analitico su i contrabbandi', in *Il Caffè*, i. 174.

[32] Pierre Remond de Montmort, *Essai d'analyse sur les jeux de hazard* (Paris, 1708), which Beccaria explicitly acknowledged in his article. For probability theory in the 18th century, the classic account is Lorraine Daston, *Classical Probability in the Enlightenment* (Princeton, 1988; repr. 1995).

[33] Beccaria, 'Il Faraone', in *Il Caffè*, i. 18–26: 19.

His example is smuggling, and the hypothetical break-even point for smugglers who risk the confiscation of part of their merchandise. In other words (and at a given import tax to be evaded by the smuggler) how large a portion of his merchandise must he smuggle in order not to make a loss even if the remaining part is confiscated? By an exercise in differential calculus, Beccaria shows that the portion needed to smuggle diminishes exponentially the higher the import tax. Put more simply, the higher the tax, the lower the risk to the smuggler and the bigger his incentive to evade. Beccaria does not offer a practical solution to the problem he had raised (which would consist in penalties on sequestered goods rather than pure confiscation of the merchandise). But he did give an example of a mathematical-analytical approach to 'the science of economics'.[34]

In Beccaria's account of the development of equilibrium prices in his lectures on political economy, he partially put his call for a mathematical language of political economy in practice. As he had done in Il Faraone, Beccaria presented the general rules of the formation of prices in a free market by means of a limited case example. In a market made up of three players, *A*, *B*, and *C*, who have different quantities of produce to trade, the value relation between the produce will result out of simple arithmetic calculation. If *A* has 12 units of grain, *B* has 6 units of wine, and *C* 9, then for *A* and *B*, the value of 2 units of grain would be 1 unit of wine, whereas for *A* and *C*, the value would be 1½. The resulting average 'price' of 2 units of grain would be 1¼. Beccaria then proceeded to extend this principle to a more complex market situation.[35]

In terms of the level of mathematics, this is of course a far cry from his previous exercise in differential calculus. But Beccaria's students to whom the lectures were addressed were not up to the task of digesting complex formulae. In fact, in the outline of his lectures Beccaria had stated that it was useless to present an abstract science to his students as 'this would be useful for a few bright minds' but not for those who need to be trained as public administrators.[36] Secondly, and more importantly, Beccaria himself still oscillated between two languages, the mathematical 'language of economic reason' on the one hand, and the Epicurean and utilitarian language of pleasure and pain on the other.[37] The Epicurean language goes back to Beccaria's first works, and in fact ties together all his philosophical works. The same account of human nature (as ultimately driven by the desire to

[34] Beccaria, 'Tentativo analitico', 173–5.
[35] Beccaria, *Elementi di pubblica economia*, 557–60.
[36] Beccaria, *Piano d'istruzioni*, 342.
[37] For the term *linguaggio della ragione economica*, see Beccaria, *Prolusione*, 375.

search pleasure and to avoid pain) is present in his legal, stylistic, and economic studies.[38] But his political economy is closer to the 'language of economic reason' than he himself may have cared to admit. Even though he could not put the new language to the test in his lectures because of the needs and capabilities of his students, he had taken a major step in the formulation of a new way to explain the economy and had inspired others to follow his lead.

Pietro Verri had postulated that the price of a product depended on the number of buyers and the number of vendors. His collaborator at the *Caffè* journal Paolo Frisi translated the axiom into Beccaria's language. If, as Verri had argued, the price P was proportional to the number of consumers C and inversely proportional to the number of vendors V, then $P = C/V$.[39]

Beccaria had proven the force of the new language in the application of differential calculus to the issue of smuggling. Paolo Frisi's translation of Verri's price theory into a mathematical formula shows that its clarity and simplicity proved tempting for political economists in Lombardy. Working separately, Beccaria and Verri had developed a new language of political economy. Both Verri's systematization and Beccaria's mathematical approach mark an advance in economic thinking. Verri in particular had achieved this by leaving the question of luxury behind. And when Beccaria explained luxury, he used the Epicurean language of pleasure and pain and not his 'new language of economic reason'. The debate that had helped them sharpen their thoughts on the economy and on 'the happiness of a nation' over the preceding years could no longer answer the new questions they had set themselves. Luxury had indeed become—as Melon had claimed at the beginning of the century—'the object of too many vague declarations'.

[38] Beccaria, *On Crimes and Punishments*, 21 and 157; *Ricerche attorno alla nature dello stile*, in Beccaria, *Opere*, 297–8; 'On Luxury', in Beccaria, *On Crimes and Punishments*, 163.

[39] Paolo Frisi, *Estratto del saggio sulla teoria della moneta del general Lloyd*, in *Scrittori classici*, xvii. 369–83, esp. pp. 375 and 378–9, where Frisi devised a similar formula for Verri's definition of the interest rate (I) as related to the number of borrowers (B) and lenders (O): $I = B/O$. Interestingly, Verri knew about, but did not take up, Lloyd's mathematical language; see ibid. 369–71.

Conclusion

Luxury and Public Happiness

The notion of luxury in Europe changed over the course of the eighteenth century. Across Europe old moral notions were increasingly replaced by new economic considerations. While this was true for Britain, France, and Germany alike, Italy offered some resistance to this trend. The Italian language added new meanings to the term without ever replacing previous notions. Some thinkers may have complained about this vagueness, but it points to something typical of the Italian Enlightenment. It provided sufficient linguistic breadth to develop debate in different, and sometimes indeed opposed, directions. The very reluctance, linguistically, to narrow down concepts such as 'luxury' offered the possibility to interpret them from different standpoints; in our case, from the position of enlightened Catholicism (as in the case of Muratori), from the moral standpoint of parish priests engaged in the quest both for economic development and for the saving of the soul (as in the case of Paoletti in Tuscany), and from the vantage point of a new analytical approach to economics (as in the case of the Milanese Enlightenment). At the same time, it allowed Italian thinkers to absorb the most varying trends of European debate into their discussion.

Across Europe luxury had long been treated as a moral issue. Only in the eighteenth century did the emphasis change. No longer reproachable or only justifiable politically as a means to demonstrate authority through pomp and splendour, luxury became the driving force of modern commercial society because it provided an incentive to work. What was originally, at the hands of Bernard Mandeville, a dilemma between moral vice and economic benefit soon became an exclusively economic concept in its transmission to France by Jean-François Melon. Similarly, the physiocrats around Quesnay, Mirabeau, and Baudeau chose to treat luxury as a purely economic phenomenon. Debate moved back, it is true, from the economy to the polity and the moral effects of luxury with Montesquieu and Rousseau. But in Italy this development received far less attention than might have been expected. When Cesare Beccaria reached the end of his lectures on political economy, he went back to the question Montesquieu had linked to the luxury debate: whether the nobility should be allowed to trade. This was a question full of 'moral, political, and economic considerations, and would require a long discussion'. But for Beccaria, the professor of political economy, this was beside the point. Economically (and this is what counted) the issue was easily solved. To ban the nobility from commerce would reduce competition. But all his teachings on political economy boiled down to the fact that this was detrimental to the economy. 'Hence economically speaking it is damaging to exclude the nobility from commerce.'[1] Montesquieu's long discussion of the political role of luxury had been brushed aside and solved in a handful of lines. Beccaria had indeed adhered to his self-imposed task 'to consider luxury economically'.

Italian debate was most at ease with the economic aspect of luxury for several reasons, mostly relating to local traditions, political circumstances, and pressing economic needs. But an important intellectual reason is the fact that Melon's economic treatment of luxury (and not, for example, Mandeville's morally ambiguous account) had been transmitted into Italy by the champion of the Catholic Enlightenment, Ludovico Antonio Muratori. His summary of Melon's chapter on luxury had made the English paradox known on the peninsula, but Muratori had done more to it. He incorporated it into his edifice of enlightened Catholicism with its emphasis on the social function of religion. From Muratori onwards Catholics accepted the Augustinian reading of luxury as necessary to the working of society and had put it to the service of public happiness. The economy was vital, but economic activity derived from a Christian impetus.

In Tuscany the development of political economy allowed for an accommodation of new economic theories into Catholic thinking. Tuscany is rightly famed for the reforms that were carried out under the rule of Peter Leopold, and Italian historiography has been at pains to demonstrate the various aspects of reform. What is often overlooked in this focus on action rather than thought is the transmission of ideas in an increasingly public culture, and the interplay between European thought and local tradition in the development of indigenous thought. Eighteenth-century Tuscany was more influenced by physiocracy than any other region in Italy. This was true on the level of government action (Peter Leopold turned physiocratic principles into legislation in the 1760s), and it is equally true for the thought of Tuscan political economists. But this was not because they 'naturally had a physiocratic mentality', as has been claimed, but rather because they found Tuscan precedent in French physiocratic teachings.[2] In fact, few theories would have seemed more genuinely 'Tuscan' in the second half of

[1] Cesare Beccaria, *Elementi di pubblica economia*, in Beccaria, *Opere*, ed. Sergio Romagnoli (Florence, 1958), i. 647–8.

[2] Norbert Jonard, 'Le Problème du luxe en Italie au XVIIIe siècle', *Revue des études italiennes*, 15 (1969), 295–321.

the eighteenth century than physiocracy as developed by Mirabeau. The reason for this similarity of minds lies in the legacy of Sallustio Bandini. Not only had the Sienese writer founded economic thought in Tuscany at the beginning of the eighteenth century and influenced all major thinkers and administrators in the course of the century. He was also—through his connection with Pierre de Boisguilbert (himself later hailed as the 'true and only precursor of physiocracy')—an early transmitter of pre-physiocratic thinking into the grand duchy. When physiocracy came of age around the middle of the century, it was easily adaptable to Tuscan thought, which had already developed in a similar direction in the vein of Bandini's teachings.

When French physiocratic thinking was transmitted into the grand duchy, the channels were typical of the Enlightenment, and indeed this is a period where it may not be too far-fetched to speak of a proper Tuscan Enlightenment. Florence was the capital city of Italian journalism, and review sections in widely read journals complemented personal networks in providing access to the most recent thinking. Inspiration from outside was complemented by change from within, which paved the way towards a more open, public culture. On the one hand, academies—which had traditionally been strong in Tuscany—gained importance in the formulation of policy. The head of the regency, for example, drew on the region's most famous agricultural academy, the Accademia dei Georgofili, as a pool of intellect to sharpen legislative projects. On the other hand, the growth of journalism provided a new forum for debate. Around the middle of the century articles in learned journals replaced ministerial memorandums as channels to propose reform. If Bandini's economic work had circulated in manuscript form among the members of the administration, discussion of his ideas was now carried out in the *Novelle letterarie*. The new forum allowed a new group of thinkers to participate in debate. No longer the preserve of administrators, economic thinking was discovered by parish priests who combined a practical approach to agriculture with a Muratorian emphasis on the Christian aspect of economic activity, which brought moral considerations back into the discussion. But, and this is the effect not only of Bandini's overpowering heritage but also of the stream of French economic writings that reached Tuscany through its journals, the language in which these concepts were expressed was no longer solely the Christian language of the moral ambiguity of luxury. Rather, parish priests accepted the battlefield on which the debate about luxury was now carried out—the realm of production and consumption, of incentives and gain.

If the language of political economy in Italy nevertheless continued to oscillate between the language of moral philosophy and an increasingly independent language of the economy, Lombardy made the most significant step in bringing about a parting of the ways. At first sight this seems paradoxical, because the most profound thinkers continued to stray beyond disciplinary boundaries, and even their most explicitly economic contributions were still part of a broader science of society. But they began to separate the various parts of this science and increasingly isolated economic phenomena in explicitly economic writings. The languages they used—and the models they proposed—to explain those phenomena were different from what had been done before. On the level of presentation Pietro Verri offered a systematic account of economics founded on general principles and the deductive method. On a conceptual level he introduced the ideas of savings, productive investment, and the interest rate as the central drivers of the economy, which replaced his previous emphasis on luxury as the engine of economic development. This new model was more than an advance in economic theory. It was also a contribution to a luxury debate that increasingly looked as if it had reached an impasse. Verri had absorbed the European discussion in his early writings and he had set the tone for debate in Lombardy by writing about the economic benefits of luxury and its role in cultural refinement. By 1770 the *economic* benefits of luxury were well accepted across Europe, but the article on luxury in the *Encyclopédie* had shown that the *moral* value of luxury was too ambiguous to allow for generalization. Verri thus refrained from considering the moral side of the argument in his mature work on political economy. Unlike physiocratic thinkers in France, who had done the same but were still struggling to tie luxury into their overall framework of the economy, Verri accepted the economic benefits of luxury, but he removed it as the cornerstone of economic development. The debate had run out of steam. Verri saw this, and decided to leave it behind.

Verri and Beccaria's decision to treat luxury predominantly as an economic phenomenon points to a general claim about the nature of the Milanese Enlightenment—the centrality of economic thought. Within Italian Enlightenment historiography, economic thought has received only limited attention. And even the historians of eighteenth-century Lombardy are by and large still more interested in Beccaria's legal philosophy and Verri's political thought than in their economic models.[3] There are good reasons, however, why political economy should have been the central concern of a large part of the Milanese Enlightenment. A declining

[3] An exception are the proceedings of the Milanese conference on Verri in 1997, where Verri's economic thought (mainly his contribution to monetary debates) does receive attention (Carlo Capra (ed.), *Quaderni di Acme*, 35: *Pietro Verri e il suo tempo* (1999), vol. ii).

economy and a shift towards agriculture in a competitive European environment imposed an overriding interest in economic development in Lombardy, Tuscany, and Naples alike. But in Lombardy in particular, the economy was the one field in which the group of idealists around Pietro Verri and Cesare Beccaria could hope to yield influence. Economic policy was an area of devolved government (in fact, Vienna left the Lombard administration considerable freedom in economic matters from 1765 onwards), whereas political and administrative reform had been monopolized in, and was anxiously guarded by, Vienna. This not only explains why Pietro Verri censored the contributions to *Il Caffè* and cut out all direct references to the political rule of the Habsburg monarchy. It also explains why he opted for the economy as the playing field on which he could be heard. What is more, the economy was a new field to conquer. The generation which had dominated public life in Lombardy until the 1760s and 1770s was trained in jurisprudence and made this the centre of intellectual enquiry. As Pietro Verri remarked in a late account of his career: 'A bit of Latin, a dreamy theology, pedantic and trivial jurisprudence: these are the only studies that were being praised; the rest was the object of hatred or ridicule.'[4]

There was thus a triple reason for the focus on political economy: it addressed the region's most pressing needs, it offered a safe route to influence without infringing on Habsburg prerogatives, and it provided a claim to power against the previous generation. To bypass the generation of his father was especially dear to Pietro Verri, who led the turn to the economy. Most thinkers of the Milanese Enlightenment followed him in this lead.

'Cultures of Enlightenment' in Regional Context

Such pronounced regional differences across the peninsula point to a wider characteristic of eighteenth-century Italy, the relationship between the cosmopolitan and the local in enlightened thought. The question whether the intellectual outlook of Italy was cosmopolitan *or* local is, I believe, beside the point. It was both. The questions that occupied the minds of thinkers from Milan to Naples were drawn from the European republic of letters. The answers they gave were different, and they depended on local intellectual traditions as much as on socio-economic circumstances.

[4] Pietro Verri, *Memoria del conte Pietro Verri in cui si espongono i motivi per i quail venne impiegato e poi dopo vent'anni congedato*, quoted in Domenico Sella and Carlo Capra, *Il Ducato di Milano dal 1535 al 1796* (Turin, 1984), 351.

Eighteenth-century Italy was an age of cosmopolitanism (Pietro Verri was most anxious to participate in a European debate and to gain 'a European name'); it was an age of reason (Cesare Beccaria made this the guiding light of his work on crimes and punishment); it was an age of reform (with the liberalization of the grain trade in Tuscany and the end of Church influence in state affairs in Lombardy); and it was an age that sought to make moral sense of modern commercial society (with Antonio Genovesi's lectures on political economy). But the local needs that determined the course of discussion across the peninsula did not lead to the development of one coherent Italian Enlightenment, but to distinct cultures of enlightenment in regional context. Despite instances of cross-fertilization it is astonishing that the Italian enlightenments existed largely in parallel, often unaware of, or uninterested in, what happened across the regional borders. In many respects, David Hume's Scotland was closer to the Milanese Enlightenment than Tuscan thought, which was developed only a few hundred miles away. At the same time, however, the Milanese Enlightenment was much more concerned with concrete matters and practical applicability. The major exponents of the Accademia dei Pugni ended their careers as administrators, and the economic debate between Beccaria and Verri demonstrates that their emphasis ultimately lay on wealth rather than virtue.[5]

Tuscany was a different case altogether. The region combined the tradition of the Catholic Enlightenment and physiocratic influence. In the last respect, it can be compared to France in the 1760s, when physiocracy dominated economic thought. But Tuscany is a case of its own, not least because it eschewed dogmatism even at the peak of physiocratic influence in the 1760s and 1770s. Influenced by theology, conscious of the specificity of its region, and particularly open to landowner interest, Tuscany symbolized what Luciano Guerci has called 'the other eighteenth century' more than other regions in Italy. The Tuscan and Lombard examples show how those regional differences can be explained. Tuscans did not 'naturally' have 'a physiocratic mentality'. Rather, the development of their thought was influenced by a local intellectual tradition that differentiated them from their Lombard colleagues. Similarly, the fact that the Tuscan elite was received much more warmly into the administration led them to gravitate towards areas where they could make a difference (such as the reform of colonial contracts and free-trade policy). Further north, dependency on Habsburg goodwill excluded political nonconformism, just as the need to

[5] For Scotland, see Istvan Hont and Michael Ignatieff (eds.), *Wealth and Virtue: The Shaping of Political Economy in the Scottish Enlightenment* (Cambridge, 1983).

differentiate from the old generation of jurists made political economy seem the most promising enterprise.

If we study the Enlightenment through its 'big texts' alone (and this is still the predominant approach in the history of economics), we lose much of its riches. Not only do we miss the intellectual context in which ideas developed, debate occurred, and themes were chosen or rejected. We also miss the local contexts, which have proved so powerful in determining the course of debates. All this is not to say that we should return to a political history of the Italian states (as Mario Mirri can be taken to argue). But it does mean that the understanding of the Enlightenment as a cosmopolitan enterprise remains incomplete unless we locate the local adaptation of cosmopolitan themes and seek to understand the regional needs and traditions which account for so much of the specific course of debate. It is a call to explain Italian intellectual life in the eighteenth century by means of distinct 'cultures of enlightenment' in regional context.

But regardless of all regional differences and regardless of different intellectual needs, there are common themes that occupied thinkers from the Dolomites to the southern tip of the peninsula. One of those, and perhaps one of the most pronounced, was the quest to find a new language in which the economic reality could be explained and economic development fostered. This language differed according to local circumstances (from an oscillation between moral philosophy and the language of commerce in Naples, to an attempt to unite the Catholic Enlightenment with physiocracy in Tuscany, and to the development of a systematic and analytical language of 'the science of economics' in Lombardy). But the underlying concerns were similar across all regions. The *Giornale de' letterati di Pisa* had stated in 1771 that public virtue and reason of state were things of the past, and that now was the age of the economy. Ludovico Antonio Muratori had argued that the chief concern of enlightened Catholicism was national wealth, or 'public happiness'. Thinkers across Italy were devoted increasingly to this theme. More than simply an 'age of reform', the eighteenth century was also an age of intellectual projects, and chief among these was to foster economic development and to put luxury at the service of 'public happiness'.

BIBLIOGRAPHY

Abbreviations

Economia, istituzioni, cultura	Aldo de Maddalena, Ettore Rotelli, and Gennaro Barbarisi (eds.), *Economia, istituzioni, cultura nell'età di Maria Teresa*, 3 vols. (Bologna, 1982).
Economisti minori	C. A. Vianello (ed.), *Economisti minori del Settecento lombardo* (Milan, 1942).
Illuministi italiani	Franco Venturi *et al.* (eds.), *Illuministi italiani*, 3 vols. in 6 pts., 2nd edn. (Milan, 1997–8).
Scrittori classici	Piero Custodi (ed.), *Scrittori classici italiani di economia Politica* (Milan, 1804).

Primary Sources

Texts and Treatises

ADAMI, ANTONIO FILIPPO, *Della necessità di accrescere e migliorare l'agricoltura nella Toscana: discorso letto in una adunanza dell'Accademia dei Georgofili 4/11/1767* (Florence, 1768).

ALDOVRANDI MARISCOTTI, CARLO FILIPPO, *Il lusso è la moneta de' poveri: dissertazione* ([Bologna, 1793]).

ANON., 'Brevi e generali riflessioni di un Inglese sopra il commercio della sua nazione', *Magazzino toscano d'istruzione e di piacere*, 1 (1754), 424–32.

ANON., *Sopra lo studio dell'agricoltura con un saggio sull'agricoltura logigiana*, in *Economisti minori*, 196–212.

Antichità illustrata, per mezzo di dissertazioni, tanto edite quanto inedite, ovvero, introduzione generale allo studio dell'antichità (Florence, 1743).

BANDINI, SALLUSTIO, *Discorso sopra la Maremma di Siena*, ed. L. Conenna Bonelli, in George R. F. Baker, *Sallustio Bandini* (Florence, 1978), 219–96.

BAUDEAU, NICOLAS, 'Du luxe et des lois somptuaires', *Éphémérides du citoyen, ou, Bibliothèque raisonnée des sciences morales et politiques*, 1 (Paris, 1767), 171–234.

—— *Principes de la science morale et politique sur le luxe et les lois somptuaires* (1767), ed. A. Dubois (Paris, 1912).

BECCARIA, CESARE, *Dei delitti e delle pene. Con una raccolta di lettere e documenti relativi alla nascita dell'opera e alla sua fortuna nell'Europa del Settecento*, ed. Franco Venturi, 2nd edn. (Turin, 1994).

—— *Elementi di pubblica economia*, in Beccaria, *Opere*, ed. Sergio Romagnoli (Florence, 1958), 379–649.

BECCARIA, CESARE, 'Frammento sugli odori', in *Il Caffè, 1764–1766*, ed. Gianni Francioni and Sergio Romagnoli, 2nd edn. (Turin, 1998), i. 39–47.

—— 'Il Faraone', in *Il Caffè, 1764–1766*, ed. Gianni Francioni and Sergio Romagnoli, 2nd edn. (Turin, 1998), i. 18–26.

—— *On Crimes and Punishments and Other Writings*, ed. Richard Bellamy. (Cambridge, 1995).

—— 'On Luxury', in Beccaria, *On Crimes and Punishments and Other Writings*, ed. Richard Bellamy (Cambridge, 1995), 161–9.

—— *Opere*, ed. Sergio Romagnoli (Florence, 1958).

—— *Piano delle lezioni di pubblica economia che si danno nello spazio di due anni dal professore di questa scienza*, in Beccaria, *Opere*, ed. Sergio Romagnoli (Florence, 1958), i. 350–8.

—— *Piano d'istruzioni per la cattedra di scienze camerali o sia di economia civile* (1768), in Beccaria, *Opere*, ed. Sergio Romagnoli (Florence, 1958), i. 341–9.

—— *Prolusione letta il giorno 9 Gennaio 1769 nell'apertura della nuova cattedra di scienze camerali nelle scuole palatine di Milano*, in Beccaria, *Opere*, ed. Sergio Romagnoli (Florence, 1958), i. 361–77.

—— *Ricerche attorno alla nature dello stile*, in Beccaria, *Opere*, ed. Sergio Romagnoli (Florence, 1958), i. 201–336.

—— 'Tentativo analitico su i contrabbandi', in *Il Caffè, 1764–1766*, ed. Gianni Francioni and Sergio Romagnoli, 2nd edn (Turin, 1998), i. 173–5.

BERTRAND, JEAN, *Essai de la législation pour encourager l'agriculture, la population, les manufactures & le commerce*, in *Mémoires et observations recuiliés par la Société œconomique de Berne* (Berne, 1765), pp. xv–139.

—— *Saggio nel quale si esamina qual debba essere la legislazione per incoraggiare l'agricoltura e per favorire in rapporto a questa la popolazione, le manifatture ed il commercio*, trans. and comm. Giuseppe Pelli Bencivenni (Venice, 1767).

BIFFI, GIAMBATTISTA, *Cose notabili accadute in Cremona dal 1° Ottobre 1777 al 24 Ottobre 1781*, in *Illuministi italiani*, 1, i. 409–15.

BIUMI, GIUSEPPE, *Piano di scienza politico economica* (1773), in *Economisti minori*, 367–89.

BOISGUILBERT, PIERRE DE, *Dissertation de la nature des richesses, de l'argent et des tributes, où l'on découvre la fausse idée qui règne dans le monde à l'égard de ces trois articles* (1704), in *Pierre de Boisguilbert, ou, La Naissance de l'économie politique*, 2 vols. (Paris, 1966), ii. 973–1012.

—— *Factum de la France*, in Eugène Daire (ed.), *Économistes financiers du XVIIIe siècle* (1843).

—— *Le Détail de la France: La Cause de la diminution de ses biens, et la facilité du remède, en fournissant en un mois tout l'argent dont le Roi a besoin, et enrichissant tout le monde* (1696–1707 edn.), in *Pierre de Boisguilbert, ou, La Naissance de l'économie politique*, 2 vols. (Paris, 1966), ii. 581–662.

—— *Mémoire sur les blés et les liqueurs* (1705?), in *Pierre de Boisguilbert, ou, La Naissance de l'économie politique*, 2 vols. (Paris, 1966), i. 411–12.

BORGOGNINI, ANTON MARIA, *Dell'utilità delle mode* (Siena, 1777).

BROGGIA, CARLO ANTONIO, *Memoria ad oggetto di varie politiche ed economiche ragioni* (Naples, 1754), in Rafaelle Ajello, Marino Berengo, *et al.* (eds.), *Dal Muratori al Cesarotti*, v: *Politici ed economisti del primo Settecento* (Milan, 1978), 1038–59.

—— *Trattato dei tributi* (1743), in *Scrittori classici*, 45, 13–299.

BUONARROTI, MICHELANGELO, 'Sul lusso dei contadini: memoria letta il dì 7 gennaio 1821', *Atti della Reale ed Imperiale Accademia dei Georgofili*, C.4 (1825), 220–32.

BUTEL-DUMONT, GEORGE-MARIE, *Théorie du luxe, ou, Traité dans lequel on entreprend d'établir que le luxe est un ressort non-seulement utile, mais même indispensablement nécessaire à la prosperité des États* (1771).

CAMINER TURRA, ELISABETTA, 'Una discussione sul lusso all'Academia Olimpica di Vicenza', in *Giornale enciclopedico* (Oct. 1781), in Marino Berengo (ed.), *Giornali veneziani del Settecento* (Milan, 1962), 478–80.

CANTILLON, RICHARD, *Essai sur la nature du commerce en général* (1755; repr. Boston, 1892).

CARLI, GIANRINALDO, *Della disugualianza fisica morale civile fra gli uomini ossia ragionammento sopra l'opera di Rousseau 'Discours sur l'origine & les fondamens de l'inégalité parmi les hommes'*, in Carli, *Opere*, 19 vols. (Milan, 1784), xix. 97–238.

—— *Riflessi sul libero commercio de' Grani* (1771), in Gianrinaldo Carli, *Opere*, 19 vols. (Milan, 1784), i. 101–48.

—— *Saggio politico ed economico sopra la Toscana fatto nell'anno 1757*, in Carli, *Opere*, 19 vols. (Milan, 1784), i. 336–67.

CARPANI, FRANCESCO, *Bilancio dello Stato col quale a priori si fa la dimostrazione del suo attivo commercio*, in *Economisti minori*, 93–144.

CARY, JOHN, *Storia del commercio della Gran Bretagna . . . con un ragionamento sul commercio in universale e alcune annotazioni riguardanti l'economia del nostro Regno di Antonio Genovesi*, trans. Antonio Genovesi, 3 vols. (Naples, 1757 [1758]).

CICERO, *Pro Murena*, trans. C. MacDonald (London, 1977).

CONDILLAC, ÉTIENNE BONNOT DE, *Œuvres philosophiques*, ed. G. Le Roy (Paris, 1948).

CORONA, NICOLA, *Riflessioni sullo Stato pontificio*, in *Illuministi italiani*, iii/2. 685–717.

D'ARCO, GIAMBATTISTA GHERARDO, *Dell'armonia politico-economica tra la città e il suo territorio*, in *Scrittori classici*, 30. 50–106.

—— *Risposta al quesito stato proposto della R. Accademia di Mantova: se in uno stato di terreno fertile faorir debbasi maggiormente l'estrazione delle materie prime ovvero quella delle manifatture* (Florence, 1780).

DE GIULIANI, ANTONIO, *Saggio politico sopra le vicissitudini inevitabili delle società civili*, in *Illuministi italiani*, i/2. 676–91.

DIDEROT, DENIS, *Correspondance*, ed. Georges Roth (Paris, 1955–70).

—— *Mémoires pour Cathérine II: Du luxe* (1773–4), ed. Paul Vernière (Paris, 1964).

DORIA, PAOLO MATTIA, *Del commercio del Regno di Napoli* (1740), in Enrico Vidal (ed.), *Il pensiero civile di Paolo Mattia Doria negli scritti inediti: con il testo del manoscritto 'Del commercio del Regno di Napoli'* (Milan, 1953), 159–229.

FILANGIERI, GAETANO, *La scienza della legislazione* (1780; rev. 1781), 3 vols. (Milan, 1822).

FORBONNAIS, FRANÇOIS VÉRON DE, *Elemens du commerce*, 2 vols. (1754).

FRANCI, SEBASTIANO, 'Dell'agricoltura: Dialogo', in *Il Caffè, 1764–1766*, ed. Gianni Francioni and Sergio Romagnoli, 2nd edn. (Turin, 1998), i. 60–72.

—— 'Osservazioni sulla questione se il commercio corrompa i costumi e la morale', in *Il Caffè, 1764–1766*, ed. Gianni Francioni and Sergio Romagnoli, 2nd edn. (Turin, 1998), ii. 655–61.

FRISI, PAOLO, *Estratto del saggio sulla teoria della moneta del general Lloyd*, in *Scrittori classici*, xvii. 369–83.

GALIANI, FERDINANDO, *Della moneta libri cinque* (Naples, 1750 [1751]).

—— *Dialogues sur le commerce des bleds* (1770), ed. Fausto Nicolini (Milan, 1959).

GALLARATI, GIAMBATTISTA, *Riflessioni sulla coltivazione delle brughiere* (1768), in *Economisti minori*, 173–95.

GALLIZIOLI, FILIPPO, 'Sul servizio personale dei contadini. Memoria . . . letta nell'adunanza de' 2 maggio 1830', in *Atti della Reale ed Imperiale Accademia dei Georgofili*, C.8 (1830), 109–18.

GENOVESI, ANTONIO, *Delle lezioni di commercio o sia d'economia civile*, 2 vols. (Naples, 1765, 1767; 2nd edn. Milan, 1768).

—— *Dialoghi morali inediti*, Biblioteca Nazionale, Naples, MS XIV-8-39; repr. in Lucio Villari, *Il pensiero economico di Antonio Genovesi* (Florence, 1958), 138–86.

GERDIL, CARDINAL HYACINTHE SIGISMOND, *Discours de la nature, et des effets du luxe* (Turin, 1768).

—— *L'immaterialité de l'âme demontrée contre m. Locke par les même principes, par lesquels ce philosophe démontre l'existence & l'immaterialité de Dieu, avec des nouvelles preuves de l'immaterialité de Dieu, et de l'âme, tirées de l'Ecriture, des pères & de la raison* (Turin, 1747).

GIANNI, FRANCESCO MARIA, *Meditazione sulle teorie e sulla pratica delle imposizioni e tasse pubbliche* (1786), in *Raccolta degli economisti toscani, scritti di pubblica economia di F. M. Gianni* (Florence, 1848), i. 9–53.

—— *Memorie e pensieri per formare tre ragionamenti sulla ricchezza nazionale* (1791), in *Illuministi italiani*, i/2. 991–1002.

GORANI, GIUSEPPE, *Dal dispotismo illuminato alla rivoluzione (1767–1791)*, ed. Alessandro Casati (Milan, 1942).

—— *Saggio sulla pubblica educazione*, in *Illuministi italiani*, i/1. 514–41.

—— *Storia di Milano (1700–1796)*, ed. Alcesi Tarchetti (Rome, 1989).

GRIMM, MELCHIOR, *Correspondance littéraire, philosophique et critique* (Paris, 1881).

HELVÉTIUS, CLAUDE-ADRIEN, *De l'Homme, de ses facultés intellectuelles et de son éducation* (London, 1772).

[HERBERT, CLAUDE], *Riflessioni sull'economia generale dei grani, tradotte dal Francese, con un discorso preliminare del Signor Abate Genovesi* (Naples, 1765).

HUME, DAVID, *A Treatise of Human Nature* (1739–40), ed. L. A. Selby-Bigge, rev. P. H. Nidditch, 2nd edn. (Oxford, 1978).

—— *Political Essays*, ed. Knud Haakonssen (Cambridge, 1994).

Il Caffè, 1764–1766, ed. Gianni Francioni and Sergio Romagnoli, 2 vols., 2nd edn. (Turin, 1998).

IPPOLITI, GIUSEPPE, *Lettera parenetica, morale, economica di un Parroco della Val di Chiana a tutti i possidenti o comodi, o ricchi scritta nell'anno MDCCLXXII concernente i doveri loro rispetto ai contadini* (Florence, 1774).

LANDESCHI, GIOVANNI BATTISTA, *Saggi di agricoltura* (Florence, 1775).

LASTRI, MARCO, *Ricerche sull'antica e moderna popolazione della città di Firenze per mezzo dei registri del Battistero di S. Giovanni dal 1451 al 1774* (Florence, 1775).

LONGO, ALFONSO, *Istituzioni economico politiche* (1773), in *Economisti minori*, 292–366.

—— 'Osservazioni su i fedecommessi', in *Il Caffè, 1764–1766*, ed. Gianni Francioni and Sergio Romagnoli, 2nd edn. (Turin, 1998), i. 115–32.

—— *Prolusione tenuta l'anno MDCCLXIX dal marchese Alfonso Longo, canonico teologo della Basilica di Santo Stefano, regio professore di diritto pubblico ecclesiastico presso le Scuole Palatine Milanesi*, in *Illuministi italiani*, i/1. 241–9.

MALLERE, DONANDI DELLE, *Saggio di economia civile* (Turin, n.d. [1776?]).

MANDEVILLE, BERNARD, *The Fable of the Bees, or, Private Vices, Publick Benefits*, ed. F. B. Kaye, 2 vols. (Indianapolis, 1988).

MANETTI, SAVERIO, *Discorso sulle mode del sig. X, recitato in una adunanza accademica dei Filantropi in Firenze l'anno 1776 in cui si parla incidentemente dell'origine e introduzione di diverse materie e cose, tanto di comodo, che di lusso, che si costumano oggigiorno*, in Clemente Bondi, *Poemetto intitolato 'La Moda', con l'aggiunta di un discorso accademico sullo stesso argomento* (Florence, 1777).

—— 'Lezione accademica', *Magazzino toscano*, 1 (1770), 3–38.

MELON, JEAN-FRANÇOIS, *Essai politique sur le commerce* (repr. Amsterdam, 1735; first edn. Bordeaux, 1734).

—— *Essai politique sur le commerce*, 2nd edn. (Amsterdam, 1736).

—— *Saggio politico sul commercio tradotto dal francese colle annotazioni dell'abate Longano*, 2 vols. (Naples, 1778).

MENZINI, BENEDETTO, *Satire* (London [Livorno], 1788).

MIRABEAU, VICTOR DE RIQUETI, *L'Ami des hommes, ou, Traité de la population* (1756), new edn. (Avignon, 1758).

—— *Les Devoirs* (Milan, 1780).

—— *Mémoires biographiques, littéraires et politiques de Mirabeau: écrits par lui-même, par son père, son oncle et son fils adoptif*, iii (Paris, 1834).

MONTELATICI, UBALDO, *Ragionamento sopra i mezzi più necessari per far rifiorire l'agricoltura* (Florence, 1752).

—— *Ragionamento sopra i mezzi più necessari per far rifiorire l'agricoltura . . . con un discorso di Antonio Genovesi* (Naples, 1753).

MONTESQUIEU, CHARLES LOUIS DE SECONDAT, BARON DE, *De l'esprit des lois* (1748), ed. Victor Goldschmidt, 2 vols. (Paris, 1979).

—— *Lettres persanes* (1721), ed. Paul Vernière (Paris, 1960).

MONTESQUIEU, CHARLES LOUIS DE SECONDAT, BARON DE, *Spirito delle leggi del signore di Montesquieu con le note dell'abate Antonio Genovesi* (Naples, 1777).

MONTMORT, PIERRE REMOND DE, *Essai d'analyse sur les jeux de hazard* (Paris, 1708).

MURATORI, LUDOVICO ANTONIO, *Dei difetti della giurisprudenza* (1742).

—— *Della pubblica felicità oggetto de' buoni prìncipi* (1749), ed. Cesare Mozzarelli (Rome, 1996).

MUTTONI, FILIPPO, *Dissertazioni intorno alle rendite dello Stato di Milano* (1760), in *Economisti minori*, 24–72.

—— *Lettera di risposta sul Bilancio del Commercio, ecc.* (1764), in *Economisti minori*, 73–91.

NERI, POMPEO, *Discorso sopra la materia frumentaria* (1767), in *Scrittori classici*, 49. 7–48.

—— *Discorso sopra lo stato antico e moderno della nobiltà di Toscana* (1748), in *Illuministi italiani*, i/2. 951–7.

—— *Memoria sulla mendicità* (1767), in *Illuministi italiani*, i/2. 967–78.

NICHOLLS, JOHN [Plumard de Dangeul], *Remarques sur les avantages et désavantages de la France et de la Grande Bretagne par rapport au commerce* (Leiden, 1754).

NOBILI, U. DE', 'Elogio del sacerdote Ferdinando Paoletti, pievano di S. Donnino in Villamagna', *Nuovo giornale dei letterati di Pisa*, 5 (1803), 9–40; 7 (1803), 65–90; 8 (1803), 5–84.

PAOLETTI, FERDINANDO, *Della teologia de' Caldei*, in *Antichità illustrata, per mezzo di dissertazioni, tanto edite quanto inedite, ovvero, introduzione generale allo studio dell'antichità* (Florence, 1743).

—— *I veri mezzi di render felici le società: appendice apologetica al libro 'De' pensieri sopra l'agricoltura'* (Florence, 1772).

—— *Opere agrarie*, 2 vols. (Florence, 1789).

—— *Pensieri sopra l'agricoltura* (Florence, 1769; 2nd edn. 1789).

PAOLINI, ALDOBRANDO, 'Discorso sul lusso dei contadini nei suoi rapporti con i costumi, e con la pubblica economia d'un popolo agrario', *Atti della Reale ed Imperiale Accademia dei Georgofili*, C.2 (1819), 452–90.

PERUZZI, BINDO DI BINDI SIMONE, *Dissertazione accademica letta nell'Accademia de' Georgofili il dì 2. Settembre 1767 sopra l'uso giusto del lusso relativamente all'agricoltura, arti e commercio* (Florence, 1768).

PIGNOTTI, LORENZO, *Elogio storico di Angiolo Tavanti* (Florence, 1782).

PILATI, CARLANTONIO, *Riflessioni di un italiano sopra la chiesa in generale, sopra il clero sì regolare che secolare, sopra i vescovi ed i pontefici romani, e sopra i diritti ecclesiastici de' principi*, in *Illuministi italiani*, i/2. 601–12.

PINTO, ISAAC DE, *Essai sur le luxe* (Paris, 1762).

QUESNAY, FRANÇOIS, *Œuvres économiques et philosophiques*, ed. August Oncken (Paris, 1888).

RE, FILIPPO, *Dizionario ragionato di libri d'agricoltura, veterinaria, e di altri rami d'economia campestre, ad uso degli amatori delle cose agrarie, e della gioventù*, 3 vols. (Venice, 1809).

RICCI, LAPO, 'Del lusso delle vesti dei contadini', *Atti della Reale ed Imperiale Accademia Economica-Agraria dei Georgofili di Firenze*, C.2 (1819), 332–9.

ROBERTI, GIOVANNI BATTISTA, *Opuscoli quattro sopra il lusso* (Bologna, 1787).

ROUSSEAU, JEAN-JACQUES, *Discours qui a remporté le prix à l'académie de Dijon en l'année 1750*, in Rousseau, *Schriften zur Kulturkritik. Die zwei Diskurse von 1750 und 1755. Französisch–Deutsch*, ed. Kurt Weigand (Hamburg, 1983), 1–58; trans. as *A Discourse Which Won the Prize at the Academy of Dijon in 1750, on this Question Proposed by the Academy: Has the Restoration of the Arts and Sciences had a Purifying Effect upon Morals?*, in Rousseau, *The Social Contract and Discourses*, trans. G. D. H. Cole, rev. and augm. J. H. Brumfitt and John C. Hall, introd. Alan Ryan (London, 1993).

—— *Discours sur l'origine et les fondements de l'inégalité parmi les hommes*, in Rousseau, *Schriften zur Kulturkritik*, 61–269; trans. as *A Discourse on a Subject Proposed by the Academy of Dijon: What is the Origin of Inequality among Men, and is it Authorised by Natural Law?*, in Rousseau, *The Social Contract and Discourses*.

—— 'Le Luxe, le commerce et les arts', in Rousseau, *Œuvres complètes*, ed. Bernard Gagnebin and Marcel Raymond, iii (Paris, 1966), 516–24.

—— *Narcisse, ou, L'Amant de lui-même*, in Rousseau, *Œuvres complètes*, ed. Bernard Gagnebin and Marcel Raymond, ii (Paris, 1964), 959–1018.

SAINT-LAMBERT, JEAN-FRANÇOIS DE, 'Luxe', in *Encyclopédie, ou, Dictionnaire raisonné des sciences, des arts et des métiers*, ix (Neufchastel, 1765), 763–71.

SAINT PIERRE, ABBÉ DE, *Ouvrajes de politique, par l'abbé de Saint Pierre* (Rotterdam, 1733).

SARCHIANI, GIUSEPPE, 'Elogio del Pievano Ferdinando Paoletti, letto nell'Adunanza del dì 28. Febbrajo 1803', *Atti della Reale ed Imperiale Accademia Economico-Agraria dei Georgofili di Firenze*, 5 (1804), 41–8.

—— *Regolamento sul commercio, arti e manifatture della Toscana* (Florence, 1781).

SEGNERI, PAOLO, *Prediche, o sia Quaresimale* (Florence, 1679).

SIMONINI, PAOLO, *Sulla ricchezza in pubblica economia* (1773), in *Economisti minori*, 422–30.

SMITH, ADAM, *An Inquiry into the Nature and Causes of the Wealth of Nations* (1776), ed. R. H. Campbell and A. S. Skinner (Oxford, 1976; repr. Indianapolis, 1982).

—— *The Theory of Moral Sentiments* (1759), ed. D. D. Raphael and A. L. Macfie (Oxford, 1976; repr. Indianapolis, 1982).

STANLEY, THOMAS, *The History of Philosophy* (London, 1655–62; Latin version, Venice, 1731).

TARGIONI TOZZETTI, GIOVANNI, *Ragionamenti sull'agricultura toscana* (Lucca, 1759).

VALENTINELLI, FRANCESCO, *Ragionamento sul lusso considerato nei suoi rapporti politici* (Ferrara, 1802).

Vasco, Tomaso P., *Piano di economia politica* (1773), in *Economisti minori*, 390–421.

Verri, Alessandro, 'Alcune riflessioni sulla opinione che il commercio deroghi alla nobiltà', in *Il Caffè, 1764–1766*, ed. Gianni Francioni and Sergio Romagnoli, 2nd edn. (Turin, 1998), i. 256–74.

Verri, Pietro, *Considerazioni sul commercio dello Stato di Milano* (1763), ed. C. A. Vianello (Milan, 1939).

—— 'Considerazioni sul lusso' (1764), in *Il Caffè, 1764–1766*, ed. Gianni Francioni and Sergio Romagnoli, 2nd edn. (Turin, 1998), i. 155–62.

—— *Discorso sulla felicità*, in *Discorsi del conte Pietro Verri dell'Istituto delle Scienze di Bologna ... riveduti ed accresciuti dall'autore* (Milan, 1781), 1–100.

—— *Discorso sull'indole del piacere e del dolore*, in *Discorsi del conte Pietro Verri dell'Istituto delle Scienze di Bologna ... riveduti ed accresciuti dall'autore* (Milan, 1781), 101–83.

—— 'Elementi del commercio' (1760), in *Il Caffè, 1764–1766*, ed. Gianni Francioni and Sergio Romagnoli, 2nd edn. (Turin, 1998), i. 30–8.

—— *Meditazioni sulla economia politica* (1771), ed. Renzo De Felice (Milan, 1998; reproduction of the 2nd edn., Naples, 1771).

—— *Meditazioni sulla economia politica*, 6th edn. (Livorno, 1772).

—— *Memorie storiche sull'economia pubblica dello Stato di Milano*, in *Scrittori classici*, 24. 108–206.

—— *Pensieri sullo stato politico del Milanese nel 1790*, in Pietro Verri, *Scritti vari*, ed. Giulio Carcano (Florence, 1854), vol. ii, app., pp. 3–38.

—— 'Saggio d'aritmetica politica', in *Il Caffè, 1764–1766*, ed. Gianni Francioni and Sergio Romagnoli, 2nd edn. (Turin, 1998), i. 198–9.

—— and Verri, Alessandro, *Carteggio*, ed. Emanuele Greppi, Alessandro Giulini, *et al.*, 12 vols. (Milan, 1923–42).

—— —— *Lettere e scritti inediti di Pietro e di Alessandro Verri*, ed. Carlo Cassati, 4 vols. (Milan, 1879–81).

Vertot, R. A. de, *Établissement des lois somptuaires en France* (1720), in Vertot, *Œuvres choisies* (Paris, 1819), v. 331–48.

Vico, Giambattista, *The New Science*, 3rd edn. (1744), trans. Thomas Goddard Bergin and Max Harold Fisch (Ithaca, NY, 1968; repr. 1991).

Visconti, Giuseppe, 'Descrizione di una famiglia rustica', in *Il Caffè, 1764–1766*, ed. Gianni Francioni and Sergio Romagnoli, 2nd edn. (Turin, 1998), i. 241–3.

Voltaire, François M. Arouet de, *Défense du Mondain, ou, L'Apologie du luxe*, in André Morize, *L'Apologie du luxe au* XVIIIe *siècle et 'Le Mondain' de Voltaire* (Paris, 1909), 153–8.

—— *Dictionnaire philosophique*, ii, in *The Complete Works of Voltaire*, xxxvi (Oxford, 1994).

—— *Le Mondain*, in André Morize, *L'Apologie du luxe au* XVIIIe *siècle et 'Le Mondain' de Voltaire* (Paris, 1909), 133–9.

—— *Observations sur MM. Jean Lass, Melon et Dutot sur le commerce, le luxe, les monnaies, et les impôts* (1738), in *Œuvres complètes de Voltaire* (Paris, 1879), xxii. 359–70.

—— *Voltaire's Correspondence*, ed. Theodore Besterman, 98 vols. (Geneva, 1953–64).

YOUNG, ARTHUR, *Travels during the Years 1787, 1788, and 1789; Undertaken More Particularly with a View of Ascertaining the Cultivation, Wealth, Resources, and National Prosperity of the Kingdom of France*, 2 vols., 2nd edn. (London, 1794).

—— *Voyage en Italie pendant l'année 1789*, (Paris, 1796).

Journals

Continuazione del nuovo giornale de' letterati d'Italia di Modena (1777).

Estratto della letteratura europea (1758–69).

Gazzetta veneta urbana (1795).

Giornale d'Italia spettante alla scienza naturale e principalmente all'agricoltura, alle arti ed al commercio (1764–6).

Giornale enciclopedico (Venice) (1774–82).

Il Caffè (1764–6).

Magazzino toscano (1770–7).

Magazzino toscano d'istruzione e di piacere (1754–6).

Novelle letterarie di Firenze (1752–77).

(Nuovo) Giornale de' letterati di Pisa (1771–96).

Dictionaries and Encyclopaedias

ALBERTI DI VILLANUOVA, FRANCESCO, *Dizionario compendioso italiano–francese* (Venice, 1774).

—— *Dizionario universale critico enciclopedico della lingua italiana* (Lucca, 1797–1803).

—— *Nouveau Dictionnaire françois–italien* (Bassano, 1796).

ALTIERI, FERDINANDO, *Dizionario italiano ed inglese*, 2nd edn., corr. and improved (London, 1750).

BARETTI, GIUSEPPE, *Dizionario inglese–italiano ed italiano–inglese* (Florence, 1816).

BOYER, A., *Dictionnaire français–anglais et anglais–français en abrégé*, 2 vols., 17th edn. (Paris, 1797).

CASTELLI, GIOVANNITOMASO DI, *Nuova e perfetta grammatica reggia italiana e tedesca* (Leipzig, 1748).

CASTELLI, NICCOLÒ, *Dizionario italiano–tedesco e tedesco–italiano*, 2 vols., new edn. (Leipzig, 1749).

CHAMBERS, EFRAIMO, *Dizionario universale delle arti e delle scienze*, 9 vols. (Venice, 1748).

CONTIN, TOMMASO ANTONIO, *Dizionario dell'eresie, degli errori, e de' scismi* (Venice, 1767).

COTGRAVE, RANDLE, *A French and English Dictionary. With Another in English and French* (London, 1673).

Dizionario del cittadino, o sia ristretto storico, teorico e pratico del commercio . . . Tradotto dal Francese. Edizione novissima. Accresciuta di moltissimi articoli tralasciati nelle altre, 2 vols. (1765).

Dizionario della lingua italiana, 4 vols. (Padua, 1828).

Dizionario filosofico della Religione (Florence, 1775).

Dizionario filosofico o sia introduzione alla cognizione dell'Uomo: traduzione dal francese (Venice, 1756).

Dizionario portatile della bibbia. Tradotto dal Francese nell'Italiano idioma. Ed arrichito di note, di articoli, e di tre carte topografiche dal P. D. Prospero dell'Aquila, 4 vols. (Naples, 1759).

EHRENREICH, JOSEPH ANTON VON, *Il Cellario Italiano, oder, Kurzgefasstes Italienisch–Teutsches Wörterbuch* (Stuttgart, 1756).

FLORIO, JOHN, *Vocabolario italiano & inglese / A Dictionary, Italian and English*, repr., rev. corr. (London, 1688).

FURETIERE, ANTOINE, *Dictionnaire universel*, new, corr. and augm. edn. (The Hague, 1694).

KRAMER, MATTHIA, *Neu ausgefertigtes Italienisch–Teutsches Sprach- und Wörterbuch* (Nuremberg, 1724).

MÉNAGE, *Dictionnaire étymologique, ou, Origines de la langue française*, new, rev. and augm. edn. (Paris, 1694).

—— *Dictionnaire étymologique de la langue française*, new edn. (Paris, 1750).

MIEGE, GUY, *The Short French Dictionary, in Two Parts. I. English and French, II. French and English; According to the Present Use, and Modern Orthography*, 4th edn. (The Hague, 1699).

Nuovo Dizionario italiano–tedesco e tedesco–italiano. Prima di Nic. di Castelli, ma ora esattamente corretto, ed a detta de' Dizionari dell'Accademia della Crusca, e del Signor Abate Franceso de Alberti di Villanuova (Leipzig, 1782).

OUDIN, ANTHONIO, *Neu und ausführliches Dictionarium von Dreyen Sprachen. In III Theile unterschieden. I. Italiän–Französisch–Teutsch, II. Französ–Italiänisch–Teutsch, III. Teutsch–Französisch–Italiänisch* (Frankfurt, 1674).

RICHELET, PIERRE, *Dictionnaire portatif de la langue française, extrait du grande dictionnaire de Pierre Richelet* (Lyon, 1756).

VENERONI, *Dictionnaire italien et français*, new edn., rev. and corr. Charlies Placardi, 2 vols. (Paris, 1749).

Secondary Sources

Addobbati, Andrea, 'I guastafeste: la legge toscana sul gioco del 1773', *Quaderni storici*, 32 (1997), 495–538.

Ajello, Raffaele, 'Carlo Antonio Broggia', in Raffaele Ajello, Marino Berengo, *et al.* (eds.), *Dal Muratori al Cesarotti*, v: *Politici ed economisti del primo Settecento* (Milan, 1978), 971–1034.

—— 'La critica del regime in Doria, Intieri e Broggia', in Ajello, *Arcana iuris: diritto e politica nel Settecento italiano* (Naples, 1976), 389–427.

Albertone, Manuela, and Alberto Masoero (eds.), *Political Economy and National Realities* (Turin, 1994).

Alimento, Antonella, 'Véron de Forbonnais tra Spagna, Francia e Lombardia', *Annali della Fondazione Luigi Einaudi*, 19 (1985), 171–94.

Allan, D. G. C., 'The Society of Arts and Government, 1754–1800', in *Eighteenth-Century Studies*, 7 (1973–4), 434–54.

Amato, Massimo, 'Il decentramento dell'economia mediterranea: il caso di Milano fra crisi e riconversione (secoli xvi e xvii)', *Rivista storica italiana*, 106 (1994), 622–50.

Arese, Franco, 'Le supreme cariche del Ducato di Milano e della Lombardia austriaca, 1707–1796', *Archivio storico lombardo*, 105–6 (1979–80), 535–98.

Argan, Giulio Carlo, *The Europe of the Capitals, 1600–1700*, trans. Anthony Rhodes (Geneva, 1964).

Augello, Massimo, and Marco Guidi, 'The Emergence of Economic Periodical Literature in Italy (1750–1900)', *History of Economic Ideas*, 4/3 (1996), 15–62.

Baker, George R. F., *Sallustio Bandini* (Florence, 1978).

Baldini, Ugo, 'L'attività scientifica nelle accademie lombarde del Settecento', in *Economia, istituzioni, cultura*, iii. 503–32.

Barbini, Giuseppe, '"Le Luxe détruit-il les mœurs et les empires?' Concorso indetto nel 1782 dall'accademia di Besançon', *Studi francesi*, 40 (1996), 319–26.

Becagli, Vieri, 'L'economia nei periodici del granducato di Toscana: la prima reggenza lorenese (1737–1765)', in Massimo Augello, Marco Bianchini, *et al.* (eds.), *Le riviste di economia in Italia (1700–1900): dai giornali scientifico–letterari ai periodici specialistici* (Milan, 1996), 69–88.

—— 'Pompeo Neri e le riforme istituzionali della prima età leopoldina', in Aldo Frantoianni and Marcello Verga (eds.), *Pompeo Neri: atti del colloquio di Castelfiorentino (6–7 maggio 1988)* (Castelfiorentino, 1992), 333–76.

Beccattini, G., 'La posizione del consumo nel pensiero degli economisti classici', in *Scienza economica e trasformazioni sociali* (Florence, 1979), 143–56.

Bellamy, Richard, '"Da metafisico a mercatante": Antonio Genovesi and the Development of a New Language of Commerce in Eighteenth-Century Naples', in Anthony Pagden (ed.), *The Languages of Political Theory in Early-Modern Europe* (Cambridge, 1987), 277–99.

BELOCH, GIULIO, 'La popolazione d'Italia nei secoli sedicesimo, diciasettesimo, diciottesimo', in Carlo Cipolla (ed.), *Storia dell'economia italiana* (Turin, 1965), 449–500.

BENEDICT, PHILIP, 'More than Market and Manufactory: The Cities of Early Modern France', *French Historical Studies*, 20 (1997), 511–38.

BERRY, CHRISTOPHER J., *The Idea of Luxury: A Conceptual and Historical Investigation* (Cambridge, 1994).

BERSELLI AMBRI, Paola, *L'opera di Montesquieu nel Settecento italiano* (Florence, 1960).

BERTELLI, SERGIO, *Erudizione e storia in Ludovico Antonio Muratori* (Naples, 1960).

BIANCHINI, MARCO, 'Ceti emergenti, riforme degli studi superiori e istituzionalizzazione dell'economia politica nel Ducato di Modena e Reggio (1750–1800)', in Giovanni Tocci (ed.), *Persistenze feudali e autonomie comunitative in stati padani fra Cinque e Settecento* (Bologna, 1988), 117–32.

—— 'Una difficile gestazione: il contrastato inserimento dell'economia politica nelle università dell'Italia nord-orientale (1769–1866). Note per un'analisi comparativa', in M. Augello (ed.), *Le cattedre di economia politca in Italia: la diffusione di una disciplina 'sospetta' (1750–1900)* (Milan, 1988), 47–92.

—— and ERICA MORATO, 'Per una storia della storiografia del pensiero economico italiano del Settecento: l'Italia centro-settentrionale', *Il pensiero economico italiano*, 1 (1993), 17–55.

BOGNETTI, GIUSEPPE, 'La teoria della finanza pubblica: il pensiero politico di Pietro Verri', in Alberto Quadrio Curzio (ed.), *Alle origini del pensiero economico in Italia*, ii: *Economia e istituzioni: il paradigma lombardo tra i secoli XVIII e XIX* (Bologna, 1996), 59–89.

BONAR, JAMES, *A Catalogue of the Library of Adam Smith* (London, 1932).

BORGHERO, CARLO, 'La polemica sul lusso nella formazione del pensiero politico di J.-J. Rousseau (1750–1753)', *Annali delle Facoltà di Lettere e Filosofia e Magistero dell'Università di Cagliari*, 32 (1969), 1–38.

—— (ed.), *La polemica sul lusso nel Settecento francese* (Turin, 1974).

BRAMBILLA, ELENA, 'Il "sistema letterario" di Milano: professioni nobili e professioni borghesi dall'età spagnola alle riforme teresiane', in *Economia, istituzioni, cultura*, iii. 79–160.

BRECKMAN, WARREN G., 'Disciplining Consumption: The Debate about Luxury in Wilhelmine Germany, 1890–1914', *Journal of Social History*, 24 (1991), 485–505.

BREWER, ANTHONY, 'An Eighteenth-Century View of Economic Development: Hume and Steuart', *European Journal of the History of Economic Thought*, 4 (1997), 1–22.

—— 'Luxury and Economic Development: David Hume and Adam Smith', *Scottish Journal of Political Economy*, 45 (1998), 78–98.

BREWER, JOHN, and ROY PORTER (eds.), *Consumption and the World of Goods* (London, 1993).

BROWN, PETER, *Augustine of Hippo: A Biography* (London, 1967).

BUCK, AUGUST, 'Die humanistischen Akademien in Italien', in Fritz Hartmann and Rudolf Vierhaus (eds.), *Der Akademiegedanke im 17. und 18. Jahrhundert* (Bremen, 1977), 11–25.

CAIZZI, BRUNO, *Industria, commercio e banca in Lombardia nel XVIII secolo* (Milan, 1968).

CANETTA, ROSALBA, 'Gli studi agronomici in Lombardia durante l'età teresiana', in *Economia, istituzioni, cultura*, i. 59–75.

—— 'L'attività di governo di Beccaria alla luce di recenti indagini: primi risultati, problemi e prospettive', in Sergio Romagnoli and Gian Domenico Pisapia (eds.), *Cesare Beccaria tra Milano e l'Europa* (Rome, 1990), 468–78.

CAPRA, CARLO, 'Gli intellettuali e il potere: i casi di Beccaria e Verri', in Antonio Santucci (ed.), *L'età dei lumi: saggi sulla cultura settecentesca* (Bologna, 1998), 211–30.

—— 'Il gruppo del "Caffè" e le riforme', in Vincenzo Ferrone and Gianni Francioni (eds.), *Cesare Beccaria: la pratica dei lumi* (Florence, 2000), 63–78.

—— '"La mia anima è sempre stata repubblicana": Pietro Verri da patrizio a cittadino', *Quaderni di Acme*, 35: *Pietro Verri e il suo tempo* (1999), 519–40.

—— 'Lo sviluppo delle riforme asburgiche nello Stato di Milano', in Pierangelo Schiera (ed.), *La dinamica statale austriaca nel XVIII e XIX secolo* (Bologna, 1981), 161–87.

—— 'Luigi Giusti e il Dipartimento d'Italia a Vienna (1757–1766)', in *Economia, istituzioni, cultura*, iii. 365–90.

—— 'Riforme finanziarie e mutamento istituzionale nello Stato di Milano: gli anni sessanta del secolo XVIII', *Rivista storica italiana*, 91 (1979), 313–18.

—— 'The Eighteenth Century, I: The Finances of the Austrian Monarchy and the Italian States', in Richard Bonney (ed.), *Economic Systems and State Finance* (Oxford, 1995), 295–314.

—— 'Un intermediario tra Vienna e Milano: Luigi Lambertenghi e il suo carteggio con Pietro Verri', *Römische historische Mitteilungen*, 31 (1989), 359–76.

CARACCIOLO, ASCIANO, 'La storia economica', in *Storia d'Italia*, iii (Turin, 1973), 533–54.

CARPANETTO, DINO, and GIUSEPPE RICUPERATI, *Italy in the Age of Reason, 1685–1789* (London, 1987).

CARRANZA, NICOLA, 'L'università di Pisa e la formazione culturale del ceto dirigente toscano nel Settecento: studi di storia pisana e toscana in onore del professore Ottorino Bertolini', *Bolletino storico pisano*, 33–5 (1964–6), 469–537.

CIPOLLA, CARLO M., 'The Economic Decline of Italy' (1952), in Brian Pullan (ed.), *Crisis and Change in the Venetian Economy in the Sixteenth and Seventeenth Centuries* (Methuen, 1968), 127–45.

COCHRANE, ERIC, *Florence in the Forgotten Centuries, 1527–1800* (Chicago, 1973).

—— 'French Literature and the Italian Tradition in Eighteenth-Century Tuscany', *Journal of the History of Ideas*, 23 (1962), 61–76.

Cochrane, Eric, 'Le relazioni delle accademie toscane del Settecento con la cultura europea', *Archivio storico italiano*, 111 (1953), 78–108.

—— *Tradition and Enlightenment in the Tuscan Academies, 1690–1800* (Chicago, 1961).

Comparato, Vittor Ivo, 'Ragione e fede nelle discussioni istoriche, teologiche e filosofiche di Costantino Grimaldi', in *Saggi e ricerche sul Settecento* (Naples, 1968), 48–93.

Corritore, Renzo Paolo, 'Il processo di "ruralizzazione" in Italia nei secoli xvii–xviii: verso una regionalizzazione', *Rivista di storia economica*, 10 (1993), 353–86.

Cusanno, Chiara, 'Fisiocrati e stampa: la strategia giornalistica delle "*Éphémérides du citoyen*"', *Rivista storica italiana*, 103 (1991), 557–98.

Daston, Lorraine, *Classical Probability in the Enlightenment* (Princeton, 1988; repr. 1995).

Demarco, Domenico, 'Il debattito settecentesco sulla popolazione in Italia', in *La popolazione italiana nel Settecento* (Bologna, 1980), 539–90.

Denis, Henri, *Histoire de la pensée économique*, 10th edn. (Paris, 1993).

Diaz, Furio, *Francesco Maria Gianni: dalla burocrazia alla politica sotto Pietro Leopoldo di Toscana* (Milan, 1966).

—— *I Medici* (Turin, 1976).

—— '"La philosophie" e il riformismo leopoldino', in Diaz, *Per un storia illuministica* (Naples, 1973), 247–88.

—— Luigi Mascilli Migliorini, and Carlo Mangio, *Il Granducato di Toscana: i Lorena dalla Reggenza agli anni rivoluzionari* (Turin, 1997).

Dickson, Peter G. M., *Finance and Government under Maria Theresa, 1740–1780*, 2 vols. (Oxford, 1987).

Dieckmann, Herbert, 'The Sixth Volume of Saint-Lambert's Works', *Romantic Review*, 42 (1951), 109–21.

Dipper, Christof, *Politischer Reformismus und begrifflicher Wandel. Eine Untersuchung des historisch-politischen Wortschatzes der Mailänder Aufklärung (1764–1796)* (Tübingen, 1976).

DuPlessis, Robert S., *Transitions to Capitalism in Early Modern Europe* (Cambridge, 1997).

Earl, D. C., *The Political Thought of Sallust* (Cambridge, 1961).

Einaudi, Luigi, 'Galiani economista', in Einaudi, *Saggi bibliografici e storici intorno alle dottrine economiche* (Rome, 1953), 269–305.

Eltis, Walter, 'L'Abbé de Condillac and the Physiocrats', *History of Political Economy*, 27 (1995), 217–36.

Epstein, S. R., 'Cities, Regions and the Late Medieval Crisis: Sicily and Tuscany Compared', *Past and Present*, 130 (1991), 3–50.

Erler, Michael, 'Epikur', in Hellmuth Flashar (ed.), *Die Philosophie der Antike*, iv/1: *Die hellenistische Philosophie* (Basel, 1994), 29–202.

FACCARELLO, GILBERT, *Aux origines de l'économie politique libérale: Pierre de Boisguilbert* (Paris, 1986).

FAUCCI, RICCARDO (ed.), *Gli italiani e Bentham: dalla "felicità pubblica" all'economia del benessere*, 2 vols. (Milan, 1982).

FERRONE, VINCENZO, *I profeti dell'illuminismo: metamorfosi della ragione nel tardo Settecento italiano* (Rome, 1989).

—— *Scienza natura religione: mondo newtoniano e cultura italiana nel primo Settecento* (Naples, 1982); trans. as *The Intellectual Roots of the Italian Enlightenment: Newtonian Science, Religion, and Politics in the Early Eighteenth Century* (New Jersey, 1995).

—— MASSIMO FIRPO, GIUSEPPE RICUPERATI, and EDOARDO TORTAROLO, 'Vita civile e storiografia: contributo per una discussione', *Studi storici*, 1 (1994), 91–8.

FÉRY, JEAN, 'Le Système fiscal et monétaire de Boisguilbert', in *Pierre de Boisguilbert, ou, La Naissance de l'économie politique*, 2 vols. (Paris, 1966), i. 53–69.

FIRPO, LUIGI, *Rousseau in Italia* (Turin, 1963).

FOX-GENOVESE, ELIZABETH, *The Origins of Physiocracy: Economic Revolution and Social Order in Eighteenth-Century France* (Ithaca, NY, 1976).

FRANCIONI, GIANNI, 'Beccaria filosofo utilitarista', in Sergio Romagnoli and Gian Domenico Pisapia (eds.), *Cesare Beccaria tra Milano e l'Europa* (Rome, 1990), 69–87.

FRASCANI, PAOLO, 'Il dibattito sul lusso nella cultura napoletana del '700', *Critica storica*, 11 (1971), 397–424.

GALLIANI, RENATO, 'Le Débat en France sur le luxe: Voltaire ou Rousseau?', *Studies on Voltaire and the Eighteenth Century*, 161 (1976), 205–17.

—— *Rousseau, le luxe et l'idéologie nobiliaire: Étude socio-historique* (Oxford, 1989).

GARMS-CORNIDES, ELISABETH, 'La destinazione del conte Firmian a Milano: analisi di una scelta', in *Economia, istituzioni, cultura*, ii. 1015–29.

—— 'Un trentino tra Impero, antichi stati italiani e Gran Bretagna: l'anglomano Carlo Firmian', in Cesare Mozzarelli and Giuseppe Olmi (eds.), *Il Trentino nel Settecento fra Sacro Romano Impero e antichi stati italiani* (Bologna, 1985), 467–93.

—— 'Zwischen Giannone, Muratori und Metastasio. Die Italiener im geistigen Leben Wiens', in Friedrich Engel-Janosi, Grete Klingenstein, and Heinrich Lutz (eds.), *Formen der europäischen Aufklärung. Untersuchungen zur Situation von Christentum, Bildung und Wissenschaft im 18. Jahrhundert* (Vienna, 1976), 224–50.

GIARIZZO, GIUSEPPE, *Massoneria e illuminismo nell'Europa del Settecento* (Venice, 1994).

GIOLI, GABRIELLA, 'Gli albori dello smithianesimo in Italia', *Rivista di politica economica*, 62 (1972), 917–62.

—— 'Il concorso di economia pubblica del 1844 all'università di Napoli ed il dibattito sul lusso e lo sviluppo delle manifatture', *Ricerche storiche*, 12 (1982), 409–44.

GIOLI, GABRIELLA, 'La nascita e l'affermazione dell'insegnamento dell'economia politica in Italia: continuità e discontinuità (1750–1900)', in M. Augello (ed.), *Le cattedre di economia politica in Italia: la diffusione di una disciplina 'sospetta' (1750–1900)* (Milan, 1988), 385–410.

—— (ed.), *Le teorie della popolazione prima di Malthus* (Milan, 1987).

GIORGETTI, GIORGIO, 'Note sul grande affitto in Toscana nel secolo XVIII', *Quaderni storici*, 14 (1970), 453–506.

—— 'Per uno studio delle allivellazioni leopoldine', *Studi storici*, 2 (1966), 245–90.

GOBBI, ULISSE, *La concorrenza estera e gli antichi economisti italiani* (Milan, 1884).

GOLDSMITH, MAURICE M., *Private Vices, Public Benefits: Bernard Mandeville's Social and Political Thought* (Cambridge, 1985).

GOLDTHWAITE, RICHARD A., *Wealth and the Demand for Art in Italy, 1300–1600*, pbk. edn. (Baltimore, 1995).

GOODMAN, DENA, *The Republic of Letters: A Cultural History of the French Enlightenment* (Ithaca, NY, 1994).

GORI, ORSOLA, 'La carestia del 1763–1767 e i suoi riflessi nel dibattito economico e politico nel Granducato di Toscana', MA thesis, University of Florence, 1977.

—— 'Mercato e prezzi del grano a Firenze nel secolo XVIII', *Archivio storico italiano*, 147 (1989), 525–623.

GREGORIO, MARIO DE, 'Prima di Bandini: tentativi di biblioteca universitaria a Siena nel Settecento', *Societa e Storia*, 19 (1996), 253–81.

GRENIER, JEAN-YVES, 'La Notion de croissance dans la pensée économique française au 18e siècle', *Review (Fernand Braudel Center)*, 13 (1990), 499–549.

GROENEWEGEN, PETER, 'Pietro Verri's Mature Political Economy of the *Meditazioni*: A Case Study in the Highly Developed International Transmission Mechanism of Ideas in Pre-Revolutionary Europe', in Manuela Albertone and Alberto Masoero (eds.), *Political Economy and National Realities* (Turin, 1994), 107–25.

—— 'The Significance of Verri's *Meditazioni* in the History of Economic Thought', in *Pietro Verri e il suo tempo: quaderni di Acme*, 35 (1999), 693–708.

GUENZI, ALBERTO, 'Il "calmiero del formento": controllo del prezzo del pane e difesa della rendita terriera a Bologna nei secoli XVII e XVIII', *Annali della Fondazione Luigi Einaudi*, 11 (1977), 143–201.

GUERCI, LUCIANO, *La discussione sulla donna nell'Italia del Settecento: aspetti e problemi* (Turin, 1987).

—— *L'Europa del Settecento: permanenze e mutamenti* (Turin, 1988).

HATCHER, JOHN, 'Labour, Leisure and Economic Thought before the Nineteenth Century', *Past and Present*, 160 (1998), 64–115.

HEMMELER BENINI, SILVIA, 'Ancora su Rousseau e il lusso', *Storia e Politica*, 16 (1977), 1–43.

HOLL, B., 'Hofkammerpräsident Gundaker Thomas Graf Stakenberg und die österreichische Finanzpolitik der Barockzeit, 1703–1715', *Archiv für österreichische Geschichte*, 132 (1976), 3–447.

HOLLDACK, HEINZ, 'Die Reformpolitik Leopolds von Toskana', *Historische Zeitschrift*, 165 (1942), 23–46.

HONT, ISTVAN, 'The "Rich Country–Poor Country" Debate in Scottish Classical Political Economy', in Istvan Hont and Michael Ignatieff (eds.), *Wealth and Virtue: The Shaping of Political Economy in the Scottish Enlightenment* (Cambridge, 1983), 271–315.

—— and MICHAEL IGNATIEFF (eds.), *Wealth and Virtue: The Shaping of Political Economy in the Scottish Enlightenment* (Cambridge, 1983).

HUNDERT, E. J., 'The Achievement Motive in Hume's Political Economy', *Journal of the History of Ideas*, 35 (1974), 139–43.

—— *The Enlightenment's Fable: Bernard Mandeville and the Discovery of Society* (Cambridge, 1994).

HUTCHISON, TERENCE, *Before Adam Smith: The Emergence of Political Economy, 1662–1776* (Oxford, 1988).

IRACI FEDELI, LEONE, 'Letture di economisti italiani dei secoli XVIII e XIX: Francesco Mengotti e il "Colbertismo"', *Annali dell'Istituto Giangiacomo Feltrinelli*, 2 (1959), 560–76.

JACK, MALCOLM, 'One State of Nature: Mandeville and Rousseau', *Journal of the History of Ideas*, 39 (1978), 119–24.

JEANNERET, F. A. M., and J. H. Bonhôte, *Biographie neuchâteloise*, 2 vols. (Locle, 1863).

JOHNSON, HUBERT C., 'Spartan Simplicity versus Decadent Luxury', *Proceedings of the Annual Meeting of the Western Society for French History*, 19 (1992), 149–57.

JONARD, NORBERT, 'Le Problème du luxe en Italie au XVIIIe siècle', *Revue des études italiennes*, 15 (1969), 295–321.

KLANG, DANIEL M., 'Cesare Beccaria and the Clash between Jurisprudence and Political Economy in Eighteenth-Century Lombardy', *Canadian Journal of History / Annales canadiennes d'histoire*, 23 (1988), 305–36.

—— 'Reform and Enlightenment in Eighteenth-Century Lombardy', *Canadian Journal of History / Annales canadiennes d'histoire*, 19 (1984), 39–70.

—— *Tax Reform in Eighteenth-Century Lombardy* (New York, 1977).

KLINGENSTEIN, GRETE, *Der Aufstieg des Hauses Kaunitz. Studien zur Herkunft und Bildung des Staatskanzlers Wenzel Anton* (Göttingen, 1975).

KOSELLECK, REINHART, 'Sozialgeschichte und Begriffsgeschichte', in Wolfgang Schieder and Volker Sellin (eds.), *Sozialgeschichte in Deutschland* (Göttingen, 1987), i. 89–109.

LABRIOLLE-RUTHERFORD, M. R. DE, 'L'Évolution de la notion du luxe depuis Mandeville jusqu'à la révolution', *Studies on Voltaire and the Eighteenth Century*, 26 (1963), 1025–36.

LAGUZZI, MARINA, 'L'alienazione dei beni ecclesiastici in Tocana sotto Pietro Leopoldo: un sondaggio in Valdinievole', *Archivio storico italiano*, 153 (1995), 335–67.

LARRÈRE, CATHERINE, *L'Invention de l'économie politique au XVIIIe siècle: du droit naturel à la physiocracy* (Paris, 1992).

LASLETT, PETER, 'The English Revolution and John Locke's *Two Treatises of Government*', *Historical Journal*, 12 (1956), 1–22.

LITCHFIELD, R. B., *Emergence of a Bureaucracy: The Florentine Patricians, 1530–1790* (Princeton, 1986).

MCARDLE, FRANK, *Altopascio: A Study in Tuscan Rural Society* (Cambridge, 1974).

MACCARELLI, TERENZIO, and ERICA MORATO, 'Il "bisognevole" e il "superfluo": occupazioni e distribuzione della ricchezza in Giammaria Ortes', *Quaderni storici*, 105 (2000), 731–66.

MCKENDRICK, NEIL, JOHN BREWER, and J. H. PLUMB, *The Birth of a Consumer Society: The Commercialisation of Eighteenth-Century England* (London, 1982).

MADDALENA, ALDO DE, *Prezzi e mercedi a Milano dal 1701 al 1806* (Milan, 1974).

MALANIMA, PAOLO, *Il lusso dei contadini: consumo e industrie nelle campagne toscane del Sei e Settecento* (Bologna, 1990).

—— *La decadenza di un'economia cittadina: l'industria a Firenze nei secoli XVI–XVIII* (Bologna, 1982).

MANETTI, GIULIO M., *La Costituzione inattuata: Pietro Leopoldo granduca di Toscana: dalla riforma comunitativa al progetto di costituzione* (Florence, 1991).

MARCHI, NEIL DE, 'Adam Smith's Accommodation of "Altogether Endless" Desires', in Maxine Berg and Helen Clifford (eds.), *Consumers and Luxury: Consumer Culture in Europe 1650–1850* (Manchester, 1999), 18–36.

MASSETTO, GIAN PAOLO, 'Economia e pena nell'opera del Beccaria', in Sergio Romagnoli and Gian Domenico Pisapia (eds.), *Cesare Beccaria tra Milano e l'Europa* (Rome, 1990), 279–328.

MAURI, AUGERO, 'La cattedra di Cesare Beccaria', *Archivio storico italiano*, 41 (1933), 199–262.

MAYLENDER, MICHEL, *Storia delle accademie d'Italia*, 5 vols. (Bologna, 1926–30).

MAZA, SARAH, 'Luxury, Morality, and Social Change: Why there was no Middle-Class Consciousness in Prerevolutionary France', *Journal of Modern History*, 69 (1997), 199–229.

MEACCI, FERDINANDO, 'La teoria della moneta', in Alberto Quadrio Curzio (ed.), *Alle origini del pensiero economico in Italia*, ii: *Economia e istituzioni: il paradigma lombardo tra i secoli XVIII e XIX* (Bologna, 1996), 91–104.

MEEK, RONALD L., *The Economics of Physiocracy* (London, 1962).

MENOZZI, DANIELE, '"Aufklärung" delle Chiese cristiane e "chrétiens éclairés": in margine ai lavori della terza sezione del Congresso C.I.H.E.C. di Varsavia', *Critica storica*, 16 (1979), 150–61.

MINERBI, MARCO, 'Diderot, Galiani e la polemica sulla fisiocrazia', *Studi storici*, 14 (1973), 147–84.

MIRRI, MARIO, 'Bandini, Sallustio', in *Dizionario biografico degli italiani*, v (Rome, 1963), 720–31.

—— 'Dalla storia dei "Lumi" e delle "riforme" alla storia degli antichi stati italiani', in Aldo Frantoianni and Marcello Verga (eds.), *Pompeo Neri: atti del colloquio di Castelfiorentino (6–7 maggio 1988)* (Castelfiorentino, 1992), 401–540.

—— *Ferdinando Paoletti: agronomo, 'georgofilo', riformatore nella Toscana del Settecento* (Florence, 1967).

—— *La lotta politica in Toscana intorno alle 'riforme annonarie' (1764–1775)* (Pisa, 1972).

—— 'Per una ricerca dei rapporti fra 'economisti' e riformatori toscani: l'abate Niccoli a Parigi', *Annali dell'Istituto Giangiacomo Feltrinelli*, 2 (1959), 55–120.

—— 'Proprietari e contadini nelle riforme leopoldine', *Movimento operaio*, 7 (1955), 173–229.

—— 'Un'inchiesta toscana sui tributi pagati dai mezzadri e sui patti colonici nella seconda metà del Settecento: le memorie di Pelli-Bencivenni, Pagnini, Tramontani e Paoletti', *Annali dell'Istituto Giangiacomo Feltrinelli*, 2 (1959), 483–559.

MOIOLI, ANGELO, 'La deindustrializzazione della Lombardia nel secolo XVII', *Archivio storico lombardo*, ser. 11. 3 (1986), 167–203.

—— 'L'economia lombarda verso la maturità dell'equilibrio agricolo–commerciale durante l'età delle riforme', in Sergio Romagnoli and Gian Domenico Pisapia (eds.), *Cesare Beccaria tra Milano e l'Europa* (Rome, 1990), 329–55.

MOLESTI, ROMANO, *Il pensiero economico di Antonio Zanon* (Milan, 1974).

MORENA, ABELE, 'Le riforme e le dottrine economiche in Toscana', *Rassegna nazionale*, 18 (1887), 211–56.

MORI, RENATO, 'Presupposti politici del riformismo di Sallustio Bandini', *Storia e politica*, 23 (1984), 301–29.

MORIZE, ANDRÉ, *L'Apologie du luxe au XVIIIe siècle et 'Le Mondain' de Voltaire* (Paris, 1909).

MOUREAU, FRANÇOIS (ed.), *De bonne main: La Communication manuscrite au XVIIIe siècle* (Paris, 1993).

MOZZARELLI, CESARE, 'Riforme e controriforme', in Aldo Frantoianni and Marcello Verga (eds.), *Pompeo Neri: atti del colloquio di Castelfiorentino (6–7 maggio 1988)* (Castelfiorentino, 1992), 391–400.

—— *Sovrano, società e amministrazione locale nella Lombardia teresiana (1749–1758)* (Bologna, 1982).

MUHLACK, ULRICH, 'Physiokratie und Absolutismus in Frankreich und Deutschland', *Zeitschrift für historische Forschung*, 9 (1982), 15–46.

NUCCIO, OSCAR, *La civiltà italiana nella formazione della scienza economica* (Milan, 1995).

O'NEAL, JOHN C., 'Rousseau's Theory of Wealth', *History of European Ideas*, 7 (1986), 453–67.

OZ-SALZBERGER, FANIA, *Translating the Enlightenment: Scottish Civic Discourse in Eighteenth-Century Germany* (Oxford, 1995).

Pallach, Ulrich-Christian, *Materielle Kultur und Mentalitäten im 18. Jahrhundert: Wirtschaftliche Entwicklung und politisch-sozialer Funktionswandel des Luxus in Frankreich und im Alten Reich am Ende des Ancien Regime* (Munich, 1987).

Pane, Luigi Dal, 'I lavori preparatori per la grande inchiesta del 1766 sull'economia toscana', in *Studi in onore di Gioacchino Volpe per il suo ottantesimo compleanno* (Florence, 1958), i. 261–313.

—— 'Le riforme economiche e finanziarie di Pietro Leopoldo', *Rassegna storica toscana*, 11 (1965), 229–46.

Panta, Lorenzo del, *Una traccia di storia demografica della Toscana nei secoli XVI–XVIII* (Florence, 1974).

Parenti, Giuseppe, *La popolazione della Toscana sotto la Reggenza lorense* (Florence, 1937).

Parisi Aquaviva, Daniela, *Il pensiero economico classico in Italia (1750–1860)* (Milan, 1984).

Pasta, Renato, 'Editoria e stampa nella Firenze del Settecento', *Roma moderna e contemporanea*, 2 (1994), 379–418.

—— 'Istituzionalizzazione della scienza e controllo del sapere: il contributo di Pompeo Neri alla rinascita dei Fisiocritici', in Aldo Frantoianni and Marcello Verga (eds.), *Pompeo Neri: atti del colloquio di Castelfiorentino (6–7 maggio 1988)* (Castelfiorentino, 1992), 217–38.

—— 'L'Accademia dei Georgofili e la riforma dell'agricoltura', *Rivista storica italiana*, 105 (1993), 484–501.

Perkins, Jean A., 'The Physiocrats and the Encyclopedists', *Studies in Eighteenth Century Culture*, 8 (1979), 323–36.

Perrotta, Cosimo, 'Il "lusso" negli economisti italiani del Settecento', in Riccardo Faucci (ed.), *Gli italiani e Bentham: dalla "felicità pubblica" all'economia del benessere*, 2 vols. (Milan, 1982), i. 171–89.

—— 'Le teorie del consumo prima di Smith: dalla polemica sul lusso all'idea di capitale umano', *Quaderni di storia dell'economia politica*, 6 (1988), 17–58.

Pesante, Maria Luisa, 'Il commercio nella repubblica', *Quaderni storici*, 105 (2000), 655–96.

—— 'Nation and Public Happiness in Two Italian Political Economists', in Manuela Albertone and Alberto Masoero (eds.), *Political Economy and National Realities* (Turin, 1994), 53–66.

Pii, Eluggero, *Antonio Genovesi: dalla politica economica alla 'politica civile'* (Florence, 1984).

—— 'Michele Ciani tra "Economia nazionale" (Ortes) e "Spirito delle leggi" (Montesquieu)', *Annali dell'Istituto di storia, Università di Firenze, Facoltà di Magistero*, 1 (1979), 151–80.

Piscitelli, Enzo, 'Il pensiero degli economisti italiani del '700 sull'agricoltura, la proprietà terriera e la condizione dei contadini', *Clio*, 15 (1979), 245–92.

Poni, Carlo, *Gli aratri e l'economia agraria nel Bolognese dal XVII al XIX secolo* (Bologna, 1963).

PORTA, PIER LUIGI, 'Le lezioni economiche di Cesare Beccaria', in Sergio Romagnoli and Gian Domenico Pisapia (eds.), *Cesare Beccaria tra Milano e l'Europa* (Rome, 1990), 356–70.

—— and ROBERTO SCAZZIERI, 'Il contributo di Pietro Verri alla teoria economica', *Pietro Verri e il suo tempo: quaderni di Acme*, 35 (1999), 813–52.

PRESSMAN, STEVEN, 'Quesnay's Theory of Taxation', *Journal of the History of Economic Thought*, 16 (1994), 86–105.

QUADRIO CURZIO, ALBERTO (ed.), *Alle origini del pensiero economico in Italia*, ii: *Economia e istituzioni: il paradigma lombardo tra i secoli XVIII e XIX* (Bologna, 1996).

RAO, ANNA MARIA, 'Organizzazione militare e modello politico a Napoli fra illuminismo e rivoluzione', in Vittor Ivo Comparato (ed.), *Modelli nella storia del pensiero politico*, ii: *La rivoluzione francese e i modelli politici* (Florence, 1989), 39–63.

RAVEN, JAMES, *Judging New Wealth: Popular Publishing and Responses to Commerce in England, 1750–1800* (Oxford, 1992).

REINHARDT, VOLKER, *Überleben in der frühneuzeitlichen Stadt. Annona und Getreideversorgung in Rom, 1563–1797* (Tübingen, 1991).

REVEL, JACQUES, 'Le Grain de Rome et la crise de l'annone dans la seconde moitié du XVIIIe siècle', *Mélanges de l'École Française de Rome* (s. Moyen Age–Temps Modernes), 84 (1972), 201–81.

RICUPERATI, GIUSEPPE, 'A proposito di Paolo Mattia Doria', *Rivista storica italiana*, 91 (1979), 261–85.

—— 'Giornali e società nell'Italia dell' "Ancien Regime" (1668–1789)', in Valerio Castronovo and Nicola Tranfaglia (eds.), *La stampa italiana dal '500 all'800* (Rome, 1980), 67–372.

—— 'Illuminismo e Settecento dal dopoguerra ad oggi', in Ricuperati (ed.), *La reinvenzione dei lumi: percorsi storiografici del Novecento* (Florence, 2000), 201–22.

RIPERT, HENRI, *Le Marquis de Mirabeau: Ses théories politiques et économiques* (Paris, 1901).

ROBERTS, HAZEL VAN DYKE, *Boisguilbert: Economist of the Reign of Louis XIV* (New York, 1935).

ROBERTSON, JOHN, 'Franco Venturi's Enlightenment', *Past and Present*, 137 (1992), 183–206.

—— 'The Enlightenment above National Context: Political Economy in Eighteenth-Century Scotland and Naples', *Historical Journal*, 40 (1997), 667–97.

—— (ed.), *A Union for Empire: Political Thought and the Union of 1707* (Cambridge, 1995).

ROMANI, MARIO, 'Beccaria economista', in Romani, *Aspetti e problemi di storia lombarda nei secoli XVIII e XIX* (Milan, 1977), 431–42.

—— 'Gian Luca Pallavicini e le riforme economiche nello Stato di Milano', in Romani, *Aspetti e problemi di storia lombarda nei secoli XVIII e XIX* (Milan, 1977), 355–91.

—— 'Il movimento demografico in Lombardia dal 1750 al 1850', in Romani, *Aspetti e problemi di storia lombarda nei secoli XVIII e XIX* (Milan, 1977), 3–47.

ROMANI, MARIO, *L'agricoltura in Lombardia dal periodo delle riforme al 1859: struttura, organizzazione sociale e tecnica* (Milan, 1957).

—— 'L'economia milanese nel Settecento', in Romani, *Aspetti e problemi di storia lombarda nei secoli XVIII e XIX* (Milan, 1977), 122–206.

ROMANO, RUGGIERO, 'L'Italia nella crisi del secolo XVII', *Studi storici*, 9 (1968), 723–41.

RONCAGLIA, ALESSANDRO (ed.), *Alle origini del pensiero economico in Italia*, i: *Moneta e sviluppo negli economisti napoletani dei secoli XVII–XVIII* (Bologna, 1995).

ROSA, MARIO, 'Ansaldi, Casto Innocente', in *Dizionario biografico degli italiani*, iii (Rome, 1961), 362–5.

—— 'Atteggiamenti culturali e religiosi di Giovanni Lami nelle *Novelle letterarie*', *Annali della Scuola Normale Superiore di Pisa*, 2nd ser., 25 (1956), 260–333.

—— 'Introduzione all'*Aufklärung* cattolica in Italia', in Rosa (ed.), *Cattolicesimo e lumi nel Settecento italiano* (Rome, 1981), 1–47.

ROSS, ELLEN, 'The Debate on Luxury in Eighteenth-Century France: A Study in the Language of Opposition to Change', diss., University of Chicago, 1975.

—— 'Mandeville, Melon and Voltaire: The Origins of the Luxury Controversy in France', *Studies on Voltaire and the Eighteenth Century*, 155 (1976), 1897–912.

ROTA, ETTORE, *Le origini del Risorgimento (1700–1800)*, 2 vols. (Milan, 1938).

ROTA GHIBAUDI, SILVIA, *La fortuna di Rousseau in Italia (1750–1815)* (Turin, 1961).

ROTWEIN, EUGENE, *David Hume: Writings on Economics* (Edinburgh, 1955).

SALLERON, LOUIS, 'Boisguilbert précurseur des physiocrates', in *Pierre de Boisguilbert, ou, La Naissance de l'économie politique*, 2 vols. (Paris, 1966), i. 41–52.

SCHLERETH, THOMAS J., *The Cosmopolitan Ideal in Enlightenment Thought: Its Form and Function in the Ideas of Franklin, Hume, and Voltaire, 1694–1790* (Notre Dame, Ind., 1977).

SCHORSKE, C. E., 'The Idea of the City in European Thought: Voltaire to Spengler', in Oscar Handlin and John Burchard (eds.), *The Historian and the City* (Cambridge, Mass., 1963), 95–114.

SCHUMPETER, JOSEPH ALOIS, *History of Economic Analysis* (London, 1997).

SCOTT, H. M., *The European Nobilities in the Seventeenth and Eighteenth Centuries*, 2 vols. (London, 1995).

SEKORA, JOHN, *Luxury: The Concept in Western Thought, Eden to Smollett* (Baltimore, 1977).

SELLA, DOMENICO, *Crisis and Continuity: The Economy of Spanish Lombardy in the Seventeenth Century* (Cambridge, Mass., 1979).

—— *Italy in the Seventeenth Century* (London, 1997).

—— and CARLO CAPRA, *Il Ducato di Milano dal 1535 al 1796* (Turin, 1984).

SKINNER, ANDREW S., 'David Hume: Principles of Political Economy', in David Fate Norton (ed.), *The Cambridge Companion to Hume* (Cambridge, 1993), 222–54.

—— 'The Shaping of Political Economy in the Enlightenment', *Scottish Journal of Political Economy*, 37 (1990), 145–65.

SOMBART, WERNER, *Luxus und Kapitalismus*, 2nd edn. (Munich, 1922).

STAFFORD, J. MARTIN (ed.), *Private Vices, Public Benefits? The Contemporary Reception of Bernard Mandeville* (Solihull, 1997).

STRUGNELL, ANTHONY, 'Diderot on Luxury, Commerce and the Merchant', *Studies on Voltaire and the Eighteenth Century*, 217 (1983), 83–93.

STUMPO, ENRICO, 'La crisi del Seicento in Italia', in Nicola Tranfaglia and Massimo Firpo (eds.), *La storia: i grandi problemi dal Medioevo all'Età contemporanea*, v (Turin, 1987), 313–37.

SZABO, FRANZ A. J., *Kaunitz and Enlightened Absolutism 1753–1780* (Cambridge, 1994).

TABARRINI, MARCO, *Degli studi e delle vicende della Reale Accademia dei Georgofili nel primo secolo della sua esistenza* (Florence, 1856).

TIRAN, ANDRÉ, 'Pietro Verri: Aux origines de la théorie de la valeur et de la loi des débouches de Jean-Baptiste Say', *Revue d'économie politique*, 103 (1993), 445–71.

TOMASELLI, SYLVANA, review of Christopher J. Berry, *The Idea of Luxury: A Conceptual and Historical Investigation* (Cambridge, 1994), *History of Political Thought*, 16 (1995), 458–60.

TOZZI, GLAUCO, 'Sallustio Bandini: economista senese', *Atti della R. Accademia dei Lincei: memorie della classe di scienze morali, storiche e filologiche*, 6/5 (1933–6), 61–141.

TRAMPUS, ANTONIO, 'L'illuminismo e la "nuova politica" nel tardo settecento italiano: l'uomo libero di Gianrinaldo Carli', *Rivista storica italiana*, 106 (1994), 42–114.

TROISI, M., 'Fonti, critiche ed influenza del pensiero economico di A. Genovesi, con un saggio di bibliografia genovesiana', *Annali della Facoltà di Economia e Commercio della R. Univ. di Bari*, 4 (1942), 1–8.

TSOULFIDIS, LEFTERIS, 'The Physiocratic Theory of Tax Incidence', *Scottish Journal of Political Economy*, 36 (1989), 301–10.

TULLY, JAMES A., 'The Pen is a Mighty Sword: Quentin Skinner's Analysis of Politics', *British Journal of Political Science*, 13 (1983), 489–509.

—— (ed.), *Meaning and Context: Quentin Skinner and his Critics* (Princeton, 1988).

TUVE, ROSEMOND, *Allegorical Imagery: Some Medieval Books and their Posterity* (Princeton, 1966).

VALERI, NINO, *Pietro Verri*, 2nd edn. (Florence, 1969).

VALSECCHI, FRANCO, *L'assolutismo illuminato in Austria e in Lombardia*, 2 vols. (Bologna, 1934).

—— 'Le riforme teresiane in Lombardia', in *Economia, istituzioni, cultura*, i. 27–40.

VENTURI, FRANCO, '1764: Napoli nell'anno della fame', *Rivista storica italiana*, 85 (1973), 394–472.

—— *Italy and the Enlightenment: Studies in a Cosmopolitan Century*, ed. Stuart Woolf (London, 1972).

—— 'La circolazione delle idee', *Rassegna storica del Risorgimento* (1954), 203–22.

VENTURI, FRANCO, 'Le *Lezioni di Commercio* di Antonio Genovesi: manoscritti, edizioni e traduzioni', *Rivista storica italiana*, 72 (1960), 511–30.

—— 'Le *Meditazioni sulla economia politica* di Pietro Verri: edizioni, echi e discussioni', *Rivista storica italiana*, 90 (1978), 530–94.

—— *Le vite incrociate di Henry Lloyd e Pietro Verri* (Turin, 1977).

—— 'Napoli capitale', in *Storia di Napoli*, viii (Naples, 1971), 1–73.

—— 'Quattro anni di carestia in Toscana (1764–1767)', *Rivista storica italiana*, 88 (1976), 649–707.

—— *Settecento riformatore: da Muratori a Beccaria*, 5 vols. and 7 pts. (Turin, 1969–89); vol. i in a 2nd edn. (Turin, 1998).

—— *Utopia e riforma nell'illuminismo* (Turin, 1970); trans. as *Utopia and Reform in the Enlightenment* (Cambridge, 1971).

VERCILLO, OSLAVIA, 'Della conoscenza di Adamo Smith in Italia nel sec. XVIII', *Economia e storia*, 10 (1963), 413–24.

VIDAL, ENRICO, *Il pensiero civile di Paolo Mattia Doria negli scritti inediti: con il testo del manoscritto 'Del commercio del Regno di Napoli'* (Milan, 1953).

VILLARI, LUCIO, *Il pensiero economico di Antonio Genovesi* (Florence, 1958).

—— 'Note sulla fisiocrazia e sugli economisti napoletani del '700', in *Saggi e ricerche sul Settecento* (Naples, 1968), 224–51.

—— 'Teoria economica e rapporti sociali', in *Immagini del Settecento in Italia* (Bari, 1980), 54–61.

VIVANTI, C., 'I prezzi di alcuni prodotti agricoli a Mantova nella seconda metà del XVIII secolo', in Ruggero Romano (ed.), *I prezzi in Europa dal XIII secolo a oggi* (Turin, 1972), 416–36.

VRIES, JAN DE, and AD VAN DER WONDE, *The First Modern Economy: Success, Failure, and Perseverance of the Dutch Economy, 1500–1815* (Cambridge, 1997).

WAHNBAECK, TILL, 'Ferdinando Paoletti georgofilo e il dibattito sul lusso nel Settecento', *I Georgofili: atti della Accademia dei Georgofili*, 45 (1998), 367–89.

WALKER, MACK, *German Home Towns: Community, State, General Estates, 1648–1871* (Ithaca, NY, 1971).

WANDRUSZKA, ADAM, 'Die Persönlichkeit Kaiser Leopold II.', *Historische Zeitschrift*, 192 (1961), 295–317.

—— *Österreich und Italien im 18. Jahrhundert* (Munich, 1963).

—— 'Pietro Leopoldo e le sue riforme in Toscana: dal diario del conte Carlo Zinzendorf', *Archivio storico italiano*, 118 (1960), 286–91.

WAQUET, FRANÇOISE, 'I letterati-editori: produzione, finanziamento e commercio del libro erudito in Italia e in Europa (XVII–XVIII secolo), *Quaderni storici*, 72 (1989), 821–38.

—— and JEAN-CLAUDE WAQUET, 'Presse et société: Le Public des "Novelle letterarie" de Florence (1749–1769)', *Revue française d'histoire du livre*, 22 (1979), 39–60.

WAQUET, JEAN-CLAUDE, 'La Composition du *Discorso sopra la Maremma di Siena*: pensée française et politique locale dans la Toscane des Médicis', *Studies on Voltaire and the Eighteenth Century*, 242 (1986), 233–42.

WEIL, FRANÇOISE, 'La Fonction du manuscrit par rapport à l'imprimé', in François Moureau (ed.), *De bonne main: La Communication manuscrite au XVIIIe siècle* (Paris, 1993), 17–27.

WHALEY, JOACHIM, *Religious Toleration and Social Change in Hamburg* (Cambridge, 1985).

WILSON, CHARLES, 'The Other Face of Mercantilism', in D. C. Coleman (ed.), *Revisions in Mercantilism* (London, 1969), 118–39.

WINCH, DONALD, *Riches and Poverty: An Intellectual History of Political Economy in Britain, 1750–1834* (Cambridge, 1996).

WOOLF, STUART, *A History of Italy 1700–1860: The Social Constraints of Political Change*, new edn. (London, 1991).

WRIGLEY, E. A., *People, Cities and Wealth: The Transformation of Traditional Society* (Oxford, 1987).

ZAMBELLI, PAOLA, 'Il rogo postumo di Paolo Mattia Doria', in Zambelli (ed.), *Ricerche sulla cultura dell'Italia moderna* (Laterza, 1973), 147–98.

—— *La formazione filosofica di Antonio Genovesi* (Naples, 1972).

ZAPPERI, ROBERTO, 'Bencivenni Pelli, Giuseppe', in *Dizionario biografico degli italiani*, viii (Rome, 1966), 218–22.

ZARIN, EUGENIO, *Storia dell'economia politica: dai mercantilisti a Marx* (Turin, 1991).

ZARONE, GIUSEPPE, *Etica e politica nell'utilitarismo di Cesare Beccaria* (Naples, 1971).

ZIMMERMANN, JOHANN, *Das Verfassungsprojekt des Grossherzogs Peter Leopold von Toskana* (Heidelberg, 1901).

INDEX

The manufacturer's authorised representative in the EU for product safety is Oxford University Press España S.A. of el Parque Empresarial San Fernando de Henares, Avenida de Castilla, 2 – 28830 Madrid (www.oup.es/en or product.safety@oup.com). OUP España S.A. also acts as importer into Spain of products made by the manufacturer.

www.ingramcontent.com/pod-product-compliance
Lightning Source LLC
LaVergne TN
LVHW101442200926
848483LV00001B/21

9780199269839